PRINCIPALS AS MAVERICK LEADERS

Rethinking Democratic Schools

Sharron Goldman Walker
Michael Chirichello

ROWMAN & LITTLEFIELD EDUCATION

A division of
ROWMAN & LITTLEFIELD PUBLISHERS, INC.
Lanham • New York • Toronto • Plymouth, UK

Published by Rowman & Littlefield Education
A division of Rowman & Littlefield Publishers, Inc.
A wholly owned subsidary of The Rowman & Littlefield Publishing Group, Inc.
4501 Forbes Boulevard, Suite 200, Lanham, Maryland 20706
http://www.rowmaneducation.com

Estover Road, Plymouth PL6 7PY, United Kingdom

British Library Cataloguing in Publication Information Available

Library of Congress Cataloging-in-Publication Data

Library of Congress Cataloging-in-Publication Data
Walker, Sharron Goldman, 1945-
  Principals as maverick leaders : rethinking democratic schools / Sharron
Goldman Walker, Michael Peter Chirichello.
      p. cm.
  Includes bibliographical references.
  ISBN 978-1-61048-348-3 (cloth : alk. paper) — ISBN 978-1-61048-349-0
(pbk. : alk. paper) — ISBN 978-1-61048-350-6 (ebook)
  1. School principals—United States. 2. Educational leadership—United
States. 3. Democracy and education—United States. I. Chirichello, Michael.
II. Title.
  LB2831.92.W348 2011
  371.2'0120973—dc22

                                                              2011004755

Printed in the United States of America

"A revolutionary look from inside our school system. When the people who really care about our schools read this book, they might bring about the very changes needed to make our public schools what they were originally intended to be—a democratic institution. What a concept!"
—**Jona Henry**, retired high school teacher

"If you have ever reflected upon our schools as complex structures and questioned the reasons our schools have evolved into stagnant organizations, this is a book that will have immense meaning for you. Chirichello and Walker have written an inspirational book of stories and reflections that capture the essence of schools as democratic, integrated, and complex organizations. It is relevant, real-life, and provides hope for those who have asked, 'Why am I doing this?' It is must reading for current and future school leaders and anyone else truly interested in improving the culture of schools and the teaching-learning process. I plan to use this book as required reading in my graduate leadership and organizational culture classes."
—**George F. Sharp**, Ed.D., retired superintendent and assistant professor, The Richard Stockton College of New Jersey

"This book is a MUST read for all potential school administrators; especially those who see themselves as 'trailblazers,' 'risk takers,' or 'innovators' who are truly interested and committed to reform. As a principal and superintendent, I would put this book on the required reading list for all of the administrators in my district. It is an outstanding practical guide for those who wish to become a successful educator."
—**George Blek**, Ed. D., retired principal and superintendent

"At last! 'The road less traveled' takes us on a fresh, new approach to the education of our children. Wonderful ideas that will strengthen and secure our democracy."
—**Roslyn Fallick**, retired teacher and school administrator

Sharron dedicates this book to her husband, Virgil, the man who helped shape her education, and to the teachers, principals, and superintendents who work together within school processes as collaborators, guiding students in the practice of democracy in the schoolhouse.

Michael dedicates this book to his three wonderful grandchildren—Amanda Charlotte, Taylor Mackenzie, and Contessa Lynn—with the hope that the schoolhouse they enter will be a place where children will have the freedom to dream as they learn how to learn.

CONTENTS

INTRODUCTION

After her school wins the coveted U.S. National Secondary Education Award, a school principal embarks upon an educational odyssey. During her journey, the school principal, Dina Macksy, discovers that the reasons for winning the award are a sham! As her school falls apart, she begins to reflect on the stagnant school organization and the ineffective prescriptions for improvement. She wonders why, as a democratic nation, American schools do not model the practice of democracy for students. The principal begins her quest to unearth the flaws in her own thinking about the way schools work in her quest to save the Republic.

The principal begins a dialogue with the great thinkers who reside on the shelves of the public library. From the ancient Greeks to the modern-day thinkers who champion their individual causes, the principal begins to understand "Newton's Flaw." She unravels that the way organizations function stems from a classical view of the universe in which the world is understood by breaking it down into parts and fixing the parts that are broken.

Being unsatisfied with this worldview and mental model, the principal embarks upon a journey to recant this view of the universe—Newton's Flaw—in favor of principles that will better serve the school as a social organization and save the Republic. The acquisition of her new knowledge transforms her worldview into Quantumland—a world that is understood by the intersection of relationships within a social system that thrives on balanced feedback loops.

Dina discovers that the school is a cooperative enterprise, which can have no discrete control center. She begins to apply the new insights gained from Quantumland to the schoolhouse. Through trial and error, she learns that schools are composed of chaotic systems in which the interrelationships between parts are more important than the parts themselves. There are no simple solutions to complex problems. High-stakes accountability measures, uniform standards, centralized control, censorship of curricula, or raising teacher certification requirements will not solve what ails schools because each focuses on a part of the system instead of the whole.

Part I of the book presents a tongue-in-cheek guide for principals in the form of rules. Principals must ask themselves constantly why they are doing what they are doing. They must begin by reflecting on their own philosophical base of *self* before they can transform anything.

Principals must begin from the inside out, through conversation and self-reflection. They must understand how classical mechanics has affected thinking about schools. They must also understand that schools must guide students toward democratic practices.

Each chapter includes conversations with great thinkers from many fields of expertise who espouse their worldviews about learning. The chapters culminate by posing reflective questions to get the reader to understand the purpose of education and schooling from the inside out. It is through this reflective dialogue that the principal begins to apply the conversations to *what is* as she moves toward what *can be*.

Part II takes the reader through the messy world of Quantumland. Moving through a series of vignettes, the reader will see how Dina transforms her thinking about learning and the purpose of schooling. Endeavoring to understand how systems really work, the principal puts her new ideas into practice and shares with the reader the lessons learned from the shelved authors in the library.

She begins to build collective capacity with all the members of the school community from the custodians to the teachers to the broader community outside the walls of the school house to enhance a process

that will improve student outcomes, academically, socially, and emotionally. The blame game gives way to analyzing the whole system rather
than its isolated parts. The principal begins to emerge as an educational
leader.

As things begin to change at the school, the principal is mindful that
lurking in the shadows are those who continue to see the school in terms
of Newton's Flaw. In the end, Quantumland meets head on with the
world of classical mechanics, and the reader is left to her own conclusions regarding the future of Principal Dina Macksy.

This story is based on our experiences as principals in public school
systems. Many events were embellished for the purpose of making a
point. The school setting and its characters are a fictitious composite of
our experiences. Any resemblance to real persons is purely coincidental.

There were so many voices who contributed to this work. They are
referenced throughout the book. The words from the voices are cited or
improvised from our writings and personal communications.

Although some of the conversations and dialogues between and
among the noted experts are embellished and imagined, they are based
on the referenced sources. The conversations represent our perspectives of translating theory into dialogues and conversations without losing the essential understandings of the noted experts whose works are
referenced in the text.

The primary texts from which the ideas are embellished in conversation are referenced in the appropriate section of each chapter when the
conversations begin. Further references to the same work in the same
chapter are not included to avoid redundancy. The imagined conversations are the best interpretations of our understandings of the cited
works and our general knowledge of the noted experts. For that reason,
the page numbers in the citations are not included.

We wish to thank all those people who hang out on the shelves of li-
braries. And thanks to all the people not on library shelves who took
the time to responds to our inquiry: *Why do countries send their children to school?* In anticipation, kudos to the educators who will think
about what the library people have said as they create democracy in the
schoolhouse as a way to further America's freedom.

THE AUTHORS REFLECT:
TAKE THE ROAD LESS TRAVELED

Collectively, we spent more than six decades in public schools, including thirty-seven years as principals. Our work spans elementary and high schools as well as urban and suburban populations. We do not propose to have all the answers to the complex questions that face school leaders day in and day out. Rather, we desire to share our experiences through stories, conversations, and reflections in hopes of stimulating the reader's thinking about our democratic ideals. We anticipate this book will offer readers opportunities to engage in conversations that will have a positive impact on their role as school leaders.

It is no secret that to achieve successful student learning outcomes, schools rely on both principal and teacher leadership. The principal must become the educational leader while teachers take on the role of instructional leaders, and that is what will make a difference for students. This notion goes beyond politics, beyond funding, beyond bashing, and moves us toward rethinking democratic schools, schools in which every student will stretch to his or her limit.

It is for these reasons that we coauthored this book. Come along and join in our journey. Take the road less traveled with us.

SPECIAL FEATURES OF THE BOOK

- The story is authentic, inspirational, and practical. It is based on our life experiences.
- As the story unfolds, the reader will understand the complexity of adaptive changes in organizations.
- The myth of principal as instructional leader will give way to a new paradigm: principal as educational leader, a more complex, daunting, but comprehensive role for twenty-first-century school leaders.
- Reflections at the conclusion of each chapter in Part I will give readers time to apply theory to their practice.
- Part I is written as a conversational dialogue among great thinkers to understand the theoretical underpinnings of democratic schools. Part II transforms theory into practice based on the day-to-day life of a principal as she transitions from *what is* to *what should be*.

- This book will be useful for aspiring, new, and experienced principals. It is worthwhile and informative for use in undergraduate courses in educational philosophy and graduate educational courses in organizational theory, understanding change as a process, and curriculum design.
- The reader is challenged to make decisions from the rules and lessons learned, being fully cognizant that the links among schooling, education, and democracy are interwoven and paramount in preserving our public schools and ensuring freedom for generations to come.

I

THE PRINCIPAL
AS CLASSICAL MECHANIC

Rule

ASK YOURSELF WHY SOCIETY SCHOOLS CHILDREN

Have you ever walked around asking strangers why any country sends its children to school? When Principal Dina Macksy was new to her job, she did just that. There she was one day, standing on the checkout line at Costco on coupon day. The lines were backed up to the rear wall and she was disgusted reading on her Blackberry about yet another gridlock in Congress.

Turning to the young woman behind her—the one with the intense look of calm on her face and the cartons of wild cherry Pepsi filling her basket—Dina asked, "Why do countries send their children to school?"[1] The young woman didn't hesitate an answer. "So that I can shop at my favorite store without having to chase my kids up and down the aisles. Why else?"

The vacuous words seemed to spew forth from her mouth in such an unexpectedly gruff tone that she made Dina think that she had somehow been uncivil by asking the question. She felt offended, not by her gruffness but by the young woman's underlying assumption that she was a babysitter for her ruffian kids.

Dina gave the young women a long, glaring look like the hero does in a pulp novel—even furrowed her brows and pursed her lips—and turned to the distinguished looking gentleman in front of her with the neatly trimmed beard. She asked him the same question.

"I really don't know why," he said. "Look around you . . . most of the people here haven't a clue about how to talk to each other and exchange knowledge that is reasoned. Schools have not taught them how to do this. They have created human, reactive clones, fodder for those who wish to control them. You are a schooler . . . your M.A. is for master of arms."

He then turned away from Dina and loaded his purchases on the conveyer belt of the checkout counter. She couldn't help but notice that his purchases consisted mainly of bottled water.

Well, anyway, when you ask a question, Dina thought, expect an answer even if you receive one you don't quite expect . . . or understand. But why even attempt to understand? The guy was an imperious eccentric. Still, the distinguished looking gentleman's response was problematic. He seemed to be deliberately obtuse, and she could not reason his meanings.

As principals, she lamented, we don't have time for analysis of such considered responses because they sometimes require us to think—*how did he know that she was an educator with an M.A. degree?* She was searching for concise answers that would be suitable for her mental framework—*what was the difference between a schooler and an educator? She didn't think schooler was a word.* She was an educator, not a schooler.

Dina continued asking the question on the lines at Walmart and Target, albeit avoiding distinguished looking gentlemen with beards and young women with the intense look of calm on their faces. She asked the question because she thought that the public's answers would provide her with direction about how to lead the workers in her schoolhouse. You see, Dina had this notion that schools were about preserving democracy. She was a bit shaken with the responses she was receiving.

No one said that we send our kids to school to preserve our democracy, which was, after all, the way Thomas Jefferson would have answered the question. Jefferson advocated public education as a means of creating an intelligent electorate capable of weighing issues and making informed decisions. We all had learned that in high school. But respondents were consigning history to oblivion.

Maybe Dina's first duty as a new principal should be to have all the classroom teachers design posters that reflected Jefferson's purpose for education, requesting that they tape them to their walls. Perhaps she should talk to the history teachers and remind them to spend more time on Jefferson.

After checking their lesson plans, she noticed that they simply allocated one-half of one class period to our third president and scribe of our Declaration of Independence, referring their students to a page in the bland, state-adopted textbook.

Because Dina was not satisfied with the queue answers, she decided to continue to ask all the smart people she knew the question. Her cousin, Dr. Michael, is a very smart man; he's a professor at a big university. He didn't hesitate.

"I would like to think that we send children to school to learn how to learn but I am not sure that's the outcome. The test phobia and focus on test preparation have all but destroyed the desire to develop creativity and risk-taking. Our schools are preparing drones rather than dreamers. If you watch *Shift Happens* on YouTube, you will be amazed with the space between what should be and what is in our schools."

Well, Cousin Michael was right about one thing. If you didn't send kids to school to learn how to learn, then how could democracy be preserved? People who can't think for themselves can be easily controlled. All you had to do was remember your world history to know that. On the other hand, the course always ended just as the Great War was beginning. And what was this space to which Cousin Michael was referring?

Anyway, Dina was convinced our democracy's preservation required thinking, informed people who had as their greatest resource the ability of continually acquiring knowledge. Plato knew how to do this and proposed training people to make the big decisions for the polis as a result of this skill.[2]

Actually, Plato was proposing what Cousin Michael said—teaching people to learn how to learn, to somehow acquire that direct perception that gives reason to reason and a direct link to truth. Both men seemed to be on the same page in their thinking, even though Plato didn't know about America and Cousin Michael had never lived in the polis, and even though Plato only wanted to embed thinking skills in a few and Cousin Michael wanted to embed them in the many.

If we send kids to school to preserve democracy by learning how to learn, why didn't people know this? Why did Dina get responses like the one she received from her friend and colleague, Gene Bilodeau who said, "We send kids to school to keep them out of jail"? Did Gene, an international educator, know that his tongue need not be in his cheek when he offered up his comment because it was not specious, historically speaking?

In the early nineteenth century, kids were sent to school because too many of them were wandering the streets and living in a state of nature, without knowledge of the social contract to guide them. They didn't know much about Jefferson either.

Other respondents said we send kids to school because we have to. Barbarra Hunter, a citizen of America and England, Raymond Grimaldi, a banking consultant, and Kathryn Conway, a humanitarian worker concurred, "It's the law."

But why is it the law? Is it a law because we want to school kids in the social contract? You remember from Philosophy 101 that the social contract was written so that we, the people, abrogated our state of nature, which was nasty and brutish anyway, and entered into discourse, negotiating terms for living together. We gave up being mean to each other in order to live in peace and harmony and, oh, to be civil to each other.

Is it the law because we don't want kids competing with adults in the labor market? Is it the law because for twelve years we can regiment children to high degrees of efficiency while removing their natural spontaneity? Is it the law because schooling teaches control and control allows others to think for us? Dina was beginning to think that maybe she asked the question wrong. After all, she was not a trained researcher.

A retired primary teacher, Roslyn Fallick, stated: "We have to remember that there is a law in our country requiring us to register children at a certain age. Therefore, parents have little choice. The purpose for this law is to ensure that all the citizens of this country will receive the required education to enable them to read and write in the English language." But would they be able to learn how to learn as they were acquiring a common language, or would they have to learn the new language first?

We have high hopes and aspirations for our offspring, which is another reason why we send children to school, some respondents said. "Parents want their kids to achieve what they couldn't achieve themselves," said Kathy Whitman, a retired administrative assistant at a California school district and mother of two grown boys. "You want your children to be well-educated and hopefully do something fantastic with their life, to be more and go further than you did."

"But if the schools don't succeed and your kids don't go further than you did, the school can be used as a scapegoat for the parents' failure," suggested Don Sorensen, a computer administrator. "If the schools don't do this, we can blame them for the failure of our children and not ourselves."

Many said school prepares kids for the world of work. Children must learn from the get-go that life is about going to a building where they remain captive all day and perform repetitive tasks in order to survive.

These respondents equated schools with learning how to survive in a factory world. Perhaps they said this because the school resembled a factory to them, just as Costco's conveyer belt at the checkout counter reminded Dina of an assembly line. When you think about schooling, there are the intermittent bells, the assembly line of the young being passed from one grade to another, the close monitoring, the regimented behavior, the standardization in making every school look like every other school even though the raw material inside the structure—the widget little people—comes with a remarkable amount of variation. Maybe someone, somewhere, did have the factory in mind when he designed schools. We'll get back to this notion later.

The socialization function of schools was high on many lists. "The success of *Homo sapiens* can be attributed to the practice of living in organized, cooperating groups," offered a respondent. "Surviving school impresses that on kids."

Might this respondent be suggesting that, if we survive twelve years of schooling, we are more likely to be civil to each other, or perhaps that we have negotiated our social contract, verified by a diploma that testifies to this event?

A young Swedish mother, Nina Thujfell, responded: "We send our kids to school to educate them so that they stand a better chance in this competitive world. I also think it's important to have common knowledge but most importantly, school teaches us to socialize and get along with each other." We want our kids to beat out the other kids, but still get along with them. That is a noble idea, but is it an achievable one?

School also has babysitting functions. For some parents, it just may be a means of getting "X number" of hours of freedom to do whatever they wish, like shopping unencumbered at Costco. Sue Faubion, a mother of three children commented, "We send them to school mostly to get them out of our hair before we totally lose our minds as mothers!"

A parent of one child, John Casciato, offered this response: "We send our children to school to have more free time to drink during the daylight hours. Isn't that obvious?" Of course, Mr. Casciato, an alternative school teacher, was joking when he said this but, if we read between the laugh lines, many of us want to get them out of our hair for X number of hours during the day so that we may return to the world of calm.

One parent thought that kids are sent to school so that the school can bring them up. "So many of us lack parenting skills," this parent said.

A retired high school teacher, Scott Cavell, echoed these thoughts. "I think that one of the main and unspoken reasons is that they—the public—believe and trust us, the educators, to do the right thing; the right thing being to do all of the stuff that they—the parents—do not have the time, skills, expertise, or patience to do. Not just teach the 3Rs but to attend to all of the issues that are fermenting out there in the greater society that make growing up and maturing more than difficult for many young people." Mr. Cavell may have been suggesting that schools must do all things for all children.

We send kids to school in order for them to learn conformity, some said, so they will be like every other child—the factory idea again. Yet others suggested the opposite. "We don't want them to learn conformity," Harm Meijer, a computer technician and native of Canada wrote. "We send kids to school to give them the opportunity to learn about society and their place in it through first-hand experiences in a structured setting. We want kids to find their place in the social clique through trial and error, not conformity, and want them exposed to kindness, cruelty, diplomacy, relationships, inclusion, and exclusion, and so on. It's the benchmark our nation has set as the minimum expectation for a quality of life available to a member of this society."

The utilitarian philosopher, John Stuart Mill would probably agree with Mr. Meijer. "The human facilities of perception, judgment, discriminative feeling, mental activity, and even moral preference, are exercised only in making a choice. He who does anything because it is the custom, makes no choice. He gains no practice either in discerning or in desiring what is best. He who lets the world, or his own portion of it,

ASK YOURSELF WHY SOCIETY SCHOOLS CHILDREN 9

choose his plan of life for him, has no need of any other faculty than the ape-like one of imitation. He who chooses his plan for himself, employs all his faculties" (Sandel, 2009, p. 51).

We send our kids to school to learn, but to learn what? "We send children to school so that they have the knowledge and academic skills that will enable them to do the most with their lives," said Jack Sides, a former Air Force pilot. Jona Henry, teacher and parent said "We send children to school to experience a world of learning; both socially and academically."

Another teacher and parent, Mary Johnson wrote, "We send our kids to school to prepare for life's journey, to learn how to read, write, and spell and to learn the latest technology."

Her daughter, Lori Edelstein, also a teacher and parent said, "We send children to school to receive an education to be successful in life. Although parents are a child's first teacher, many are not equipped to teach their children the wide range of subjects taught in school."

A financial consultant, Judith Sides, offered this. "We send our kids to school to expand their minds and open them up to new ideas." Teacher Linda Gilbert said, "We send kids to school to create a passion in them."

Some respondents thought they could not properly answer the question because they had no children. A former actress, Laura Shewman, said, "Since I have no children, I'm probably not the best one to ask, but I would think it's a variety of reasons: To learn facts—reading, writing, history, math. To learn to socialize like making friends, working as a team, obeying orders when necessary, playing nice, being patient and enduring boredom—things like that."

Laura continued, "We send them to school to learn values, although I really think that role belongs to the parents/family caretakers. I do feel that children and later older young folks do absorb values from their teachers and school figures of authority like coaches. And those values can be positive or negative depending on the figure of authority. But in the best sense, I would expect a child of mine to learn some degree of responsibility and other personal values from a school situation."

Laura hit on important ideas about schooling. Jefferson would have been proud of her. Concepts such as teaming, shared values, and positive figures are important components of a democracy. People who are childless are still entitled to their opinions because we live in a democracy where all opinions are considered—at least that's the theory.

One parent summed it up this way: "We send our kids to school because we believe that schools are good places and teachers are good people and that kids will be better off for the experience and, because we have to."

Gene Bilodeau added, "We believe that education will improve the general state of man and we believe that educated people have a better chance at happiness and prosperity."

Well, Aristotle would have applauded Mr. Bilodeau's statement. Aristotle said that happiness is the meaning and the purpose of life, the whole aim and end of human existence (Loomis, 1995).

We send kids to school for many reasons: to provide free babysitters, because it is the law, because it performs a socialization function, so that kids will learn something, so that kids will be like the others—or not be like the others—but we can't forgot that one of the most salient reasons is to preserve our democratic way of life.

Our culture represents a set of beliefs, which form the basis of our freedoms and continues only when there exists a thinking, informed, and vigilant citizenry who have the ability to reflect beyond the limitations of their own insights. If we, the citizenry, forget those beliefs because we no longer know how to learn how to learn, then we abandon our way of life and invite the mob, led by people who pursue their own clandestine interests, to rule us, achieving a way of life we did not set out wanting to achieve. Freedom requires constant vigilance. It just can't be taken for granted.

Maybe a lot of people have forgotten this or simply never knew it because democracy is something we don't see schools practicing. Schools may teach democratic concepts in the history classrooms but Dina wondered why schools did not model those concepts throughout the whole schoolhouse. In fact, why aren't schools buzzing about with classrooms where student creativity and spontaneity were the rule, not the exception, where the thought and practice of democracy were melded together?

Maybe it has something to do with that space Cousin Michael talked about between what is and what should be.

REFLECTION

Now that you've read about it, what do you believe? Why should Joe, Maria, Kim, and Enrique send their children to school? Have you given this question much thought lately? It should drive what you do, day in and day out, in the hallways and classrooms, in your conversations with teachers and parents, in your meetings with custodians and secretaries, and in your interactions with students.

It should be the focus of your vision and school's mission statement. It will give your professional life a purpose. It will become the story you will share with your staff and shareholders[3] over and over again. It will become the focus of your professional work.

Take a moment to think about it. Grab that pen or go to your computer, and reflect on the statement: I believe society sends children to school because . . .

NOTES

1. All the people who ventured an answer to this unscientific survey regarding why we send children to school are real people who said that they had never been asked that question.

2. If you want to know more about Plato, read *The Republic and Other Works* by Jowett (1973).

3. We used the term shareholders rather than stakeholders to emphasize the collective capacity of the school's community of professional practice.

Rule

FLUSH OUT YOUR
THEORY OF ORGANIZATION

We can't really rely on others to tell us why we send our kids to school, although we can integrate their answers into our own thinking as we build our own theories. W. Edwards Deming once said that without theory, we can only copy (Delavigne & Robertson, 1994). He had a theory about the connected nature within all systems. We don't use this theory in schools because nothing in schools is connected.

A psychology professor, Seymour Sarason, described a theory as a necessary myth we construct to explain what we don't completely understand (Sarason, 1990). He had a theory that people must know themselves before they can affect permanent change in an organization. Few principals bother to understand what he means because they are too busy falling in behind the latest bandwagon, just as Principal Dina Macksy did.

Then there are the scientists with their theories. Take the classical physicist, for example, who has this theory about a neat and orderly universe whose origins can't be explained by a craps game. Now take his colleague, the quantum physicist, who thinks otherwise—it's not so neat and orderly, and perhaps it can be explained by the roll of the dice.

The point is each of these physical mechanics has a theory that explains to them how the universe works. They may not agree with each other, but they will continue to observe the stars and collect data that support their own beliefs, constantly exploring commonalities. If just once the data do not fit the theory, they know their theory is wrong.

That's what Einstein meant when he said "No amount of experimentation can ever prove me right; a single experiment can prove me wrong" (Famous Quotes). Einstein's relativity theory is just that—a theory—but so far all the data out there confirm it, even if many of us don't understand what is being confirmed out there.

Another example of how theory works comes from Newton. We don't float into the outer atmosphere because of something he called gravity that keeps us in our place. Although it's true we can't see gravity, we know that it is there; the idea of gravity is a good theory because it explains with regularity and predictability why we don't float into classrooms, although we know some high school students who do!

Once Newton got the idea about gravity, Einstein explained to us how it actually worked, tweaking Sir Isaac's theory by explaining away the slight perturbations in Mercury's orbit with his theory of relativity. But that's another story and another one most of us don't understand.

The problem with principals is that they don't really construct theories: we just use what Plato called marketplace banter to explain the state of our schools—like Dina did when she asked people why they send kids to school without questioning why they thought what they thought. It is dubious whether principals know that their organizations are, like the universe, a complex system of people and actions that work interactively to produce *something*.

Dina's theory is that *the something* should be a thinking individual who understands how to learn because the preservation of our Republic depends profoundly upon an intelligent citizenry. Unfortunately, her two decades of working in the system and working on it still produces inconclusive data to support this theory. Einstein was much better at theory building, and Newton too. They both knew that by using logic one could learn, but by using imagination, one could soar.

As stated in the previous rule, Dina gave you her theory about the purpose of schools—general as it may be—*principals function to perpetuate democracy*. Our founding fathers thought that if all their haggling and backroom drama were to mean something, children would have to learn that living in a democratic society meant that the experience of being able to choose was better than having someone else do it for them. Education serves the state and thus serves the people—in a democratic fashion.

Schooling is a tool that serves the people, enabling them to know how to make good choices that benefit not only each individual, but also all of those with whom we live. In fact, in a truly better world, our choices would be about the common good, not our own good. At least that's what philosopher Immanuel Kant might say. His thinking is hard to understand, but he proposes that if we do things with selfish intent, like have concern about ourselves, we aren't really free (Tarnas, 1991).

But think about the ineffable pleasure principals attain when they give and ask nothing in return. Think of the elevated plane on which they find themselves standing and the freeing feeling they have. Think about them as they hand each member of the senior class a diploma, announcing that these self-actualized students have met state certification requirements and are ready to lead the world.

Principals are proud that their graduates believe in the collective capacity of people to solve problems. They are proud that these graduates know how to evaluate ideas and confront challenges. They are proud that these graduates are concerned with the common good and the dignity and rights of others. They are proud that these graduates have processed democratic living and the values inherent in life, liberty, and the pursuit of happiness. They are proud that these graduates can dream as Cousin Michael envisioned in the previous rule's text they would.

Anyway, returning to the land of reality, Dina's theory was a myth. That explains why she did not make things happen in her schoolhouse. But she will not discard her theory. If she did, she would undermine her belief about living in a free society.

As Mr. Sarason might say, her theory is incomplete. The purpose of this conversation with principals, then, is an attempt to complete it, flesh it out, and maybe learn from the missteps in the process. For example, why did Dina believe that we send kids to school to preserve democracy? Don't we just send them because it's the law? Don't we just send them to abate incarceration rates and save the taxpayer money?

Dina's theory was incomplete when she moved into the principal's office. More to the point, it wasn't even there. She had no theory of why we educate students; she just knew that it was the principal's job to do something to the students, sort of like going to an alchemist and asking him for the brew that would allow her to award students the state-certified diploma that said that she had done her job.

If too many of her students floated away from school because the schoolhouse gravity could not take hold of them, it meant the alchemist's concoction failed, and the superintendent, Mac Avelli, would look at the graduation rates and point fingers at her at evaluation time. He had no theory either.

She wondered if principals, in general, were like her—out of touch with theory, out of touch with research, with reflection, introspection, and complexity. Did they say things, as she did—like *research says*—to impress their teachers and assure them that the substance of what they say is more important than the presumed authority with which their words are spoken?

Perhaps the term *research says* is a principal's mantra to disguise what is really unknown. Because it is written, it must be right! Real change never occurs because principals don't have the time to think about what they are thinking about. They just react to what they are thinking. They usually base their problem solving on their experience, which is absurd when you think about the fact that the quality of their experiences may not have always been that good or appropriate in a particular setting. Dina's New York background, for example, might have helped her in an inner city school in the Bronx but would prove limiting at a school in Beverly Hills.

Principals must recognize that they don't always have to use experience to discover what they are seeking. Plato knew that, and that is why he separated experience from real knowing—he just didn't trust the experience. Before we were born, we knew the truth of all things, but when we came into this world as a mortal, we forgot. That's what Plato said.

Principals sit in their cavernous offices warmed by the fires behind them—the very fires that throw shadows on the walls. They watch the shadows and think that what they are seeing is reality. But the real reality is behind them at the entrance of the office, where the sun is shining. If they watch the shadows, they won't realize that there is something missing in their school. Of course principals' offices don't have fireplaces, but you get the point. So then we just have to find the conduit that will allow the *principals' knowing* to come into them so that they can turn around, walk out of the office, and unlock the secrets to preserving democracy and save the Republic. That Plato was quite a guy!

There is, however, one thing that Dina's experience affirms—we have to search for a theory about organizations that can live up to the ideals of our founding fathers and Plato's process of discovery—that is, if the man is right. Couldn't our beliefs be embedded within us instead of wandering out yonder waiting for us to catch up to them?

Nonsense—the great man was smart. And he said we couldn't use the beliefs of the marketplace because they are opinion, beliefs without much foundation, experience without much quality, or as Plato might say, experience is deceptive. What we experience every day is a shadow of reality.

Similarly, Dina believes that schools cannot operate according to the whims of superintendents and school boards, but rather by theories that are universal to schools and natural to the people who inhabit them. After all, learning is natural even if we do it in unnatural settings—settings that encourage passiveness and submissiveness. Of course, principals have to be able to find those universal theories and at the same time hold on to their jobs.

Add this to the fact that principals never examine their way of knowing; often they don't ask themselves, after signing their first one-year contract, about the nature of their new existence. They don't ask themselves opaque questions that echo in the murky corridors of the schoolhouse, such as, "What is this school about that I am now living in seemingly twenty-four hours a day?"

To be sure, Plato questioned his surroundings, didn't like it very much, and moved himself into higher real estate property. Today we call it the *ivory tower*, a place in which college professors still live—no offense to Cousin Michael—so maybe it did him some good detaching himself from the sycophants of the bandwagon who still flail around in the moat, trying to keep their heads above water because they never asked themselves why they are wet—while Plato and Cousin Michael always stay dry.

Thinking about the nature of our environment is very important because, if we don't, we might still be battling it out in caves at a time when we still haven't negotiated the social contract. Eons ago, the Ionians, early Greek-type people, constructed a theory about their environment. If they could conquer their environment, they could control it instead of it controlling them.

To do this, they had to construct a new way of knowing, a new way of thinking. That is, they had to conjure up the courage to say to the high prophets of the temple that superstition no longer worked in explaining the world. There had to be a better way—a more knowing way. So these ancient Greeks fiddled around with the shape of things.

They theorized that within water there were these globular atoms that slipped and slapped over and under each other, making water slippery. That's why it's hard to hold water in our hands. Fire atoms are sharp and jagged. That's why we don't touch fire—it hurts. And with geometry, the world perspective began to change.

Instead of accepting what the temple priests told them, the Ionians began exploring for themselves (Burke, 1985; Tarnas, 1991). So you see, questioning our environment leads to a different way of shaping it.

What does matter is that we have to have a theory about how things work in order to run—*maybe the correct word is lead*—an organization. We also need contrivances of thought to do this. While Plato removed his experience from knowing, Aristotle thought there was no knowledge without including it.

Plato is probably right in that there are certain truths that exist about all people, truths that cannot be based on what we know solely because we don't know that much. But since we don't know that much, a combination of experience and introspection creates the thoughts of the mind in combination with the experience and introspection of others, which means that Plato may not be as right as he thought he was. At least, that's what Aristotle thought.

Why spend all this time with these notions about the place of theory in our organizations? Simple. Without theory, we get Sisyphus. Of course, with it we can get him anyway, but at least with a theory, we can explain to the superintendent why the boulder landed on us again.

Sisyphus is the Greek guy who put all his physical and mental weight against a boulder, pushing it up a hill, only to watch it fall down again. No matter how hard the poor guy tried to change things, nothing worked in the long run. Poor Sisyphus. He tried so hard and, boom, down the boulder rolled, sometimes missing him narrowly and sometimes steamrolling right over him, crushing him until he was stretched ever so thinly across the schoolhouse ground, looking up at all those people walking over him.

The story of Sisyphus is a story about hapless work, and we know that the Greek mythological character doesn't really die, although he could eventually have suffered a heart attack.

Principals don't have to fill the Greek's shoes, but this is how it happens. Every time Dina unfolds a new educational plan and gets it going, it somehow escapes from her grip, doubling right back on her.

She once had this great theory about how to keep the campus clean. It was always littered because the students were too lazy to throw their trash in the trash cans. At least that's what she believed after observing the students, talking to their parents, and listening to the marketplace gossip.

Her theory was that a clean campus would help in strengthening her school's academic standing. So Dina told—yes, *told*—teachers to take their third period class out every third week and help the custodian pick up trash. This would teach the students civic responsibility, the campus would look cleaner, and the custodian would have less work so that he could have more time to clean up the graffiti in the bathrooms. She only had one custodian at the time.

As the students learned civic responsibility, she reasoned, the streets would be cleaner, and would soon replicate the pristine walkways of Switzerland, where test scores demonstrated that the kids there were smarter than American kids. With cleanliness would come a calm feeling that would permeate the campus, allowing students to study, relieved of the stress of a dirty campus.

Good idea, right? No, wrong. Science teacher, Mr. Quintin Waver said it all with his vitriolic rant: "I'm tired of taking learning time away from my physics class to pick up somebody else's trash. The students feel the same way! Let the custodian do what gravity has forced down on this earth!"

There she was, crushed just like Sisyphus, seeing too late the boulder crashing down on her. Someone had sprawled across it in alpha, beta, sigma lettering something that looked like it said *low morale* and in larger letters, *stupid idea.* But she was too embarrassed to share this out loud with anyone. There she was, lying prone on the ground again, exasperated because she had constructed a theory about the change process from pure sophistry.

In the absence of theory, no matter how we try to make things better, problems always pop up here and there again. After we solve one problem, another springs up. Dina was always so exasperated with that undulating, invidious snake that she kept running after under the thin layer of carpet in her office. When she stomped her foot down on it in one place, it would pop up in another place.

Like her colleagues, she had read the research and attended all the relevant workshops about principals as change agents. But she wasn't changing anything by telling everyone to pick up the trash on the school grounds. She was only producing a greater morale problem and taking time away from academic learning.

Why did she think that a clean campus would lead to heightened learning? Because she once taught in Africa where education attainment levels were low and slum environments high. Using the quality of her experience, she made this presumed connection between litter and learning.

How often do principals ask themselves how they know what they know and why they do what they do? How do they change their way of knowing and develop brilliant theories to underscore the real purpose of education, which Dina still thinks is preserving our American democracy? At the same time, how do they develop what Aristotle called the natural abilities of all people, *although his concept of democracy was not quite what our founding fathers had in mind*?

First, they have to discover the source of their own thinking by going to a meeting; you see, when principals don't know something in education—and they want to leave the schoolhouse—they go to a meeting. At this particular meeting, they will learn how the old physical theories of a mechanical universe are no longer relevant and how new physical theories of Quantumland are replacing them. They will be introduced to new ways of perceiving aggregates of people and particles. They will also learn that our schooling processes have produced a great division between people and the physical world, engendering school theories that are out of this world. They will learn how a theory can propel them into a new world of knowing. They will begin to have a realistic theory of organization.

REFLECTION

Reflect on the character Sisyphus, the Greek guy. How many times are you going to push the boulder uphill only to see it roll back down again? And then you repeat the process over and over again? It was Albert Einstein who said that doing the same thing over and over again but expecting a different result is a sign of insanity. Are you exerting a great deal of energy to push something uphill but, time after time, it seems to roll back down? Recall Dina's pick-up litter campaign.

Take a moment to reexamine cause and effect relationships. Then imagine what you are thinking is only the tip of the iceberg. Look deeper, look at patterns, relationships, structure, and unlikely causes. Challenge your mental model that often relies on solutions related to your prior experiences. They may not be relevant. Because it worked in Africa, it may not work in your school. How can you get that boulder to stay on top of the hill and not roll back down again?

It is time to begin to develop a realistic theory of organization. As you begin, you will understand how your theory will propel you into a new world of knowing!

Rule

PROBE THE
MECHANICAL UNIVERSE

It was at a meeting that the keynote speaker sullied Principal Dina Macksy's developing beliefs about education and schooling. It was a big meeting, a national convention of administrators of education held in San Diego. Dina was very glad that it was located there because, as we all know, San Diego has great beaches, and she really liked the beach. She went, not expecting to learn anything new because she had just become a new principal of a small, rural high school and she didn't realize that she didn't know anything.

Her theory on organization resided in the world of classical physics. Like Newton, she believed that her organization worked like a large, mechanical clock. When the clock broke down, all she had to do was look for the part that was not working and fix it; it was mostly the teacher parts that needed the fixing.

Dina's predecessor, who was promoted to the assistant superintendent's office, was kind enough to hand her a list of the teachers who needed fixing. She didn't question why he left them for her to fix; she was still excited about being out of the classroom and no longer a slave to the factory whistle—it was really the bell—that rang every forty-five minutes. She abhorred this bell because just as she felt an intellectual climate warming over the classroom, time was up and she had to spot check the desks of those students who were not yet part of the climate change.

But now she was the leader of her organization. It was her job to keep this great, mechanical clock in working order. She had to make certain each of the parts worked and that all teachers had clean desks. In that way, she would keep her school looking good and in precise working order, making the superintendent, the school board, and the public happy.

Notice that she thought nothing about the students in this process. That's because schooling is about children, but not about making them happy. Principals know it's about children because they make teachers hang posters in their classrooms that affirm that children are this nation's most important resource. Principals remind teachers of this on a daily basis.

What Dina didn't know was that clock keepers were an invention of the Middle Ages, and that school really *was* about making children happy. She didn't know this because her thinking never advanced beyond the Middle Ages and maybe because every time she saw her reflection in the mirror, she saw other, more experienced principals who she wanted to be like as she grew up in principal-land.

Dina was more interested in painting landscapes rather than portraits, trying to be like someone else rather than discovering herself. She was the clock keeper, and as long as she kept the clock in timely order, she kept her job, just like all those other principals. She liked her job, and it made her feel important.

But why didn't she ever ask herself why she began each day thinking of her school as a clock? What embedded beliefs made her think that to fix the school all she had to do was fix the part not working?

If you asked her why she thought that controlling the clock was important, she would have thought reflectively and said something Newtonian like, "That's the way it has always been done. The universe is like a great big clock and the clock is kept running by fixing its parts. When each part does its work, there is balance in the universe. All that there is to know is in the clock. It's our job to preserve its orderly operation."

In her mind she accepted this statement, even though she didn't understand the relationship of the universe to a clock. However, the metaphor suited her purposes and gave her direction, no matter how aimless it appeared.

Now at this point, we need to know something about Aristotle's teleological reasoning. The term *teleological* comes from the Greek word *telos*, which means purpose, end, or goal. If we reasoned in teleological fashion, we would ask ourselves what the purpose was for thinking of a school as a clock.

In addition, once we knew the purpose, would we finally see the alignment problem we were having? That is, if schooling was about children learning how to use critical reflection and analysis to evaluate ideas; about children concerned with the common good and the dignity and rights of others and the values inherent in life, liberty, and the pursuit of happiness; about children who Cousin Michael said should be dreamers—could we continue to view people like the cogs and gears in a machine?

If you're a movie buff like Dina, you might remember the 1936 movie *Modern Times*. In the movie, Charlie Chaplin's character, the Tramp, finds himself working inside a machine—actually he is a part in it. His job is to use his wrench to tighten bolts so that the cogs and gears of the machine move in clock-like tempo and precision.

Dina didn't ask herself if she might be behaving a little like him. Nor did she ask herself if her function as a clock keeper interfered with her vision to carry on education in the Jeffersonian spirit. How could she? She was too busy reacting to events. She didn't realize that *Modern Times* was really now.

When to schedule the fire drill, how to find the student who wrote ungodly references about her mother in a Latin-based language on the bathroom stall, why a certain teacher didn't clean the graffiti off his desks—these questions had to be answered or the school would fall apart. Still, in the deepest recesses of her mind, she knew that something was wrong with the way she perceived school.

Now back to the meeting in San Diego. It was really a big meeting where thousands of principals sat together, suffered the pontifications of a keynote speaker while eyeing the clock, waiting for the hands to strike the appropriate time to escape. The keynote speaker, Ms. Margaret Wheatley,[1] walked onto the stage and began her address to two thousand school administrators. Dina was sitting in the rear of the auditorium, near the door, eyeing the hands on her watch because she thought fifteen minutes was more than enough time to appear respectful.

Ms. Wheatley, in a very small voice, began by stating that we model ourselves and our ideas after a world that no longer exists. She continued her keynote by stating that the ideas that we are stuck with are generations old. Many of them are in need of retirement because they no longer serve to explain the world in which we live. We need only to look to the world of nature to see that this is true. There are new principles of nature being discovered that suggest that we do not always live in a mechanical universe.

She continued by stating that the world does not always run like a timepiece. There are times when events cannot be determined based on linear thinking. There are times when change is abrupt and not predictable. There are times when we cannot break things down to basic components in order to find the cause of the problem.

In one paragraph of her speech, she had shredded apart every belief Dina held about her job as keeper of the clock. But Dina continued to listen to the speaker with rapt attention. Besides, it was raining outside and it wouldn't be pleasant at the beach!

Ms. Wheatley continued her keynote, stating that we are beginning to discover that there are inseparable particles in nature, changing and mating spontaneously. We are beginning to understand parts are wholes and wholes are parts.

Like a shattered piece from a hologram or a single human blood cell, we know that the parts are contained in the whole and the whole is contained in the parts (Wilber, 1985). Each contains the ingredients of the other. Each can change without warning. Although the mechanical universe is static, this new universe is composed of self-organizing systems that are complex, self-inventing, and ever-changing.

As the speaker's voice gained momentum, a pudgy, broad-shouldered principal who looked like the great character actor Sydney Greenstreet (Kasper Gutman) in *The Maltese Falcon*, distracted Dina. He grunted like the men with high testosterone levels do at the gym while lifting in midair nine hundred–pound weights. Dina was making mental contact with the idea of unity, feeling her soul merge with this new unity Ms. Wheatley was teaching her about, and this principal was separating her from it.

She watched him rise out of his seat—Ms. Wheatley had not yet spoken for fifteen minutes—pull up his pants with both hands, straighten his string tie, and mumble, "Jeez Louise, I thought this was an educational conference! What does physics have to do with education?"

Well, maybe he was right, Dina reasoned, but it was still raining outside and the speaker was posing thought-provoking and daunting questions. The departing principal didn't understand that Ms. Wheatley was not giving her audience a physics lesson: she was telling them how organizations work—about their indivisibility.

If the audience could master what she was sharing with them, they could affect democracy, allow students to dream, raise student achievement levels, and save their country from its doomed status as just another Roman Empire wanna-be. And, they could do this without playing the blame game and really look good in front of their superintendents, their school boards, and the public.

The speaker seemed to be talking about a medieval mindset that Dina and many other principals had adopted and failed to question. She was impressing upon principals that they needed to break away from thinking that their job was to tighten cogs and gears so that the school could perform its movements and tasks with clock-like tempo and precision.

Still, Dina could not imagine how one fixed anything without breaking it down to its essential parts and fixing the parts that were broken. Fixing the part fixed the system. Even Aristotle was on her side about that. He taught that everything must and could be broken down to its essential parts until there was only one. Maybe she had misunderstood his teachings. That was possible. Sometimes we only hear what we want to hear—the parts that complement our beliefs.

Back at the beach, the sea gulls fluttered through the air, beckoning Dina to their coastal enclaves, occasionally hovering over the stretch of sand reserved for her. But they were becoming more distant as Ms. Wheatley continued to speak. She went on to say that even the celestial bodies don't work as rationally as we once thought. Things don't happen the way we think they do. Everything is entangled, not separate, not discrete, not acting on its own.

Dina was out of breath with Ms. Wheatley's thoughts. Being able to predict, not being able to predict, entangled, not acting on its own— what was she talking about? We live in a neat and orderly world. We could unlock nature's secrets by slowly peeling away each layer like an onion.

The keynote continued with Ms. Wheatley's framework. She implied that principals are using old ideas to solve new problems. These ideas emerged from the minds of great thinkers who lived centuries ago. Their world was different from ours. Their ideas were useful in discovering the nature of things in the context of their time and their understandings, but today we know that their truths may not be the solutions to the problems of our time.

Could that be why things change but don't really change in schools, Dina asked herself? Was William Blake right when he suggested in his short poem, "Jerusalem," that we don't create new systems, we just become enslaved by another man's?[22] Is that what former school superintendent Larry Cuban (1990) meant when he asked why school reform was always the same?

Educator Richard Gibboney (1994) asked if, as educators, school leaders were looking at the world of human relations in education through a prism that was not entirely applicable to the modern world. When you think about it, Dina thought, schooling hasn't advanced very far using this old prism. If a person from the past century visited the schoolhouse, would he see much that looked different?

Ms. Wheatley continued speaking, telling the audience that sub-atomic particles did not always follow the laws of cause and effect. Dina recalled the story of the breakdown of radium. She remembered the science teacher at her school, Mr. Quintin Waver, telling the students that every sixteen hundred years, one-half of all the radium atoms in the world disappear, but we don't know which radium atoms are going to disintegrate and which radium atoms will not. We can even predict how many atoms in a piece of radium are going to disintegrate in the next hour, but we have no way of knowing which ones are going to disintegrate. There is no physical law that governs this selection. Which atoms decay is purely a matter of chance (Zukav, 1974).[3]

Not being a scientist, Dina was not sure what Mr. Waver was telling her at that time, and she did not know what Ms. Wheatley was telling her at this time. What rose up in her conscious mind was her daily *things to do* list that she carried around on her green clipboard: first period, evaluation of Mrs. Indika Trench; second period, meeting with parents; third period, classroom visits; fourth period, lunch duty; fifth period, special education meeting; sixth period, superintendent's visit.

Dina's secretary, Mrs. Hogarth, had prepared this perfectly planned list but she forgot—or was it Dina who forgot—that in an instant the perfectly planned list becomes entangled with the belligerent parent, Mrs. Otto Rageous, waiting outside her door who objects to her son being suspended because he etched words *everybody uses* on a desk.

"And who's going to supervise him at home?" Mrs. Rageous asks. "I have to work." So there goes Mrs. Indika Trench's evaluation and the dog and pony show she had prepared for the principal's amusement because bantering and jousting with Mrs. Rageous would take the entire period—and the next.

Maybe Ms. Wheatley was right—principals couldn't always predict what was going to happen next and the effect it would have on their daily checklist. She insisted that the way things worked was not always orderly and predictable, as the past three hundred years had led us to believe. Our old lenses could no longer be used for viewing, probing, and understanding, what she termed *this new Quantumland*, where the rules of nature did not always follow the rules of cause and effect.

Dina was fired up by her new zeal yet confused by the vision of this undetermined and uncertain Quantumland. How did one begin to live in a world that lacked order . . . where effect did not always follow cause . . . where predictability was only a possibility . . . where the universe would not reveal its secrets to us without making ourselves part of the equation . . . where wholes were indivisible and could not be defined by individual parts . . . where the whole was more than the sum of its parts. Was objectivity being thrown out the window?

She was captivated by the idea that principals were seeing the world through a lens that no longer had corrective value. Apparently she was the only one seeing this. The more Ms. Wheatley spoke, the sparser the audience became. After the requisite fifteen minutes, educators were moving up the aisle toward the exit signs. They failed to see what the keynote speaker was suggesting: that there was a relationship between this Quantumland and the entangled, messy way in which their schools operated.

This new Quantumland demanded that Dina recant the natural laws she learned. She could no longer predict whether parts would behave a certain way, once she used her wrench to fix them. The idea that she couldn't always blame the part when the system failed—instead having

to review the system in which the part was involved—was a new way
of looking at organizations and a strain on her already overactive mind.

How could she focus on this new thinking when there was the screaming, tempestuous, Mrs. Rageous in her office, who spewed auguries of
foul tidings if the "principal didn't acknowledge that her mind was as
dense as the desk on which her son wrote"?

But as Dina listened to Ms. Wheatley, the synapses kept firing questions. Could it be that organizations broke down repeatedly because
principals concentrated on fixing the parts and ignoring the whole?
Could it be that it wasn't understood how the parts of organizations
worked together to create the whole? Could it be that the whole, not
the parts, should really be the focus of a principal's attention? Could it
be that we would have to stop blaming teachers when something didn't
work and instead look at why a particular teacher's test scores were low
in the context of the school system in which she was situated? Her ideas
were becoming more abstruse by the moment.

Could it also be that Dina brought her biases to the litter challenge
because she perceived the problem through her eyes alone? She looked
at the parts of her school—the students, the teachers, and the trash—
and thought that by fixing these parts, the problem would go away.

Could it be that she might have handled the problem by looking at
the interacting events in the environment that created the trash: Were
there enough trash barrels? Did students know that throwing trash on
the ground gave the custodian, whom they liked, more work? No, to
save time, she told everybody what to do. People don't like to be told
what to do, and those who do may choose to join the Marines.

Dina's beliefs about running an organization were being undermined
by the tectonic plates in her head, rubbing against each other and slowly
erupting into a massive earthquake. She had a headache and was becoming frustrated, almost despondent, with this line of thinking because
she didn't know what she believed. A fearful malaise overtook her as
she raced around the schoolhouse, reacting to situations based on the
limited quality of her own thinking.

Should Dina really concern herself with the integrative nature of
matter? Didn't she really believe that the world and she were separate
entities and that she could discover new ways to treat it by discovering
what knowledge she had before she was born and then throwing down

the life preserver to the flailing arms in the moat? This line of thinking was uncomfortable. She was pouring into her head, not her body, matters she didn't understand. She didn't have a frame on which to hinge these new concepts mentally.

Democracy's greatest strength is its ability to act in unconventional ways. Instead, Dina was fixed into a certain rigid way of thinking—thinking that could not be distinguished from the thinking of other principals who validated her thoughts because they were all thinking the same thoughts about how change is enacted. But, Ms. Wheatley said that yesterday's ideas do not work today. We need to sharpen our minds and design new tools to meet the new world in which we are living. But we must first admit that our ideas and the world in which we live may not always be in alignment with each other.

It was hard to make this admission. Like most principals, when something goes wrong in the system, Dina blamed the behavior of the parts for the dysfunction. If the part is improved, the system will function correctly again. Improving a part can improve the whole.

But was there truth to be found by separating things out? "You risk your skin catching the killers and the juries just turn them loose so that they can come back and shoot at you again," a character says to the hero in the great existential film, *High Noon*. "Why do you do it?"

"It's the whole thing," is the hero's opaque response.

Dina thought more and more about parts and wholes. She knew she was now on the cutting edge of an educational journey, becoming aware of an organizational construct that fused together a whole new way of thinking about how principals and school organizations interacted. But before she could mount a new template on school organization, she had to know more about the old one and its relationship to school governance and democracy if she were to save the Republic. So she told her teachers she was going to another meeting, this time at the city library.

REFLECTION

Have you ever tried to tighten cogs and gears thinking that would restore clock-like precision in the schoolhouse? Do you continue to focus

on the parts without considering the possibilities of interrelated parts
to wholes, unpredictable possibilities, and often undiscovered causes?

Think about your most recent *quick fix*. Did you use *antique frame-
works* to solve your daily challenges? What if you began to think about
it in the context of *Quantumland*, a new conceptual framework? How
would that affect your approach to the seemingly insurmountable challenges that confront you day in and day out?

NOTES

1. The ideas developed in this chapter were from notes that one of the au-
thor transcribed from a keynote address given by Margaret Wheatley at a national principals' conference. The ideas were expanded and interpolated from
Wheatley's book *Leadership and the New Science.*

2. William Blake's poem may be found at http://www.poetry-archive.com/b/
jerusalem.html.

3. Actually the story was told by Zukav in *The Dancing Wu Li Masters*, p. 60.

Rule

EXAMINE HOW YOU KNOW
WHAT YOU KNOW

After the meeting with Ms. Margaret Wheatley, Principal Dina Macksy found herself pacing up and down the corridors of her school, hearing violins playing as she slipped deeper and deeper into a quagmire of despair, the violin music mounting to a crescendo and forcing tears to well up in her eyes.

She was happy being her school's leader; that is, until she heard Ms. Wheatley say she was doing everything wrong—well, maybe not doing things wrong but doing things the way they had always been done. If she wanted to enact real change in her schoolhouse, she would have to listen to how the orchestra played together instead of always hearing the individual players.

Then it happened—she could no longer make even simple decisions, like the rule she enacted that said that students could not eat in the classrooms. She didn't know how to approach problem solving from any perspective other than control, especially when a junior named Jon Deway asked her why she made such stupid rules. "I can't think on an empty stomach," he said.

Well, in the past she would have said: "Because, little kids like you deposit the food on the floor instead of in the wastepaper basket, which gives the teacher and the custodian more work and causes the exterminator to make more trips to school because more than the usual little buggers are creeping into the classrooms. Besides, it's the rule and I'm the rule maker."

Somehow, she didn't feel that response was . . . well, responsible. Kids have growing bodies and those bodies do need fueling at different times during the day; that is, they acquire hunger at different times and she could not predict those times for all those kids.

Anyway, who was she to decree that thou shall not satisfy one's need for nourishment in the classroom? Couldn't she have approached the problem from a different perspective than an omnipotent autocrat?

In a democracy, the people come together, debate, weigh issues, and then make decisions. We believe that each person has the capacity to learn and can act on his or her thinking. So why was she the only one doing the thinking, deciding on the rules and detaching herself from the people upon whom she was putting the rules? Didn't an Italian guy named Niccola Machiavelli do that? Her superintendent, Mr. Mac Avelli, always quoted him. "He who wishes to be obeyed, must know how to command."

Well, it was in her job description that she run the school. Her name was at the top of the chart that read *Chain of Command for the School*. Furthermore, she had an advanced degree that certified she knew more about running an organization than anyone else at her school.

Sometimes the teachers thought they knew better, but they didn't have the advanced degree. The teachers and students working in the processes could not help to work on them because they couldn't see beyond their classrooms, they were just the cogs and gears of the organization, singular parts isolated from the other parts that occasionally needed Dina's wrench to work better.

But she felt disturbed each time she used that wrench. She must have innately known that nothing that she was doing made sense to her feelings about democracy. In a democratic organization, aren't the lines of communication open? Aren't decisions based on cooperative interaction, not somebody ordering you about? Couldn't many minds working together make better decisions than one mind working alone, especially if all those minds had similar goals for their students?

When she first entered the principal's office, she discovered that it didn't work that way. Superintendent Avelli told her what to do. If she said she would like to run his dictates by the teachers, he said that she was being indecisive. For example, one day he pointed out to her in his austere tone that all teachers would have to clock in and out of work. She said that teachers were not factory workers and she was not the manager of the factory.

"Why not ask the teachers," she proposed, "if there were a better way to make certain they were on time? Let's tell the teachers we have a problem and see if they can solve it." She suggested this, even though she wasn't convinced that there was a problem.

The superintendent, she reflected, probably talked to some vendor who convinced him that this time clock, which cost thousands of dollars to install, would make the workplace more efficient.

"Indecisive," he scowled. He wouldn't let her put her democratic beliefs into practice. However, she knew what the teachers were saying. The science teacher, Mr. Quintin Waver, was very emphatic. "Clocking in to work is very demeaning and unprofessional. I will not be treated like a blue-collar worker instead of a college graduate. This is outrageous!"

He was right but Superintendent Avelli was higher up on the *Chain of Command* chart. Didn't he know that the teachers would tell the students about the new clocks? As a result, the students would learn that in a democracy, people do not come together, debate, weigh issues and then make decisions. In fact, like an autocrat, he was taking thinking away from the people.

Dina was the leader of a sham organization because she was the only one who made the important decisions. She was like her superintendent, the part that looked into the machine and adjusted its cogs and gears.

For example, when she decreed that every teacher was a teacher of reading—her teachers had to improve their students' state reading scores—she expected to find in every classroom and lesson plan, even physical education, some indication that teachers were emphasizing reading and vocabulary. She was being democratic because she was allowing teachers—yes, allowing them—to use any method they chose to do the job. She even gave ten minutes at the faculty meeting to discuss how they would do this. Wasn't that being democratic?

Ms. Wheatley had really played with her mind, so she decided to go to another meeting that could perhaps help her to clarify and adapt

Wheatley's thinking to the schoolhouse. The city library was the site for the meeting. The topic of the forum was "Epistemology and the School Principal—Understanding the Sisyphus Dilemma." She wondered what epistemology meant; didn't it have something to do with philosophy, and then the Kasper Gutman thought—what did philosophy have to do with schooling?

As Dina entered the library, she saw an audience of principals surrounding a number of men sitting at a long, large conference table, like the oval one that important people sit at in the Cabinet Room at the White House, the one always shown on the evening news or in pictures on your web browser.

Nametags identified the names and profession of the men at the table. It was a good thing because some of them looked like they had leaped off the library shelves and into their chairs. Some were dressed in attire that appeared antiquated. She wondered if their ideas were as well.

A principal, with deeply etched lines in his long, sad face, was sitting at one end of the oval table. His deep-set eyes had a tired look about them. His nametag revealed him as Mr. Sid Aphus, principal of Corinth High School.

He began speaking as soon as she sat down. "Every time I unfold a new educational plan and got it going," he told the others at the table, "it somehow escapes from my grip, doubling right back on me."

Of course, Dina quickly identified with what Sid said. Remember the trash cans? And after the trash cans, there was the big award her school won—we'll tell you about that later.

"It is exasperating," he continued, sucking in his chest and wetting his lips. "In the long term, I never seem to be able to enact permanent change.

"I want to see the people in the system constantly working on it in order to improve what we are doing but it does not happen. I don't know why . . . maybe it's because I don't trust them to move beyond their own self-interest. But we must all realize that America can't survive unless there is a citizenry who, through knowledge and insight, will know how to continually work for democracy for all of us . . . work for the common good, Jefferson said.

"Schools are instrumental in shaping society toward nobler ends. If America is to survive, we are in need of a citizenry capable of evaluating and analyzing before making decisions that impact our country . . . we have need of a citizenry who have the thinking ability to continue the dreams of our founding fathers."

Sid paused before continuing again. "Sometimes, I feel like I have constructed a view of the change process from pure sophistry because I don't know how to produce such a citizenry. I don't know how to create processes that replicate democracy for students . . . processes that are embedded in the practice of it. I work so hard only to find myself doing the same thing over and over again without ever achieving the results that will maintain American democracy. Our country is as fragmented as our schools. It feels like things are just falling apart and we have no way to stop it."

Sid was lamenting something greater than Dina did when she made the decision that a clean campus would save America. He was asking how we all, as a free people, decide that a clean campus is necessary, and if it is, the processes that are needed to achieve that goal. But Dina was confused.

Ms. Wheatley said that Dina had to look at her school from a different perspective. But Dina didn't know how to find meaning in some of the words she heard used—process, democracy, control, macro and micro worlds, subatomic particles, classical and quantum mechanics, parts and wholes.

She didn't know how to integrate them into the whole to affect positive and permanent change, bringing together our nation and furthering its theme of democracy. She just wished she was smarter, and that her first-grade teacher, Miss Levi Ethan, hadn't emphasized phonics over meaning.

"I want to enact change that has positive, long term effects," Sid maintained. "Why can't I do this? Could it be that this isn't possible because of the way in which I run my school? But I don't know any other process that is as expedient and efficient than separating the organization into smaller parts and making those parts work up to their potential through mechanisms of control.

"People have to be told what to do or they don't do it. I told my students what to do when I was a teacher and now I tell the teachers what to do. Maybe if I put my beliefs about leadership on the table, I can understand why I think that I have to lead by ordering people about. It's not democratic." His head oscillated in one direction and then the other as he spoke, his voice falling an octave.

"Raise your hands," he said, turning to the audience of principals, "if your school has been recognized at one time as an outstanding school."

Dina raised her hand. Her school had won national recognition as an outstanding school during her third year as principal. But as Sid indicated about change, the changes she made didn't last for long. Like the trash can imbroglio, what initially looked like it would work didn't because the part of the system she fixed had little relational value to the whole. That is, the parts in the system weren't talking to each other.

"Then you know what I'm talking about." He looked at Dina when he said that. "No matter how we lead the change process, problems always pop up here and there. After we solve one problem, another comes forth. Like the rest of you, I've read the educational textbooks and literature. I attended all the relevant workshops about principals making a difference. But, everything that I have learned is separate and isolated from everything else that I have learned. And the talk is always about how to improve the parts in the system.

"But there is no unifying thought that looks at how the parts in the system relate to the other parts and how all the parts are related to the whole system. That is, we don't know how to look at the interconnectivity in the system and examine the results it is producing. We have no single unifying theory of governance in the schoolhouse and because we don't, we constantly go on rock climbing expeditions."

"You are looking for a single theory that would unify the entire physical world . . . a theory of everything," mumbled a man with white hair that looked like it had just been shocked through and through by a passing electromagnetic field. His voice sprang up from under the table where he was said to be doing a mind experiment. "I know exactly what you mean. I couldn't find it either."

"That's exactly what I'm looking for in order for democracy to survive," Sid said enthusiastically. "I need a theory of everything that unites all these disparate, educational ideas. You see, democracy cannot survive without an intelligent electorate, and school governance has outdated theories on how to produce this. Maybe I have to look outside of education for the answers I am seeking. There is so much missing in my thinking."

The library became silent until a man with a British accent said, "There is indeed so much missing in your thinking, Principal Sid Aphus." His nametag identified him as Mr. John Locke, philosopher (Locke, 1947).

"It's your mind . . . you are not its true owner," he said. "You have borrowed your thinking from others without full knowledge that you have done so and without understanding the assumptions that underscore the thinking you have unknowingly allowed others to pour into you. In other words, Principal Sid Aphus, you have not examined how you know what you know."

Sid sat there stone-faced. Dina wondered if he felt as mindless as she did.

Wait a minute, she thought. Nobody was in her head but her. The solution to the trash problem was her own, wasn't it. Or was it? She based the solution on control. Why? Nah, her ideas were her own—as limiting as they were. But she had to admit that her leadership style was a result of the *that's the way it always has been done* syndrome. So maybe her ideas were not her own, she ruminated, and if they were borrowed, she needed to understand who the loaners were and the underlying assumptions of these borrowed ideas.

Newton (White, 1997) had talked about the mechanical universe in which we live. If the universe was mechanical, like a clock, did Dina view human beings as people who could be controlled—told what to do—programmed? Did she mass people together in her mind, arrange them in time and space, and understand them as she would the parts in a machine? She wondered who had poured this idea into her head.

"Perhaps your ideas come from me," a man in a white toga said. He was reading her thoughts and she wasn't even sitting at the table. That was scary. His nametag identified him as Mr. Democritus of Abdera, philosopher (Tarnas, 1991)—one name was all he needed—just like modern-day rappers.

"So few people acknowledge me anymore or even know who I am," he said, using his fingers to brush off the thick layer of dust covering the whole of his toga. "I put forth the idea that everything in nature is composed of material particles that are disconnected, invisible, and irreducible. I called these particles *atomos*.

"When a problem in the system confronts you, you look for the part in the system that is in need of repair. You disconnect the part from the system and focus on fixing it in isolation of all the other parts, thinking that if you fix the part, you fix the whole.

"Can you view the world of social relations from a physical point of view? Can you atomize people? I don't know . . . don't live in your world. But I can enlighten you about the men who stood upon my shoulders. However, allow them to speak for themselves because I am beginning to lose my voice." He was coughing as he said this; it must have been the cloud of dust in which he was now enveloped.

"Yes, allow me to elaborate." The nametag read Monsieur Rene Descartes, mathematician and philosopher (Dicker, 1993). "Nature can best be understood in the language of mathematics once you realize that nature is without feeling but extremely complex. To understand it, you must understand the mathematical laws that explain the infinite number of particles, which mechanically collide, and aggregate. These particles do not move in an utterly random fashion but obey those fundamental laws imposed on them by God. Everything in the physical world can be understood through its divisibility and logical order."

"Why mathematics?" Sid asked. Dina was just as puzzled. How can numerical processes explain anything about the real world? How can math save democracy?

"There is no uncertainty in numbers," Monsieur Descartes explained, "only truth. Nature is a great machine ruled by mathematical principles. The machine creates the laws for all matter in this universe. Once we find the secrets of how individual parts of the machine operate, we can control and manipulate it. You see, there is a natural order in nature that is simple, predictable, and universal and can be broken down to its inalterable essence."

So maybe it was Democritus and Descartes who poured into Dina's head the idea that schools and the people who populate them are like machines that could be controlled. It was a steely theory—soulless—but totally objective, like Mr. Spock, the Vulcan officer on the starship *Enterprise* who had divorced himself from feelings in order to remain objective instead of pouring himself in the hazy world of human relationships. Plato did that too, removed emotions from pure thought—maybe Plato was really a Vulcan?

"Thank you, Monsieur Descartes," said Mr. Isaac Newton, scientist, nodding his head in agreement and addressing the audience of principals (White, 1997). "You see, I gave a picture of a mechanical universe that operates like a giant clock, each part of the clock doing its part to make the whole work. The clock functions independent of perceptions, assumptions, and ideas about the universe. It doesn't care what we think because its laws are like mathematics . . . they are there whether humans exist or not.

"I chuckle when I think of that little fellow in the movie *Modern Times* . . . Charlie Chaplin . . . greasing the parts of the machine to keep it in working order. God doesn't have to do that. It's all so natural. The laws of mathematics make it so.

"I see this perplexed look on your face Principal Aphus. Perhaps the knowledge I provided you is old learning that needs to be adapted to your world and examined in the light of new discoveries in physical laws?"

"Yes, you must update yourself, Newton," mumbled the guy with the shocked hair. He was now sitting upright on a chair at the table. His nametag identified him as Mr. Albert Einstein, scientist (Isaacson, 2007). "By just observing the experiment, we put ourselves in it and that changes it. Everything has to be looked at relative to everything else. Your view, Newton, was too rigid and deterministic. Just by looking up at the stars, you influenced what you were seeing."

"I hardly think the ideas of scientists can be relevant to me as an educator," Sid said in a fit of pique.

Dina thought he was behaving like Kasper Gutman, reluctant to continue learning how to learn. And then in kicked the *eureka factor*! Dina realized what Sid didn't understand.

You see, when Sid looks at his school, she reasoned, he sees a system that is not always controllable, even though he imposes control upon it, forcing events to happen, holding his breath, hoping they will happen as he has planned, that cause will follow effect as Newton and others said it would.

But when Sid looks up to the sky, he sees a balanced system where all things move uniformly and there is eternal regularity and continuity. In the cosmos, he sees predictability. He sees a Great Creator who gave us an elegant universe where all known phenomena of celestial and terrestrial mechanics are united under one set of physical laws.

We could live in this perfect, mechanical, terrestrial world, Sid thinks, if we just knew how to unlock its scientific secrets. Why couldn't a school work more like the cosmos, he asks himself? Perhaps because the physical and social worlds contained different relational values between the parts themselves and the parts and the whole.

Newton interrupted her new thoughts. "I was able to unlock the mysteries of the universe systematically by understanding each part, but the key to the lock always has to be turned . . . objectively. If we approach a problem rationally, rational solutions will follow. As in the schools you lead, principals can understand and work with their systems by breaking them down into discrete parts and understanding and knowing the state of each part."

"Well, that is certainly what I have been doing, Mr. Newton," reflected Sid. "But your theory doesn't always work . . . maybe that's because people aren't machines even if I treat them as if they were."

These great men had given school leaders many approaches through which they could look at school problems, Dina reflected. Do we approach the problem in the same way Plato would have, removing ourselves from it, viewing it from a distance, knowing that we know better than others? After all, our special certification says we do.

Do we approach the problem, as John Locke would have: follow what is written on our inner white sheet of paper—the tabula rasa theory that both he and Aristotle favored—and do what has always been done?

Do we approach the problem as Newton would have—merely unlock the secrets of the universe one by one because all things in nature are already known—or like Democritus—keep breaking the problem down until the indivisible piece causing the problem is found?

It seems we had been using all these approaches in school governance with little, permanent effect.

Yes, we change things, Dina continued thinking, but never contemplate the change we are hoping to achieve, or where the knowledge of the change derived. Ah! That's what epistemology means—knowing how we know what we know, the nature of knowing. It's almost as if we have taken reason away from people so that they could be kept in their place.

Machiavelli, our first political scientist, was an expert at doing this, as was the Catholic Church. That's why Martin Luther got in trouble with the pope. He wanted all people to be able to read and interpret the Bible for themselves, and the pope didn't believe in synergetic thought. He wanted to keep people in their place.

As Dina was thinking democratic thoughts, Mr. Werner Heisenberg, whose nametag said he was a quantum mechanic, appeared to be engaged in verbal sparring with Mr. Albert Einstein.

"While I concur that it is all relative, Mr. Einstein," he argued, "you must agree that nature can't always be pinned down. There are so many parts looking for connections. Some things are not so clear-cut, with cause always following effect in a rationale fashion. What I mean is that everything cannot be planned in advance, carefully, precisely and in great detail. We don't always know how A plus B equals C" (Wheatley, 1992).

"Rubbish!" balked Mr. Einstein, "God does not play dice with the universe. All results are a product of cause and effect working in a neat and orderly fashion. Nothing happens by chance."

"But can everything be planned in such a cause-and-effect fashion when we are dealing with people?" asked Sid, looking a bit bewildered. "What I am hearing is that Mr. Einstein's view on how we understand natural systems is not as rigid and deterministic as Mr. Newton's, but less flexible than the quantum mechanics of Mr. Heisenberg, who proposes that we can't always keep tabs on all things.

"In social systems, I would think that the latter is particularly true. Both Mr. Einstein and Mr. Heisenberg agree that, in order to understand how systems work, we have to put ourselves in the equation and understand its interconnecting nature. Nothing operates in isolation of something else and when we remove something from the system—isolate it—I would guess we change the system. I need to know more about parts theory in order to know if the ideas that have been poured into my head from Democritus, Descartes, Newton, and all the others really do have application in school governance."

Do theories about the operation of the physical world have relevance in school governance and the perpetuation of democracy? The thought lingered with Dina as the speakers in the library continued their dialogue.

REFLECTION

Are you looking for a single theory that would unify the entire physical world—a theory about everything? Or are you willing to acknowledge that you cannot keep tabs on all things, and sometimes the solutions cannot be pinned down?

When you think about how you know what you know, which of the great thinkers who participated in the debate would support your beliefs? Is it Wheatley, Locke, Newton, Democritus, Descartes, Einstein, or Heisenberg?

Rule

MODIFY THE THEORY OF
THE MECHANICAL UNIVERSE

The dialogue at the library meeting continues. "My experience has been that we fix problems by assigning blame . . . the assumption being that if I point the finger at the right target, the system will be saved," said Principal Sid Aphus.

"Why do I think this? Is it because of eons of thought about the way things work? Unlike you, Mr. Einstein, I have never thought much about my role as relationship builder. I am like Mr. Newton, a divine mechanic whose job is to set operations into motion and create an environment in which I observe. When something goes wrong I fix it."

"Let me explain something to you, Principal Sid Aphus," a man at the table called out. "I don't have the celebrity like the men from whom we have just heard. . . . I am a bit more contemporary . . . the name is Seymour Sarason, professor of psychology at Yale University . . . but we must see how their thinking is linked to ours in order to know ourselves better (Sarason, 1990).

"If you don't establish this linkage, you won't see a complete picture when attempting change, perhaps because you isolate yourself from the problem when you are really in the problem. Mr. Einstein made earlier reference to this. You must know yourself in order to find relational value with others."

As he spoke, Principal Dina Mackey began to put the words and sentences she had been hearing together. How many of us principals realize how our theories of organization—those of us who have more than an "everybody does it this way prescription" for running our organization—are a product of past thinking, thinking that was contrived in a different time and context than ours? Mr. Democritus gave us the idea that everything in nature was composed of material particles that were disconnected, invisible, and irreducible.

Then along came Mr. Descartes who proposed that nature could be better understood by breaking it up into the smallest possible fractions. And Mr. Newton took his celestial thinking about the universe and gave us terrestrials a worldview that was reductionist, deterministic, fixed, and mechanical. That is, since the machine was already working, all we had to do was find out how each part worked in an objective and reductionist fashion.

Mr. Einstein suggested that the complete picture of the machine could only be understood by our relative position to it; that is, we are a part in the experiment. But things were not as objective as Mr. Newton suggested, and we could not detach ourselves from what we were observing.

So, she concluded, it is from all these great thinkers that we received a mechanistic paradigm of the classroom. We learned how to arrange and control time and space, separate teaching from learning, and reduce learning to an individual rather than a collective experience. Of course, others came along later in time who continued moving these concepts along. She guessed she would probably be introduced to them later.

Mr. Sarason interrupted her thinking, even though she felt he was in her thinking. "To demonstrate how these theories worked, I need a volunteer from the audience. Would one principal in the audience volunteer and tell us about their first three years as principal?"

Pick me, pick me, Dina chanted to herself as she sprang to her feet. "Sure. I remember it so well, Mr. Sarason," she began. "It was my first day as the new principal. I was happy. I recall waking up in the morning and sitting at the edge of the bed with this exhilarating feeling of being the one in control of my school. Great things for kids were going to happen now that I was at the helm.

"With great joy, I went to work. I walked around. It was six o'clock and the campus was empty except for Dog, a tricolored beagle who could be found sleeping each morning at the schoolhouse gate waiting for the scents from the cafeteria to awaken him. I walked around surveying my new territory . . . it was larger than the last rectangular piece of leased property in which I operated in as a teacher.

"Seven o'clock came. I greeted the teachers, staff, and students as they walked up the ramp to the front gate. They returned my greeting with congratulations and smiles. It felt good to be principal. Another hour passed. I pinched myself. I was still the principal. I was still walking around. I was still smiling.

"The next day something terrible happened. The greetings and smiles had dissipated. Now I was supposed to do something that would create a positive change for all those people who came to my school. After all, they depended on me to make the world a better place for them and preserve democracy.

"The exhilarating feeling morphed to anxiety. Alone, standing in the middle of the campus, I was assailed by a shocking question. How do I go about making all these people do what I wanted them to do . . . if I ever found out what it was I wanted them to do?

"Common sense and all those administrative courses I had taken reminded me that the first thing a new principal does, Mr. Sarason, is find out what the school is all about. I asked anybody I saw what they thought the purpose of schooling was. They gave me all kinds of answers but not one connected to my belief that schools should be about maintaining our democracy.

"So then I changed the question and asked a new one. What did this school want to be when it grew up? What did this school expect of me?

"I asked teachers. The more confident ones said that I should just leave them alone and do my job. Not helpful. Wasn't my job connected to theirs?

"I asked students . . . just leave us alone and show up at our football games. No help there. I asked a school board member whom I saw at Costco. 'Don't hassle the teachers and students like the last principal did.' Still no help. How could a principal affect change if people just wanted to be left alone?

"I asked the school board president what he wanted for the high school. 'We want all things for our students,' he said. His answer reminded me of all the answers I received when I asked about the purpose for sending kids to school.

"I asked Superintendent Mac Avelli. He said, 'You heard what the school board president said. He wants all things for students. So give it to him. Think of a plan which does all things for all students.' His tongue was not stuck in his cheek when he said this . . . nor did I walk on water . . . barely even treaded it.

"So I fell back on my experience as a teacher and my assumptions about the classroom, elevated to the principal level. I was the divine mechanic, in control of this universe, and each person had to do his or her part to affect positive change. In addition, when you are in control but don't have a prescription for change, head for the medicine cabinet because without a prescription you lose control. Inside the medicine cabinet are a hundred and one prescriptions for what ails schools."

She stopped for a moment, collecting her thoughts, and then continued. "Your school has a reading problem . . . try a phonics program. If phonics doesn't agree with your philosophy of how students increase their reading scores, try the whole language pill. Scores in math are low. The new math may still work. Have a discipline problem and believe that sparing the rod spoils the child? Implement corporal punishment. Don't want to produce bruises on the bottom? Try assertive discipline. Distribute the prescription in the prescribed doses and you solve your problems. One size fits all.

"As a teacher, Mr. Sarason, I experienced new principals introducing new programs. Their programs were euphemistically referred to as the *principal's new idea*. The principal opened her medicine cabinet of wonder drugs that she had collected from workshops. She ran her finger under the titles typed onto the plastic containers. Her finger stopped its lateral movement when it came to the label she knew was right for her school, her teachers, and her students.

"The *principal's new idea* became a directive to the faculty. Implementation meant the staff would stay after school and attend workshops that would instruct each of us on how to use the prescription. When we returned to our classrooms, the principal traversed his universe, making certain each part in his system was doing its part.

MODIFY THE THEORY OF THE MECHANICAL UNIVERSE 49

"Some teachers liked the new pills they were distributing. Most did not. They saw no homologous relationship between the prescriptions they utilized in their classrooms and the principal's antidote for what he considered the school illness. The principal didn't realize that when pills are ingested, it somehow affects the *me-me* and *me-we* relationship of the entire school community.

"The teachers also saw that as a result of applying the principal's new idea, other problems were occurring in their classrooms and spilling out into the principal's office. It was the snake under the carpet rearing parts of its undulating body here and there and everywhere throughout the school.

"One problem created another. It didn't matter. We all knew that the expiration date on the prescription would elapse or the principal would find a new job. It always seemed to me that principals liked climbing up career ladders . . . when they were not climbing rocks. We would then return the pills to their plastic containers and place them alongside the other plastic containers in our desk drawers.

"I must admit I was skeptical about looking through the medicine cabinet, but that's what principals did. There were so many education companies hawking their product. I knew that by using common sense, I could find the right prescription that would make my school better."

"But it sounds like you were guessing at the problems," responded Mr. Sarason.

"I would never have guessed at problems to understand the cosmos," added Mr. Newton.

"Without theory, we just copy," said a new voice, a Mr. Deming, whose name tag identified him as a physicist/organizational theorist.

"I thought I knew what the problems were," Dina continued. "I made a list of all the parts in my school system that needed fixing. I didn't think about the why of it all. I mean, when you see a problem, you react . . . you fix it.

"The teachers equated soporific teaching with pedagogy, creating listless listeners in the classroom. Kids who don't listen find other things to do, which augmented discipline problems. In addition, the scores on state tests, announced in the local newspapers each spring, were a constant source of embarrassment. And our student bathrooms were always unclean . . . and there was trash on the campus. I could go on and on with the problems confronting my school.

"But then I found the elixir, Mr. Sarason. It was a prescription for developing comprehensive schools to which I turned. The label stated that it could cure all our problems. It had treated successfully all sorts of problems in many schools in the nation. It could work in my school as well. I removed the prescription from the shelf, studied the instructions, declaring to the faculty that this will cure us of our school problems.

"I was once again like a teacher shaking the rattle, content with the vigorous action of a new program I was going to implement in my classroom. I was in charge and would tell . . . yes tell . . . each person how to do his part in making the system better. I never once thought that any teacher would not take the prescription and give the pills to their students."

And the prescription worked. Dina began to see results. She monitored each phase of her planning and when somebody took a detour, she called that person into her office. She played the blame game. Dina reminded the guilty person that each one of them in the system had to do his or her part for the whole system to improve. When the parts work, the system works.

"Within three years of implementing my plan," she continued, "my school was recognized as one of 272 exemplary schools in the nation. Why? I thought it was because I had sedulously read the label on the plastic container, meticulously followed its directions.

"I was invited to the White House for the school's achievement. In a Rose Garden ceremony, the secretary of education said to the 272 proud principals, 'Each of your schools had good leadership, strong principals, high standards and expectations, and had effectively addressed problems.'

"The president of the United States stepped out through the portico doors of the White House and congratulated us. A documentary film was made about our school's efforts. Newspapers and magazines lauded our achievements.

"When I arrived back in my office, I found an avalanche of congratulatory letters on my desk from school administrators, business leaders, and even the governor of the state.

"There were the requests from principals of other schools and writers of books who wanted to know the one thing my school did that led to our success . . . send more information concerning your program for teachers analyzing standardized test scores with students . . . we would like a copy of your promotion retention policies . . . we are looking for ways to augment the team concept.

"Like the barker in a circus sideshow, they all echoed the same call . . . tell us how you did it. Tell us, tell us, and tell us so we can apply what you did to our system. Tell us and we will use your template to create a great school.

"Well, while it felt good to read all these letters, there was something troubling about it all, Mr. Sarason. And it was the last letter I read that had me doubting myself and left an indelible malaise within me. It was from a principal in New Jersey.

"He wrote that one attribute of an excellent school is that of constant self-analysis in order to continually improve. Continuous improvement means understanding the nature of the constant interaction of the people and events of an organization. It seems that everything depends on everything else to function well. A principal has to have a good sense of who she is to understand it all. She must really know her school community. She has to be more of an Einstein with a little Heisenberg thrown in than a Newton in the way she perceives the world. However, by knowing this, she is able to guide all her shareholders to the same page. When you have done an excellent job, everybody feels it."

Dina paused, then continued almost in a whisper, "But everybody didn't feel it. It was then that I knew something was wrong. The wrongness jumped out at me. The fact was I had no team, didn't know my teachers, and had no theory that I could articulate about the change process other than that I am in charge.

"I had won the educational lottery but was still poor. I looked into myself and felt the joy of being the best. I looked outside myself and was repelled by its solo effort. I knew the success would not last. It couldn't. How can something last when you are the only one playing the game?"

"That is certainly true," said Mr. Sarason (Sarason, 1990). "Without a more complete picture of who you are and why you think the way you do, you wind up dictating change. Ask yourself who you are and why you believe what you believe. If you can do this, you will find out how incomplete your mental image is of yourself and the change process. Everything you do is dependent upon your construction of the world."

"Who you are and what you think," explained Ms. Margaret Wheatley (Wheatley, 1992), who had only just seated herself at the table, "your personal philosophies, do not belong to you but to those who long ago informed your thinking. You sometimes adapt belief systems from another time to yours. Perhaps that is why, as educators, you do the same things over and over again."

Dina always believed that she was in control of her world. She was like a god who operated a part of the universe. She believed Mr. Newton gave her that idea. She could fix the school with the right plan as long as she controlled the system.

If she approached a problem rationally, rational solutions would result. But she was beginning to understand what Mr. Einstein was saying. All people and events in an organization influence one another. We have to understand these influences or the problems just continue as they did—and still do at her school. She really didn't solve any problems because of the limited relationship she saw between the system and herself.

"You have to begin by understanding the array of relationships, the network of interrelated parts, and how they work together to achieve goals," said Mr. Sarason. "This time around," he told the principals, "when something goes wrong, instead of blaming a person, look at the system to see if there is a flaw in the design.

"Put yourself in the equation. Maybe the flaw is with the process that has been set in motion and not the people working in the process."

Was there a flaw in Newton's thinking, Dina asked herself? Maybe she needed to introduce herself to herself so that *she* could know *herself* with a great deal more perception and understanding. Mr. Sarason had stated that we have an incomplete picture of ourselves. Perhaps it was time to complete the picture.

REFLECTION

When a problem occurs in the schoolhouse, do you run to the medicine cabinet and look for the right prescription bottle that will fix it? Do you look out the window to cast blame or into the mirror? Think of your early years as principal. How many prescriptions did you try? Are you still looking for the right prescription to subdue the pain? Were you successful when you treated the illness as a cause rather than a symptom? Did you explore ways in which you focused on the process more than the illness?

Perhaps most of us are still living in the context of a mechanical universe. Maybe we believe that everything depends on us—the super-principal approach!

Rule

KNOW THYSELF

At the meeting in San Diego, Ms. Margaret Wheatley had introduced Principal Dina Macksy to changes in the microworld of particles, but she continued living in the macroworld of people. Dina couldn't make sense of how all those atoms floating around in Quantumland connected to her becoming a democratic leader in her schoolhouse, although she was beginning to give more thought to what the speakers at the library said about living in a mechanical world.

Still, she felt again like Principal Sid Aphus, going nowhere and doing nothing to model how a democratic organization could affect positive change for the Republic. She continued obeying the commands of Superintendent Mac Avelli.

She bellowed them out to the Avelli in a swift and decisive fashion so that Avelli did not rate her as indecisive on her annual review. But after listening to the speakers at the forum and now understanding that she had to unload eons of Western thinking that was no longer useful in viewing the world in which she now lived, she felt her despair lifting.

You see, she had a plan, a thoughtful plan. All she had to do was to know herself and the people who had influenced her worldview with a lot more depth. If she could do this, she could share the information with Superintendent Avelli who would then also understand the why of it all.

Dina felt like she was about to experience an incarnation, performing a miraculous intervention into school leadership, the effect of which was to liberate all administrators from the cold, steeled, and detached world of Newtonian thought.

First, she would discover the identity of all the other thinkers who had poured their thoughts into her head, forcing her neurotransmitters to send faulty messages about the way in which schools should be structured and governed. Then she would seek understanding about how she had applied their thinking into her practice.

Dina felt like a vacuum cleaner ready to suck from her three pounds of protoplasm thoughts that were no longer useful in building a democratic school. "Knowing where you are coming from determines what you do and develops the frame upon which a person views the world," Mr. Sarason had said. "What people choose to do and, in particular, the competencies they choose to develop, depend very much on their self-image" (Sarason, 1990).

Einstein added, "A person who reads only newspapers and at best books of contemporary authors looks to me like an extremely near-sighted person who scorns eyeglasses. He is completely dependent on the prejudices and fashions of his times, since he never gets to see or hear anything else. And what a person thinks on his own without being stimulated by the thoughts and experiences of other people is even in the best case rather paltry and monotonous" (Einstein, 1954, p. 64).

Dina had stayed current on the change process, paid attention to the prescriptions of the hawkers and university types—no offense again, Cousin Michael—but never asked them why they thought their cures were the best for saving her school. She just figured they must know what they were doing because they were smarter than she was and, besides, other schools were doing what they were doing.

So, she had to be less paltry and monotonous and think about why she thought that schools should practice democracy. Why did she think that the arrangement of the school into separate classrooms populated by children who were age graded and staffed by teachers whose job was to treat all their students as if they were the same was the best setting in which to educate Jefferson's common man?

Why were so many deficient students or dropouts produced as a result of this arrangement? Why did educators think that demanding that kids be quiet created a more meaningful school experience? Why did she think that, unless schools were modeled on democracy, students could not be taught that which Cousin Michael referenced—learning how to learn?

Was democracy about bringing people together or separating them? Why was she suddenly feeling as if the schools were not democratic because those in power wanted to make sure that they remained in power?

You could do that by separating people into smaller groups, she reflected. "Divide et impera," Julius Caesar is thought to have said. "Divide and conquer." Was there a conspiracy going on that said the common man had to remain common and in his place. Was the arrangement of the furniture in the classroom was part of that conspiracy? Aristotle thought people should be put in their place. Look what happened to him and the polis.

Dina still felt strongly that the pursuit of knowledge was accomplished via the deep perception that comes from engaging in the transcendent thought that Plato contemplated. But she was now beginning to also think that who she was and what she did could not be separated from the deep perception lurking in the darkness somewhere out there in never-never land.

She had no idea how to find it. That is, she did not know how to separate truth from experience, so go ahead, call her the "E" word. Yes, she was becoming an EMPIRICIST, putting herself in the equation, throwing objectivity and Plato to the wind, her idol crumbling before her.

The road before her was murky. So, she returned to the library, ambulating up and down the rows of the bookshelves in various rooms. It seemed kind of out of date to go to the library when she could have Goggled the answers she was seeking.

She could have also used Sparks Notes—it could have easily been Cliff's—but you see that's what leaders always seem to do, shake rattles for momentum and look for the swift and decisive answers to their questions. She wanted to meet firsthand the people who had influenced her thinking. She had met some at the forum and that was a good start, but it was only a beginning.

Anyway, for now Dina wasn't making the quantum leap between what they said and her school practices. She, as yet, had little to hinge their thoughts to in her mind because as the vacuum cleaner sucked out an old thought, she had little if any frames of reference on which to hang the new. *But is that what she really wanted the sucking machine to do? Didn't she just want to redefine or perhaps modify the old with the new?*

Besides, the thinkers sitting on the shelves seemed so alone, the pristine pages of their tomes showing few signs of being leafed and fingered. So, she told her teachers that she was going to another meeting, and through the rumor mill she found out that they thought she was going to too many meetings. She also heard that they were happy when she left the building because she wouldn't be in their classrooms judging them. It was a win-win situation for everyone.

The first question she posed to the people sitting on the shelves was this: *Why, as a principal, did she think that solving problems was a piecemeal event?* Why did she approach problem solving from a parts perspective? Why did principals enact change piece by piece, step by step?

The science teacher, Mr. Quintin Waver, who became tempestuous when Superintendent Avalli asked that he sign in using a time clock, once stated that there were too many moving parts in education for them all to move together. Was he right?

She was hoping that the shelf dwellers would call out their explanations from the library's education stacks but that initially didn't happen. Instead, a Prussian named Max Weber fell from the stacks in the sociology section.

"I introduced what you call bureaucracy in order to make the workplace objective," he declared. "You see, in my day, to be hired you had to know somebody and how can you objectively evaluate a crony or in-law? My idea was to technically rationalize the workplace by placing in authority those who had knowledge of it, side stepping the favoritism issues. I established order in the workplace (*just like Descartes and Newton had done in the cosmos, Dina thought*) by creating a division of labor based on knowledge and skill.

"All workers from the top to the bottom followed the same rules and regulations, and supervisors rated their job performance objectively. This labor division meant that problems could be traced to the source. (*Democritus and his atomos theory were at work here.*)

"In the factories, the product was broken down into smaller parts and each worker worked on doing his part to create the final product. (*Democritus again.*) Those who knew best how to manage became managers.

Because leadership was objectified and based on knowledge, *only a chosen few should lead. (Plato and Aristotle would have applauded this.)* Managers were given legitimate authority over the workers. Leadership was not about power but authority.

"It is important that workers know who their boss is.

"For example, in the school that has a template similar to the one I put over factories, each teacher should always respect the chain of command; that is, as principal, you receive orders from your superintendent and you give them to the teachers who then give them to the students. People should give orders only to their own subordinates and receive orders only through their own immediate superior.

"In this way, the superintendent can be sure that directives arrive where they are meant to go, and knows where responsibilities lie. The chain of command must be respected for the organization to function with efficiency. It is management's job to make sure the worker does as he is told" (Ouchi, 1981; Weber, 1968).

Superintendent Avelli believed this, Dina told herself. He installed the time clocks. I created procedures for litter collections. We believed that we knew what was best for the school to work, *but we were not Plato.*

"And I analyzed the task of each worker in order to increase his capacity to produce," interjected an American mechanical engineer named Frederick Winslow Taylor (Taylor, 1915).

She was now wandering the shelves of the engineering library, perplexed by the connections she was beginning to see between the factory and school. Superintendent Avelli gives her a directive and expects that she will deliver it to the teachers. But what results from that directive depends on how it is heard and interpreted and the conversations people have about it. People in organizations don't leave their ability to think and reason at the door.

She wondered if Mr. Weber had thought about how individual worker interactions affected the entire workings of the workplace when he created his template for organizations. She knew Mr. Taylor had not.

"Human beings can be physiologically programmed to be efficient machines," Taylor continued to say. "I task analyzed the motions of workers performing their assigned tasks, studying the time it took them to accomplish it. I was able to show them how to do the job . . . tightening up their individual processes . . . without increasing fatigue."

As a result of his work, analyzing each part of the specific task, he was able to ascertain how to get the most production from the workers. Methods for getting the job done were standardized, and all workers did work in the way they are taught.

It sounded like Dina had used this concept called technical rationality when she *Hunterized* (Hunter, 2004) the teachers at her school. If a teacher she was evaluating didn't include the magic words that would produce great learners in her lesson plan, words like objectives, anticipatory set, guided practice, input, checking for understanding, modeling, closure, that teacher was not being technically rational and was doomed.

One has to ask, Dina rued, how in these closely monitored, disciplined, structured, standardized, and controlled environments minds that are not exercised could keep freedom from crashing down on itself?[1]

Of course there were positive reasons to Taylorize the workplace. Once upon a time in America, there were a multitude of people called craftsmen who produced a total product from start to finish. But, with a growing population, supply no longer met demand. Unskilled people looking for jobs in the new factories and immigrants who were flooding American shores and could not speak English needed only to be shaped into a Taylorized process in a Weber workplace in order to produce what America needed.

That is, people who couldn't read, write, or speak English could be taught how to work on a part of a product—rote learning. All they had to do was see, do, and constantly replicate a repetitive action, as Dina's first-grade teacher had done. She had the class read the word list and recite their math tables over and over again while in their rows of assigned seats.

The job of work didn't have to make sense to the worker. Many workers, each working on a specific part of a product, doing the same thing over and over again, in a set amount of time, increased American production. The immigrants and newcomers from the farms flocking to the cities received wages they might never have received in their native land. This was good. They didn't have to know anything, just fit in a particular slot.

Weber and Taylor tried to be totally objective in arranging the workplace. Breaking things down into parts meant that the workplace would be neat and orderly and each worker would know his or her job. When a part was deficient, it was easy to assign the blame. It was management's job to make sure the worker did as he or she was told.

Just as Newton thought that the universe could be explained as a great universal clock, scientific managers like Weber and Taylor took the processes they wanted to understand apart, explained the behavior of the part, and aggregated their explanation of the part into an understanding of the whole system.

If the system didn't work, the part was at fault. And, what is important here is that the part was to blame because no one had the imagination to ask how the deficient part related to other parts or the system as a whole. It was like Mr. Waver said, maybe there were too many parts or perhaps too little thinking.

When a teacher is not producing the test results that will make the school look good, the teacher, the part, is blamed. She has not done her part and that's why the system is producing low scores. And, because teachers are not doing what they were told to do by their supervisors, it must mean low test scores nationally are the product of poor teaching. So the problem can only be fixed by raising teacher certification requirements.

If that doesn't work, point fingers at the universities for their failure to produce quality teachers who will augment test scores. If that doesn't work, point fingers at a new target—how about principals? They are going to too many meetings and not doing more to *Taylorize* the teachers in their schools, even though Taylor was updated with Hunter. Take a part of a system, assign it blame, aggregate the behavior of the part to explain the behavior of the whole system, and bingo, what do we have? Reform over and over again.

Scientific managers never asked the workers how they thought the job could be done more efficiently because workers were seen as machines that could be tailored to specifications by pouring limited, step-by-step instructions into them because they could not think at more complex levels. It's kind of how we treat the kids in our classrooms when we only ask them simple questions.

It was Taylor who said, "I can say, without the slightest hesitation that the science of handling pig-iron is so great that the man who is . . . physically able to handle pig-iron and is sufficiently phlegmatic and stupid to choose this for his occupation is rarely able to comprehend the science of handling pig-iron" (Montgomery, 1987, p. 229).

Nobody back then thought the workers in the process could learn how to learn; if they could not think, they could not learn. All the managers had to do was show and tell workers what to do. All workers had to do was watch and commit to memory the instruction, performing the task repetitively. The idea that reason belonged to a select few was promoted in factories bearing the Weber-Taylor banner *and also by Plato, Aristotle, Locke, and certain other elitist thinkers.* We were back in another time again.

As Dina completed her thoughts she realized that she had just morphed into a quantum state. Suddenly she did not know exactly where she was in the library. She couldn't pin down her position. She was here, there, and everywhere at once, and sages were confronting her from various library stacks.

Abruptly, Mr. Douglas McGregor (Heil, Bennis, & Stephens, 2000) was in her face. "What are your assumptions about human nature? Do you trust people?"

Well, she believed that people were good and wanted to do a good job when they came to school—the teachers, that is. But Superintendent Avelli didn't agree with her about this, calling her naive. "People can't be trusted to do the right thing and have to be controlled. That's why I have to be the center of their universe. If I'm not, they will ruin the goals I have set."

"Do you know thyself?" Socrates asked, lunging at her like a bolt of lightning from the philosophy library. And then the faces of a group of miniature men looked up at her from the stacks of education research books piled high upon a cart, chanting phrases like mindscape, personal mindset, and self-image, all which meant to say that she had to expand her thinking and understand her own mental attitude if she wanted to affect democracy and save the Republic.

It was not enough to know the source of her thinking. It was like Mr. Sarason had said: if she knew where she was coming from she could determine why she does what she does and develop the frame upon which she views the world.

"It's called a mindscape that slowly evolves. We are not always conscious of it," said a Mr. Sergiovanni, one of the chanters (Sergiovanni, 1987).

"I call it a personal mindset," said a Mr. Fullan (Fullan, 1991). "One develops this over time and it determines the action one performs."

"Self-image, mindscapes, mindsets are all similar to a mental set or frames," concluded a Mr. Senge (Senge, 1990), "that form our world-view. We have to look deeply into the mirror in our minds to understand why we understand what we understand."

So this "know-thyself" perspective states that you must understand the design of your own *inner* system before designing change in another. No wonder, Dina thought, the litter theory failed to create a clean campus!

"That's correct," Mr. Sarason said, reading her thoughts. "But before anything can change, you have to construct a conceptual framework that connects to your inner ideas. You have to know what your beliefs are and how those beliefs entered your mindscape . . . how the beliefs emerged in order to judge them critically, to rethink them and, to find their connections . . . and if appropriate, change them."

At this point she was a bit confused. It seemed to her that the library was replete with research about leadership and studies on the state and behavior of man. It was devoid of studies on the way one practically views or thinks about change.

Nobody ever asked her why she thought everybody picking up litter would solve the litter problem. If they did, maybe she could have found connections between her deeply ingrained beliefs about democracy and schooling and the deeply ingrained beliefs and ideas of others. Then she could have stuck her head in the trash can even sooner than she did!

Suddenly, Mr. Fullan entered her mindscape. "The principal directs the change process, so the job falls to that person."

"And the way the principal goes about enacting change depends upon the construction of the world the principal develops," Mr. Sarason added.

A Ms. Lieberman suggested, "Principals live their beliefs" (Lieberman & Miller, 1984).

"And because they live their beliefs," Mr. Sarason interjected, "it is important that a principal, as a change agent, be familiar with the assumptions, premises, and theories that are brought to her office and guide the educational journey at a particular school site. Without critically reflecting upon individual actions, leaders will continue to accept things as they are and have always been."

In conceptualizing the school organization, one needs to ask where one is in relation to that setting, Mr. Sarason had proposed. Examining the *inner* frame means exploring the assumptions brought to the role of management by the school leaders. *Was this the self-analysis in which the New Jersey letter writer had referred, she asked herself?*

To make operational the *know-thyself* perspective, she began asking herself how she constructed the world. We sometimes live beliefs that have not cognitively surfaced. What we believe is not always known by us. She didn't realize how Newton, Weber, and Taylor, as well as other well-meaning people, had shaped her thought until Ms. Wheatley nudged her tens of billions of neurons and trillions of synaptic connections.

Dina had tapped into a mass of interlocking, interstitial, chemical, and electrical clutter and then, in one moment, out from the snarl, a singular fiber of thought flopped that would help her to redefine her will, consciousness, behavior, and personality. The thought was simple—*know thyself.*

So she returned from the quantum stacks of the library to the ordered, new forum that was just beginning, more confused than ever. That's how it goes when you are *getting to know you, getting to know all about you.*

REFLECTION[2]

Ghandi said that we must be the change we wish to see in others.[3] Leading by example is the most enduring form of leadership.

Like the potter, we have the power to shape our own life. Get to know yourself. Listen to your inner voice. Live what you value and believe, listen to the conversations of others. Find the connections. This is the pathway to becoming an authentic leader.

When you look into the mirror, who do you see? Do others see the same person, or is your reflection an illusion? What do you value and believe? What shape is your life taking? Are you authentic? Do others see who you see? If so, why? If not, why not?

First and foremost, *know thyself.* Once you are successful at this and begin to peel back the layers, your real image will emerge. As this image emerges, ponder your core values and beliefs. What are they? And always remember, you must be the change you wish to see in others!

NOTES

1. Nobel Prize winner, Huerta Mueller (1993) demonstrated in *The Land of Green Plums* what happens when the mind is not allowed its freedom and is controlled by outside forces that dictate and manipulate it, forcing fear to drive one mad. And, Hannah Arendt (1963) in *Eichmann in Jerusalem* describes how evil is created when the mind lacks the ability to reason and think. Evil, she surmises, is the product of thoughtlessness.

2. This reflection was adapted from Chirichello and Richmond (2007).

3. This quote and others by Ghandi may be found online at: http://quotations.about.com/od/gandhiquotes/tp/10_gandhi_quote.htm.

Rule

UNDERSTAND THE
ONTOLOGY OF CONTROL

Returning to the forum at the library, some of the distinguished visitors at the long oval table had left while others returned to their dusty places on the shelves. Before the break, Principal Sid Aphus had announced that it was his intention to begin a second dialogue about the principal's role in the maintenance of American democracy, a topic that was high on Principal Dina Macksy's interest list. Maybe such a discussion would nudge her mind into "knowing" mode and help her to establish why she thought that schools had to be democratic.

Hearing the topic, new personalities sprang from the various sections of the library, taking seats at the oval table, while others retreated between their book jackets. "I feel somehow that our schools . . . and our profession in general are a threat to American democracy," Sid lamented on returning to his seat. "I'd like to think that once upon a time in education students were inculcated with the values that the founding fathers thought, through universal public education, were necessary to preserve democracy . . . values like freedom and liberty.

"Of course, I sense that preceding a statement with *once upon a time* is indicative of a fairy tale. Whatever the case, there is a connection between the preservative power of those values and the organization and governance of our schools. I am beginning to think that if the connection is not put on the table, it will be lost, and like Rome, our Republic will fall. Only this time the barbarians at the gate will be us. We will let it happen because, as Mr. Einstein always said, the thinking we use to solve problems is the same thinking we used to create them.

"I practice control in the governance of my school," he continued. "I go to meetings, read the latest research, and climb on the bandwagons of those programs I think will make my school better. I create a plan of action and tell the teachers that they will follow my plan. If they don't, their evaluations will reflect the indiscretion. I don't ask for their suggestions because I don't think they have the same view of the school from the classroom as I have from my office. That is, their job is to focus on their classroom. My job is to focus on the schoolhouse. We are separate entities."

"You mean that you spend most of your day in the tower and the teachers spend most of their day in the moat?" Plato affirmed, sitting on the top of the stacks, his ashen, bare legs drooping over the books, his chin resting in the palm of his hand as he peered down on Sid.

"Yes, something like that," Sid said. "It's simple . . . the system works and students get schooled. So, that being said, why do I have this disquieting feeling that, although my students are being schooled, they are not being educated . . . especially to take on the responsibilities of democracy?"

Dina discerned that he was taking that mirror Mr. Senge talked about, turning it inward, and unearthing his internal pictures of the world, making sense of the images he saw, rationalizing them, looking for the links between the thoughts.

"I grew up in the big city," Sid continued, "and I have early memories of school in those very formative years of intellectual growth. I was so eager to attend school. Each day from the fifth floor apartment window, I would look down on the street and watch my older sister come home from the big, red fortress-like public school building with the black iron fencing surrounding it.

"When she came through our apartment door, I would beg her to read the stories she had read that day from *Fun with Dick and Jane*. I didn't find the stories very interesting but I was in awe of my sister's ability to create sounds from those black configurations on the white pages. What was the magic learned in school that allowed her to do that?

"In my neighborhood, the adults, many of whom spoke with foreign accents, told children that education was an elevator, which would lift them to higher stations in life . . . going to school took people out of the factories and helped them rise above their station. I was eager to go to school, learn, and rise above my station because it was thought to be a good thing. Reading was an important first step in elevating oneself above one's station."

Sid backed up in his chair, seeing in his mind's eye further images of his past. "It was the first day of school. I can still see children whining and screaming, their short arms stretched tightly around the lower limbs of their mothers, their heads buried in the folds of their mothers' dresses. Those who didn't cry were stoned faced and bleary eyed, not knowing what to expect.

"The pain of separation was difficult for some youngsters, but not me. I was eager to begin the process of learning and deciphering those black configurations on the white pages of the books that my sister carried home and elevate myself to a higher station in life. The teacher, Miss Levi Ethan, asked the parents to leave the classroom. 'The children will soon be adjusting to their new environment,' she told the parents in her austere, omnipotent voice, her arms folded above her chest.

"As soon as the parents were out the door, we were told to line up in nice straight rows—boys on one side of the room and girls on the other—neat rows and columns of wooden desks with their iron legs bolted to the ground, separating us from each other.

"Miss Levi Ethan had arms that flailed," Sid chortled, "and when she spoke, they were constantly in motion . . . all four pairs of them. She arranged us on the line by height . . . the shortest in the front.

"I remember a boy named David yelling that he didn't want to stand on the lines the teacher made. They were stupid lines so he wouldn't stand in them and she couldn't make him. His mother had said to listen to what the teacher said, so David's recalcitrance was an act of profound defiance. She told him in a very shrill voice to shut up, sit down, and be quiet. 'Good, little citizens should be seen but not heard,' she scolded.

"The shrill voice emanating from the teacher frightened me."

Sid paused, his face becoming dour. "When David ignored her inference about being a good citizen, her voice again shrieked across the room but this time she extended one of the four arms, pointing and wiggling her index finger straight at him. It seemed to be the longest index finger in the world. For a while, David was seen, but not heard.

"In the quiet of the room, it seems to me that each of us was then assigned a brown wooden desk that contained on the right upper corner a dried inkwell with a metal flip-top that was no longer useful except to tinker with while the teacher practiced tranquilizing teaching methods on us . . . she talked, we listened.

"It was so quiet in the classroom after all the yelling was over. I feared looking to the right or left of me. As I sat in the disquieting air of the bleak, first-grade classroom of ordered neat rows, I was unknowingly being taught about how one behaves in an autocratic state where the rules must be obeyed if you were to become a good, little citizen.

"I remember David so well, because he refused to accept the rules of the classroom. In the lunchroom, I overhead Miss Levi Ethan talking to Principal Mac Avelli, about him.

"'He's so restless,' she told him. 'I sat him in back of the room so I don't have to hear him when he kicks at the legs of his chair and pounds his fists on the surface of the desk. Sometimes he even just gets out of his seat without raising his hand and runs around the room screaming that I can't tell him what to do. He has a say in how the rules are made. He's an American. I yell at him until I feel my face flushing but yelling does no good. He still does what he wants. You have to do something about this problem, Principal Mac Avelli.'

"I hated when Miss Levi Ethan yelled at David because her shrill sounds frightened me," Sid lamented. "I became worried about making mistakes and my body tensed anytime I felt her eyes on him. It was hard to absorb what she was trying to put into my head. I was afraid that if she called on me for an answer to her questions, I would get it wrong and be yelled at too . . . even though I wasn't doing anything wrong and was eager to learn.

"I remember when she did call on me, I was so afraid of giving an incorrect answer, that I made no utterance, just holding my breath and feeling the heat of my face slowly rising. That worked for a while. She said she would just call on someone more alert. She made me feel stupid."

Maybe that's how I came to believe in Plato, Dina thought. I didn't think that anything I sensed make any sense and therefore truth could only be found by looking outside myself, like at the Supreme Court, where judges made objective decisions or our elected lawmakers who made wise laws.

Sid continued his story. "One day, as we marched in a straight line into the classroom from the lunchroom, I became aware that David was no longer with us. He was being moved to the classroom down the hall . . . that strange classroom where kids from all different grade levels were mixed together. The teacher in that room yelled at the students even more than Miss Levi Ethan yelled at us!

"Somebody had asked our teacher why the kids in that room were different from us. She said the students in that class were special. Principal Mac Avelli had put David in that room with the other kids who refused to be good little citizens.

"Special was supposed to be something good so I was confused. But I knew that I didn't want to be in that class with all the special kids. I didn't want the special kind of attention they were getting. I wanted the gold stars on the piece of paper given to me by the teachers when my paper was neat or my punctuation was correct or when I obeyed the rules, which of course, I always did. My mother liked it when I got those gold stars. She always said good things to me when I brought them home.

"It's ironic," Sid said, frowning, "but I can never remember why I got the gold stars . . . just that I did. I wanted the teacher's smile and my mother's good words. I did not want the yelling. If I followed the rules and did my job, I received those rewards. It felt good being selected to erase the blackboard or collect the test papers. I even began to speak in class and answer questions.

"When my mother asked me what I did in school, I proudly said that the teacher picked me to be board monitor. Besides receiving the honor of performing the task, it took me out of my seat and relieved the tedium of being bolted to wood for so long each day. I was now walking between the rows of desks a little freer than the other kids were. 'You are learning how to be a good citizen,' the teacher told me as students gave me glaring looks.

"As the years passed, I learned that there was an unwritten social contract that students negotiated with their teachers in each classroom . . . in every school, in every year.

"If I followed the rules, shrill voices would not shatter my day. If I lined up properly, listened to teacher talk, marked the worksheet correctly, and came to school each day on time, my reward would be good marks and happy teachers . . . and I would become a dutiful citizen.

"Gradually I also learned that getting good grades had value. A good grade made me feel smart in a world that was supposed to reward smartness. An A grade meant that I had followed the rules and regurgitated correctly the words on the page. Rewards would one day follow."

But Sid, thought Dina, would you ever find truth and knowledge and save the Republic?

"My first-grade classroom worked like the factory my father reported to every day. Just as there were the workers and the manager, in school there were the students and the teacher. The teacher ruled the students.

"She set the tasks and the standards for what the students were to do, usually without even thinking about what the students could bring to the curriculum. She controlled students with a barometer of fear . . . as it rose in the classroom, the joy of discovery, so innate in small children, declined.

"For Miss Levi Ethan, teaching was about controlling. Her belief was that only regimented, highly disciplined students could bring forth the information that she poured into their heads."

Sid shrugged his shoulders. "It wasn't her fault . . . it was the way the system was set up to mass educate students so that America would have an enlightened . . . and alert . . . population. She was just doing her part.

"People like me still encourage that part. A good classroom is a disciplined one. But, we paid an enormous price for this, sacrificing so much of our creative and natural curiosities that we brought with us to school . . . and that had the potential to do all things for all people. For much of the day, we lived in an artificially arranged society that was created so that the children and the teacher could live together, each child being thought of as a product to be standardized as information was poured into his or her inert head.

"It was as if the teacher had given each boy and girl a box as each one entered through the doors of the first-grade classroom. She told them to empty into that box all that they felt and knew. The box was closed and wrapped and as each one of them pressed their little finger down over the knot, the teacher pulled the string tight. She then took the box away from them, one by one, row by row.

"The box was shelved and stored for twelve years. Hardly anybody ever saw it again. And then one day it was gone. We had learned how to be good, little citizens who bartered away spontaneity for gold stars and anesthetic minds."

As Sid was speaking, Dina noticed that various shadows of people were jumping up and down from the bookshelves, even over and through one another, from many sections of the library, scrambling for a seat at the table.

A man with intense eyes and thinning grayish-white hair named Mr. Thomas Hobbes—a philosopher we read about in high school, along with Locke and Rousseau—said, "Come, come now. Bad behavior in the classroom is most unacceptable. The teacher has a legitimate right to stop David from his brutish acts because they impinge upon the rights of others to learn. She represents the rules that were established by the school. These rules have to be established because in a state of nature, children are brutish . . . evil. What must life be like in the absence of rules? Many Davids running around the room."

"But did David have his say in the construction of the rules?" asked Mr. Locke. "If the teacher has all the power, does it lead to abuse as Principal Sid Aphus noted . . . mental abuse where students fear giving wrong answers. In other words, does unlimited governance by the teacher lead to abuses?"

"You mean does the school become a Leviathan," asked Mr. Hobbes (Hobbs, 1996), "an uncontrollable monster which abuses the people with whose well-being it is charged?"

"Well, if you ask me, children are born neither good nor bad," Mr. Jean-Jacques Rousseau said. "They model what they see. It is the teacher who turns the students into recalcitrant creatures by imposing artificial rules that do not reflect natural social relations. We were not meant to be rowed and columned even if this structure does help to maintain order and discipline."[1]

"At the expense of creativity, cooperation, and the dynamics of social interaction, Mr. Rousseau?" asked Ms. Lucille Lindberg (1954), a twentieth-century educator. "By not teaching students how to make rules together, the teacher is not involving the students in the practice of democracy. My professor at graduate school, Mr. E. Thomas Hopkins, taught that children grow when they are guided in an enlightened atmosphere. Classrooms where children have no input . . . where the curriculum is fixed and determined ahead of time by the school . . . preclude them in reaching their intellectual capacity."

"Dummkoff! You are simply dummkoff!" shouted Principal Nick Chez. He was the principal at Berlin High School, a new charter school that had opened across town. His lower lip was quivering as he spoke. "Children bring little knowledge with them to the classroom. It is principals and superintendents who have the knowledge of how to control things. Children . . . they are still in the state of nature when they come to us because they watch too much television, have uncontrolled use of the computer, and parents who lack parenting skills."

"We can train people as I did with my dogs," Mr. Ivan Pavlov, a noted Russian psychologist, chuckled (Todes, 2000). "Dangle incentives . . . watch them salivate. It works. Rewards and punishments . . . it always works to keep children in control. Let them salivate . . . that's my motto. If you can condition them, you can control them . . . and then they are ready to learn. But I don't think you should throw candy at them anymore . . . obesity issues . . . you know . . . a problem of your time."

"Should I remind all of you that's what I too discovered," Mr. Taylor said proudly. "People are easily programmable. We can make them do almost anything we want as long as we keep them ignorant . . . and give them candy. We need thinkers at the top, not the bottom of the hierarchical chain . . . men like Plato, who are objective about all things."

"Quite right," Plato said sharply, out of breath, pacing back and forth on the high stacks, his fingers laced in a tight hold behind his back. "People who lead must be sent to the tower to learn how to transcend the knowledge of the people in the moat and acquire the higher forms of knowledge. They are the individuals who must lead. Not everybody can do this."

But how does democracy survive, Dina asked herself, if we focus on conditioning people at the expense of what Cousin Michael called learning how to learn? How do we guide children in transcending their intellectual potential if we keep them in their place and control them?

REFLECTION

Is your school an artificially arranged society—one that you created—like a box, so teachers and principal can live together? What do you demand that teachers empty into that box—perhaps attributes like creativity, resourcefulness, and spunk? Is conformity more important than creativity? At the end of the day, who gets your gold stars and what happens to students like David, students who do not conform, who challenge, who probe?

NOTE

1. Thomas Hobbes wrote *Leviathan*, in which he gave us his concept regarding the state of nature. He believed that people were born "bad" and in the state of nature would not emphasize civility. Jean-Jacques Rousseau disagreed with him, saying that humans were born neither good nor bad but were influenced by the people in their environment. Locke argued in his *Second Treatise on Civil Government* that men give up certain rights in order to live together. What all three have in common is their advocacy of social contract theory.

Rule

NEVER ACCEPT THE CONVENIENCE OF CONTROL

"Not everybody is equipped to do the thinking jobs," Aristotle and Locke chanted in unison. "And even in a democracy you need the people who do what they are told . . . you need the pig-iron workers."

Well, you see, that's another thing that bothered Principal Dina Macksy. Are schools arranged in such a way to keep people in their socioeconomic place instead of elevating them to higher stations, as Principal Sid Aphus was taught growing up? Do we deliberately stifle what Cousin Michael called dreaming? Do we unknowingly program them through control without realizing it? Or do we realize it and accept the convenience of control?

What's the one thing that you as a principal don't want to see when you enter a classroom? Think about it . . . you twist the knob on the door, gingerly entering room 22. If the room is filled with student chatter and cross-talking like the ladies on the popular morning television program *The View*, you assume that teacher has a discipline problem.

You don't analyze the chatter or what the teacher is doing because the last education book you read said that a principal needed only one minute to conjure up what was happening in the classroom. Really? Can you so easily analyze the *hazy world of human relationships* (Gibboney, 1994)?

"Why bother thinking about the people who inhabit space in your organization?" Principal Nick Chez uttered, the narrow slits of his eyes glaring fervently at Sid.

"Their only motives are self-interest. They don't know how to cooperatively learn . . . nor do they want to take the time to learn how to do this . . . cooperatively." He chuckled at his witticism. "'Just leave me alone and let me do my job,' is their mantra as they shut their doors in your face.

"I need to control them because they have never seen American democracy at work in the schools," he continued. "Don't you think it would prove perilous to give democracy to people who don't know how to use it?"

Nick shook his head from side to side, folding his arms across his chest. Here was a cold and remote principal who overvalued his accomplishments, Dina suddenly thought.

"I don't trust people," he continued, "because they don't know how to think and reflect on that thinking. I run a charter school . . . a place where parents want their children to be and where my teachers want to be. It is my job to keep them all secure. Teachers want to feel secure, and they want someone to provide that security. Above all, they want to be left alone.

"I well understand that in their present state they will tolerate a modicum of control knowing that I can keep them secure and will leave them alone as long as they follow my directives.

"However, when you get something, you have to give something. By being controlled, you relinquish your ability to acquire greater depths of knowledge . . . you and your students . . . than you would acquire if you had acted together in a thoughtful manner. I know this on a very conscious level, but I suppress this thought because of what the unconscious tells me will happen if I let go of the leash."

Nick stopped, wetting his lips, before continuing. "My teachers never deviate from the prescribed curriculum. My school runs as precisely as a clock. The bell rings and all my students, like objects on a conveyer belt, move in sync, exiting one classroom and entering another. No one lags behind . . . sluggards are quickly dealt with.

"Knowledge is acquired if we pursue it in a neat and orderly way . . . as Mr. Newton has suggested . . . as detached, rational human beings living in a fixed, deterministic environment. I willingly exchange short-term results for the long-term disaster."

"Quite right you are," said Mr. Plato, out of breath after climbing down from his stacks and rushing again to his seat. "There are only a few able to locate truth and knowledge, and as leaders, that is your role."

"Now wait a minute!" Sid shouted, shaking his index finger at Nick and then up at Plato (the latter had again retreated to the apex of the stacks). "It seems to me what your elitist thinking suggests is that we as principals must control the schoolhouse in order for schooling to occur. But what about education? Can democracy survive without an educated polis?"

A tall, slender man wearing a red waistcoat and tinkering with something at the table that looked like a portable copying press interrupted Sid. Not removing his eyes from his contraption, Thomas Jefferson asked, "If students do not feel free to express and share ideas in the classroom, asking questions in order to develop, formulate, and refine their ideas, how can an American culture, premised on the expression and sharing of ideas, be perpetuated?" (Doyle, 1976; Pulliam, 1982).

"If we don't educate students in the experience of democracy, Mr. Jefferson, the result is an acceptance of democracy without experiencing it. You know the ol' saying—if you do not use it, you will lose it." The speaker was educator Mr. John Dewey (Dewey, 1961).

"Controlling environments engender fear," said Alfie Kohn, a modern writer on human behavior (Kohn, 1986, 1993). "It is only commonsense that for people to ask questions, they cannot fear the asking. Knowledge expands when people are not in fear of questioning."

"I believe that the founding fathers strongly advocated universal public education in order that citizens make wise political decisions for maintaining our democracy," stated Sid. "Yet all I do is instill fear in teachers when I tell them that they must teach to the state tests and a high percentage of their students must pass if they want to retain their jobs.

"My superintendent, Mrs. Levi Ethan, tells me that nothing should interfere with raising our school's reading, writing, and math scores. 'We do want to look favorable in the newspapers,' she tells me.

"I reiterate to her until I am blue in the face that looking good in the newspaper is less important than educating students. This current emphasis on basic academic skills is a historical aberration. It would never have occurred to the founding fathers that instruction in reading, writing, and arithmetic alone would guarantee good citizenship. 'Tell that to the state,'" she shouts.

"I am so fearful that these last generations no longer know how to express themselves or share ideas or for that matter know how to question societal problems. If they don't question, they accept. This notion places our nation in peril and demonstrates how democracy can be lost to people hoping to achieve their own personal agenda."

"Your anxiety is well-warranted." The rather pale man who made this statement was wearing a brown suit of broadcloth with gold buttons engraved with eagles. He stood up when he spoke. The audience did as well. They were showing their reverence for our first president. "Revisit my first message to Congress, where I advocated that the people be taught to value their own rights and to distinguish between oppression and the necessary exercise of lawful authority" (PBS, 2009).

"Your address warned, sir," said Sid, "that, because public opinion would influence public policy in a democracy, it was essential that public opinion be enlightened."

"And I said that public education was needed to prepare voters to exercise wise judgment," added Mr. Thomas Jefferson (Brookhiser, 2006).

"I felt and still do that it is less important for schools to know the president's term of office and more important that they be prepared by the schools to think critically about candidates and their positions, and then choose wisely. I felt it important that citizens understand their duty to their neighbors and country."

"I am greatly troubled," uttered an early advocate for public education in America. His nametag identified him as Mr. Horace Mann (Cremin, 1980).

"Many years ago I traveled in Europe, stopping in Prussia where there existed universal basic education. But this alone did not ensure democratic values. Prussian students were highly literate but supported autocracy. I concluded that schools in a democracy could not be held accountable for academics alone but must inculcate democratic moral and political values so that literacy would not be misused."

As they further dialogued, Dina found herself walking the corridors of her school. All she could now see was a giant factory where relationships between individuals were held together by the dynamics of control—the antithesis of democracy. The superintendent tells her what to do, she tells the teachers what to do, and the teachers tell the students what to do. She rarely sees a lively exchange of ideas in the classroom or at faculty meetings.

Moreover, we all know what community meetings are like, she thought to herself. People argue as if they forgot the social contract and retreat to a nasty and brutish state where everyone grunts and scratches. Could it be that people no longer believe that, to have freedom they must give up a little of themselves and submerge themselves in the common good?

How meaningless are the terms participatory management, site-based management, middle school concept, cooperative learning, and parent involvement without any knowledge about the workings of democratic processes steeped in democratic thinking?

Sid must have been reading her thoughts. "The last time I visited classrooms at my high school I was overwhelmed how every classroom looked like every other classroom," he explained. "The teacher was in the front of the room and the students were seated in neat rows in a quiet and orderly fashion. The teacher was a teller of information and the students were expected to listen and learn what was being poured into their heads.

"I saw few patterns of behavior that showed our students engaged in the practice of democracy . . . group problem solving, group decision making, and active engagement in dialogue. I saw few instances where ideas were being exchanged.

"I noticed one teacher trying to teach his senior government class the rules for brainstorming but the seniors had a difficult time staying with the rules. They preferred to shout out responses. Anarchy was more of what I saw in that classroom. I saw open dialogue between a few students in a few classes, but it was about the nature of the Saturday night football game.

"I hear so many of my colleagues say that they don't care what the government does as long as it leaves them alone," he said ruefully. "Maybe people who say this don't understand that democracy is a group process and they can't be left alone . . . unless they don't want to live in a free country.

"I just don't think that people understand anymore the nature of democracy and the fact that if they want to retain it, they must commit to practicing it. Teachers see no workplace models, and students, who spent so much of their formative years in school, even less so.

"Not long ago I asked a group of students what was meant when we talk about the democratic process. Included in their responses were phrases like *each citizen is entitled to a life of liberty and the pursuit of happiness.* They even used words like a *republican theory of government, constitutionalism, popular sovereignty,* and *political representation.*

"They were volunteering meaningless words with which they had no practical experience. Will they know what democracy looks like when they see it in action, or will they mistake it for a shouting match? When leaders abuse power, will they know it?"

"They cannot," said Ms. Lucille Lindberg (Lindberg, 1954). "There has to be interaction between people as a result of processes of open communication that are taught and experienced. Critical thinking cannot occur if children think that all they have to do is regurgitate right answers."

"If we allowed students to help make decisions regarding school organization or allowed too much dialogue in the classroom, it would lead to chaos," Nick guffawed, breaking into laughter. "Besides, it would take time away from teaching to the state tests. In my school, I know what is best for my teachers and students . . . and their parents."

Lucille jumped out of her seat, the veins in her neck bulging. "And as a result education does not occur at your school!" she cried.

"Our state test scores are among the highest!" he said, sneering at Lucille's rejoinder.

"Yes. But can your students think outside the test? Can they engage in decision-making processes? Democracy has no value unless we know how to live it," she blared. "Democracy is a group process. It is learned by doing. And schools must teach students to do it from the first day of school on."

"That's absurd!" Nick retorted, banging his clenched fist on the table. "Are you suggesting, Ms. Lindberg, that we give teachers and students, and I might add parents, lessons in group dynamics? My teachers hardly have time now to cover everything in the curriculum that the state mandates we cover. I don't have time for one more thing!

"I asked the history department at their last meeting to tell me what democracy in the classroom might look like. I could see them snickering at the question. 'Chaos,' they clamored almost in unison.

Students today don't know how to dialogue. They are too impatient. Fights break out."

"But how will students learn democracy if it is not practiced to some degree in the classroom?" asked Lucille.

"Democracy is not something that can be practiced in the schools." Nick responded. Students want to be told the rules and left alone. They are machines that need to be molded to our specifications. As I said, they would rather be controlled. And one more thing. Some of my students have gone on to win elected office . . . become supermen. They were supported by important and powerful people . . ."

". . . who now manipulate them!" said Lucille, the neck veins still popping up through her skin.

"I'd like to return to an earlier point that was made," said Sid, attempting to return calm to the room. "Let me share my mindscape with you . . . a mindscape that reminds me of what freedom means." The room turned silent.

"I learned about freedom, but not from the schools. From the schools I learned the words of democracy like the students do today, but from the streets I learned what was meant by it. After school, I joined the cacophonous, cluttered ranks of people who moved up and down, back and forth, around and across the city pavement. There was a pattern to their movements, even though I couldn't positively know what street I would travel next. I felt like Robert Gilmore's Alice, in his book *Alice in Quantumland* (Gilmore, 1995).

"'The quantum mechanic took his turn at the billiard's table . . . and made a vague stab with his cue. After her previous recent experiences, Alice was not really surprised to discover that the ball shot off in every direction at once, so that there was no part of the table where she could say definitely that the ball had gone, though equally she could in no way say where it actually was. After a moment the player went over and peered into one of the pockets, then reached in and drew out a red ball' (Gilmore, 1995, p. 32).

"It was like that on the streets where the sun filled me and I could never predict with accuracy which streets I would travel and how one street would connect to the next . . . it all just happened. There were no neat rows, no neat way of doing things. The streets were a web of interweaving alleys, avenues, apartments, stores, parks, and subways . . . all these interconnecting parts revolving around our curiosity, our natural spontaneity.

"Living was dynamic and unpredictable. There were no bells to mark the moment. Life was spontaneous and I was able to discover new realities by simply walking, watching, listening, and connecting . . . constructing new mental images of life . . . finding systems with common roots that supported each other.

"Everything was interconnected and created a complex harmony of life entangled and enmeshed in activity, which worked together to continually evolve and change. As I wandered those streets after school, my mind attempted to make sense of and integrate the activities that occurred.

"The problem was that I had no guides to help me interpret the activities, and I had to depend on myself and my limited understandings to provide meaning. I couldn't talk about the activity in the classroom because education was not what school was about.

"The learning on the streets was different from the learning in the schoolhouse. In the schoolhouse, I sat in the assigned seat and did work that was unconnected to any reality I knew. Dick was having fun with Jane, and two and two made four, but who were those people and what did those numbers mean?

"I brought knowledge to the classroom. . . . I knew the names of many streets and how they received their names, I knew the names of the people who lived on the fifth floor of my building, where they worked, and the names of their children. None of them had names like Jane or Dick.

"But no teacher asked us about the streets or about the people we carried in our minds to school. No teacher asked us to create stories about Mr. Dewey, the city librarian who taught us all about the numbers placed on the books, or Joe, the policeman who pointed fingers at people we should stay away from . . . 'Drugs,' he said.

"Students were asked to check this knowing at the door as they worked rote problems and answered simple questions. The ladder of thinking went straight up. Before I could analyze, synthesize, and evaluate, I had to have knowledge, understanding, and be able to make applications.

"'The students may not advance to step two until step one has been completed,' the teacher told parents. Thinking skills were something I worked in sequence toward, and only after drill and practice with lower order thinking could I progress.

"Year after year, it was drilled into my vacant, inert head . . . which really was not all that vacant or inert. It just wasn't making connections with anything in school because one street of thought was not connecting to another. When I finally circled the right answer on the right page, I was rewarded with a grade and a smile from the teacher. She was thrilled that I finally *got it*.

"Classrooms were Pavlovian factories that sequestered students, who when stimulated, responded. But not on the streets. On hot summer nights, people came out of their apartments and sat in circles in front of the building. They talked to each other, they talked at each other, they talked about each other, they talked at the same time, they argued when they didn't agree.

"There were no rules posted other than the sign that said no loitering in front of the building. They didn't talk about the rules and there didn't seem to be any. They didn't sit in neat rows and sneak a word with the person behind them. They didn't recite words: they spoke them and looked at each other as they spoke.

"I sat with these people, afraid to speak because of our obedience training at school. I was uncomfortable facing them because I was used to seeing the back of another person's head. But, there was an excitement that they generated when they spoke about politics and baseball games. They didn't have to raise their hands when they spoke. They just spoke when they felt like it. And, what they said sounded unrehearsed.

"One day, one of those people facing me asked, 'Do you think a Superman is the answer to our problems?' I froze. I had read Superman comic books but my teacher said comic books were bad. Suddenly, I didn't know how to create thinking words. I didn't know what the right answer should be, so I said nothing. The person who asked me the question just smiled. He didn't yell at me and tell me that I had to be more alert. He just smiled . . . a kindhearted smile that made me feel good inside . . . that said it was okay not to respond.

"I listened some more and slowly found the courage to enter the conversation. After that, I heard people say, 'that kid is sure smart.' They were talking about me! With them, I learned that sometimes there were no right answers. People had opinions and stated them while other people listened, debated, and cajoled. They allowed me into their conversations and never once said that I was wrong . . . or stupid."

Sid's mindscape propelled Dina to dive into her own thinking about freedom and control. She found a recounting in one of her early diaries.

In first grade, we practiced reading as if we were workers on an assembly line in Dad's toy factory. We were reading up and down the rows and columns, paragraphs from *Fun with Dick and Jane*.

Each kid read his part. I used to figure out what paragraph I would have to read by counting how many paragraphs and readers were before me and jumping to it. I prayed I would know all the words. If you didn't know all the words, the teacher would make you sound them out in front of the whole class. Once, I asked Judith, the girl next to me, what a word was in the paragraph I was going to read. I was scared stiff the teacher would see me talking and yell at me.

Today, Mrs. Router, my eighth-grade English teacher, did this round robin reading thing again in class. Once again doing what I had done in the first grade, I began to count people and paragraphs because I was scared stiff I wouldn't know all the words. When my turn came, I read the words perfectly. Mrs. Router said I did a good job.

My first-grade teacher used to tell me that I needed to study harder. I was glad I read all the words correctly and remembered the method I had used in the first grade so that the teacher did not embarrass me in front of all the other kids. The teacher rewarded me for reading aloud all the words, but I sense that I didn't read very well. Wasn't reading words more than sounding them out?

How could I be rewarded for reading well, when I didn't understand what I was reading?

After reading her youthful diaries, Dina was beginning to understand that her ideas about control had been shaped by educators, as Nick and she too had bought into its ideas. There were many parts to this concept called teaching, but control was elevated to the forefront, acting only to impede learning. But she had submitted to the practice.

She just had to do her part and study harder, the teacher said. She wondered if there was another way to gain the knowledge of the universe and save the Republic.

She also concluded that she was rarely present in those classrooms, even though her attendance was good, because the conversations were not shared. And without those shared conversations, what was poured into her head was filled with such ambiguity that it was difficult to discern the truth.

Her teachers always reminded her to use her head in the classroom and her body on the playing field. They emphasized cooperation but winning, working hard but having fun. "Go out there and have fun," they clamored as she moved off the bench on to the basketball court. But how can you have fun when you are so worried about the disapproving look on their faces if you miss the basket?

She felt like a person who had been partitioned into two halves, each half fighting the other. Schooling had permeated her thinking with prompts that fought each other. Conversely, she learned that the body had a limited relationship to the mind, that competition had a higher priority than cooperation. It was more important to beat than to be beaten (Kohn, 1986).

The prompts being taught didn't remind her of a democratic society where everyone was supposed to work together to form a more perfect union. While fun became synonymous with feeling good about oneself, losing became synonymous with attaining bad feelings. This agenda built fear of failure into its program.

As a result, as a child, she had to learn how to defend herself from the residual humiliation that accompanies losing. She concluded that, as children, we are born into a heavenly world. But at an early age, the learning and joy are bludgeoned by the demon called schooling, transmuting them into something that they were not. Goliath always stared down at David. How could children survive in a world, where at the age of five, heaven was usurped by a yin-yang disconnect?

"Democracy takes time to think about and practice," Sid reflected, as Dina concluded her thoughts. "But I have tried. Sometimes I announce a course of action and report it to the faculty. Sometimes I test the waters by making a tentative decision, presenting it to the teachers for their reactions, before making the final decision. Other times, I solicit suggestions about the possible courses of action and then seek a solution."

"But all of those scenarios are based on control," said Lucille. "If you wanted to practice democracy you would provide all the individuals who are affected by the problem opportunities to work together on it."

Sid reflected, "Maybe you're right. I remember a colleague of mine . . . an older gentlemen . . . telling me about the student riots in 1968, especially in France when students marched on the streets in masses. France at that time was a very rigid, formalistic society.

"Anyway, the workers, who also demonstrated, knew their objectives but the students did not. Neither of these groups supported each other, but my colleague, who had been attending the Sorbonne at the time, recalled that what he remembered most about that spring was not the resulting violence . . . the police beating up students . . . but people talking with each other.

"French people talk with great ardor. During the riots, people talked in the streets—students and workers, students and their teachers and professors, workers and teachers. People not part of the demonstrating groups joined in the conversations. I was told that for the first time in a very long time people were talking to each other. With the demonstrations, my colleague felt an overwhelming sense of freedom because people were talking."

"This did not occur in our university classes," my friend told me. "Teachers and students never talked to each other."

Sid concluded, "So I must ask myself, why do we not insist upon this talking in the classrooms and hallways of the schools? Why do we insist on control and sacrifice thinking to a test? If by nature we are a free people, why do we shroud the schoolhouse in the dynamics of control?"

"Convenience," someone at the table murmured.

REFLECTION

In *Leading with Soul*, Bolman and Deal (2001) tell a story about a stream that comes to the edge of the desert. It hesitates to flow further, knowing that if it does, its waters will disappear into the hot sand.

But the wind shouts to the stream that it will be absorbed by its powerful air currents that surge across the desert. The stream will evaporate and be carried by the wind. When it reaches more fertile ground, it will fall to the earth as moisture. It will become a stream again, more powerful than before.

Just like the stream that gave itself up as it approached the sweltering desert sand, you must loosen your control over others. You will gain power by giving it away.

Power is like a boomerang. Toss it into the air, and it will return to you. How will you give away your power so it comes back to you? Are you willing to retreat from command and control to collaboration and collegiality? Will you continue to shroud the schoolhouse with the illusion of control?

Rule

KNOW THE DIFFERENCE
BETWEEN PARTS AND WHOLES

"**P**erhaps we practice control and are controlling," said Principal Sid Aphus, "not because we believe it is the best way to organize the schoolhouse, but because it is the only way we know to take masses of kids and school them.

"I would imagine that the schoolhouse had to be structured so that the job of teaching and learning could be accomplished in an efficient manner. Breaking things down into smaller parts helps us to manage what we can't otherwise handle. The problem is, as we learned in our first dialogue, breaking things down into smaller parts takes our focus away from understanding the entire problem."

"Think about ancient cultures, Principal Aphus," said Mr. L. Thomas Hopkins (Hopkins, 1941). His nametag identified him as a twentieth-century educator.

"They did just that. For example, when there was a problem in the Greek societal system, the Greeks pointed fingers and blamed it on a person or persons for offending a particular god. If the crop failed a particular year, the people would aggregate their understanding of the crop failure to an explanation of why Demeter was angry with the farmers."

"Yes, I am seeing that it is easier to take what we know," reflected Sid, "aggregate that knowing to the cause of the crop failing . . . in my case poor test scores, and make sacrifices at the local temple . . . firing teachers and principals.

"We break something down to manageable size . . . the size our mind can handle. Look at how we manage the curriculum. Why is subject matter so disparate? Why do we take the science out of math, the social studies out of English, and the geography out of history?"

"I am partially responsible for that," Aristotle recounted (Loomis, 1995). "It was my belief that all things in nature could be broken down into its singular, unconnected essence. I think Democritus and several others gave me that idea."

"It may be that because of that thinking, Mr. Aristotle," Mr. Hopkins responded (Hopkins, 1941), "the Romans divided the educational curriculum into many disciplines. And the Renaissance period expanded the notion of the divisibility of systems. They broke human activity down into learning, working, and playing" (Hopkins, 1941).

"That's correct," said Mr. Russell Ackoff, an organizational specialist of this century (Deming Library, 1987–1989). "Renaissance man took the mechanical universe of Isaac Newton and analyzed it on a part-by-part social level. For example, they organized what we do every day . . . human activity . . . into learning, working, and having fun. So a child goes to school and is expected to learn but not have fun or work. A principal goes to her job and is expected to work but not learn or have fun. And both attend football games where they can have fun but are not expected to learn or work."

There was silence in the room. People were thinking, connecting.

Then Mr. Hopkins started up again. "And the division continued," he said, his voice softening as if lamenting the fact. "As we divided human activity, we divided our own thinking and became further removed from understanding the world as a connected whole.

"Take the disciplines for example. During the eighteenth century, natural science grew out of philosophy, and during the mid nineteenth century it became a separate discipline of study. Physics and chemistry stemmed from the natural sciences. And, from evolutionary theory sprang biology, zoology, and botany. Disciplines were divided and, like the Aristotelian tunnels, developed farther and farther apart without interconnecting tunnels, becoming indivisible essences that were immutable."

"This division continued during the Industrial Revolution," Mr. Ackoff continued (Ackoff, 1981), "where the idea that organizational systems could be understood in the context of individual parts had its roots. Mr. Weber and Mr. Taylor have already testified to this.

"Whereas one person or a small group of people prior to the Industrial Revolution controlled the means and management of production, the new technology established methods of control. This separated the planning of the product from the execution of the product. Once again, breaking things down into parts was the worldview for understanding how to deal with and control the whole."

When you think about it, Principal Dina Mackey thought, with this new economic technology, individuals never had the opportunity to see the finished product—kind of like schools.

"Let me explain further," said Mr. Adam Smith, an eighteenth-century political economist (Bendell, Kelly, Merry, & Sims, 1993). "The goal of production was to reduce the variance and provide for uniformity of each unit of production. We called it uniformity of product by variance reduction. The goal was to use methods which yielded little or no variance."

"As I previously stated, I broke down the organizational parts into manageable components," said Mr. Weber (Ouchi, 1981), "where each component could be observed and therefore controlled.

"I created job divisions and hired workers based on job skill and evaluated them based on their performance level. I impressed upon them rules, regulations, and loyalty to the job. My goal was increasing production, not building social clubs. By dividing the management of labor in a systematic manner, I could control the workforce."

"Your plan spilled over to the schoolhouse," said Sid. "For example, management is by mandate—top down. The organization is divided into smaller and smaller chunks—the schools are divided by grade levels, the students sorted by age, the curriculum by subjects, the classrooms always divided into rows and columns. Each teacher is certified by the state to teach a specific area and each administrator a particular level of grades.

"How can we ask people who come through the schoolhouse every day to leave their array of social, cultural, and psychological baggage outside the door so they can be objectively rated only on what we pour into their heads and on how well we reduce the variance between them in order to control them . . . objectively? Can the human mind be asked to perform in this detached manner and yet understand that freedom is about maintaining cooperative interaction?"

"Well, it certainly all makes sense to me," Principal Nick Chez said stoically. "My grandparents came to this country from Germany. They could not speak English. They left their farm and arrived in New York City, the great urban center of the world.

"Because they had limited skills, they searched for jobs in the factories. Industrialization and the scientific revolution were in high gear and they needed jobs. A worker who had no skills and could not speak English could be taught to do the job if it was broken down into parts. And that's what my grandparents did. They worked in the factories, doing the same repetitive task six days a week, fifteen hours a day. It was a harsh system, but without it they would have starved."

"But your grandparents were human beings," Sid said, compassion keynoting his tone. "How can you depersonalize the workplace?"

"It made sense," Nick answered. "Mr. Descartes had informed us that man was like the springs and wheels of a clock. Figure out how each part works and you perfect the timepiece. Production increased. The system was neat and orderly, just like the cosmos."

Two education historians, Mr. David B. Tyack and Ms. Elisabeth Hansot, who had been sitting quietly, perked up (Tyack & Hansot, 1982). "Let us not be oblivious to the fact, Principal Aphus, that there were good reasons for depersonalizing the workplace. In the 1800s, educational leaders were trying hard to professionalize themselves," said Mr. Tyack.

"They saw the organizational model of scientific management," Ms. Hansot continued, "as a way of doing this. Scientific management provided a mechanical template for warehousing large numbers of children and providing them with a universal education. The factory model and its system of control appealed to the public because the public were themselves working within such a structure and they understood it."

"One task of the educational leader," added Mr. Tyack, "was to see that the teacher converted the raw material . . . the child . . . into a new American product called citizen. Like his factory manager counterpart, the educational leader worked on making the teacher more productive through, for example, preparing detailed lesson plans. As the principal *Taylorized* the teacher, he was also inspecting the raw material as it was conveyed from grade to grade through a system of periodic testing."

"I became the Frederick Taylor of education," said Mr. Franklin Bobbitt (Tyack & Hansot, 1982). His nametag read "turn-of-the-century educator." "As Mr. Taylor believed that efficiency depended upon the work processes being separated from the hands of the employees and managed by the managers, I believed that the teacher had to be told the school's expectations and the methods and resources to be utilized. And of course, children should be arranged by age and slotted for the appropriate grade. How else could we sort children . . . size maybe?"

"With these wonderful sorting methods," Nick explained, "teachers and children could be uniformly molded so as to have little variation. It doesn't sound like these new educational leaders trusted the teachers any more than I do."

It sounded like someone was thinking about pig-iron again, Dina thought.

"Well, you must view their educational beliefs in the context of the time, as Ms. Margaret Wheatley suggested," Mr. Tyack said (Tyack & Hansot, 1982). "Educational leaders were trying to professionalize education and remove it from the political arena.

"Doctors had advanced their technical knowledge by dividing the body into parts and specializing in healing each part. Factory owners had advanced their technical knowledge by dividing the means of production into planning, implementing, selling, and delivering."

"The new educational leaders," continued Ms. Hansot, "used scientific management to design a school planned and staffed by specialists where children were sorted and slotted into age-graded programs, provided textbooks, and taught by certified teachers."

Dina was beginning to realize the idea of scientific management took complex systems like schools and broke them down into individual parts. The function of each part was analyzed independently of the other parts.

There were the children who had to learn a curriculum taught by teachers who had to be told how to do this and a principal whose job was to make certain they did this in the proscribed manner. The focus was on managing the process. When all the individual parts did their individual jobs, the designed product would receive the awaited stamp of approval at the end of the assembly line. But somebody forgot that the design of people unlike the design of widgets cannot be replicated. So, as the raw material was passed from one conveyer belt to the next, chinks developed and the machine had to be stopped, analyzed, and fixed . . . again and again and again.

"We view management from a parts perspective without even thinking about it, and that is a good thing," said Nick. "Of course I always think about it, attempting to refine my employees and students. I just introduced Madeline Hunter's 'Essential Elements of Instruction' to the teachers (Hunter, 2004). In another month, every teacher will begin his lesson with an anticipatory set. There can be no variance in this. The system works best when each part of this factory-like enterprise does its job as defined by the job description."

But why, Dina asked herself, didn't the new professionals choose a democratic model for schooling . . . a model that didn't treat people like parts of a machine . . . a model that applauded the individual and combined experiences of people? Was it because the interests of the new professionals and the new industrialists coalesced? The educators wanted universal education, and businessmen needed workers for the factory. One hand helped the other.

"I was an early advocate of public education," Horace Mann affirmed. "I did not believe in the class system or even the existence of classes. But I know what you're thinking, Principal Aphus. You're thinking that I sold out education to business interests. That may be true, but my motives were pure. I wanted all kids to be educated even if it meant using a factory design."

"Let's face it," Mr. Tyack said, "industrialists and professional educators were scheming together. The organization and curriculum of schools evolved to meet the needs of developing capitalism" (Tyack & Hansot, 1982).

Dina reflected after listening to the various views she had just heard. Horace Mann thought that the purpose of universal education was to transmit American democracy. However, she sensed that a model of schooling was chosen that accomplished just the opposite.

As Ms. Wheatley said, we have to look at why people do things in the context of their time (Wheatley, 1992). The early educators didn't think as much about the variance in people as they galvanized their thoughts about school systems. They thought more about a structure where a lot of children could be sorted and slotted and prepared for democracy in an American society.

So we again return to the question of whether the factory template we have inherited is compatible with educating our youth and with fostering our experiment in democracy. Can a schoolhouse, which has become the Goliath to the David, do this? Some say it can. Why? It's the way things are always done.

REFLECTION

The greatest sin of analytical thinking goes back to the Renaissance, when human activity was analyzed and divided into three categories: learning, working, and playing. But can the human mind be asked to perform in this detached manner and yet understand that freedom is about maintaining cooperative interaction?

Think about all the assumptions that have separated the parts from the whole in your school. Now reverse these assumptions. What if they were all false and you had to undo them? What impact would that have on your school? What would be different about teaching and learning? What would change in your role and responsibilities?

Now you are beginning to get the idea; the whole is greater than the sum of its parts!

Rule

UNDERSTAND INTERACTIONS: PEOPLE, DATA, SYSTEMS, AND THEORY

At an early age, Principal Dina Macksy concluded that children learned the workplace rules that governed learning at the expense of what Cousin Michael called learning how to learn. How could a child focus on creating dreams when lurking behind every corner of the schoolhouse were Principal Nick Chez and Superintendent Mac Avelli?

They based their rules of leadership on the creation of as little variance as possible between and among children—and teachers. They had taken Adam Smith's sense of widget production to heart.

In such a controlling atmosphere, the child's natural sense of self-discovery readily acquiesced to being structured by the norms of the schoolhouse. Rarely challenged were the interweaving nature of schoolhouse rules, the child's intellectual development, and the operating processes in the schoolhouse.

Schooling was about parts, the most salient part to learn was called control. Control was divided into *either-or* behaviors. Of course, as Principal Sid Aphus said, we lived in a more natural world after school, but the schoolhouse reached well beyond its boundaries. It reined us back into the world of certainty, where everything was fixed and determined before we got there, minimizing anything that we could have brought to the learning table from the outside.

As we grew, we became so used to believing what we were told that we forgot to think about the relevance of the telling. Mr. Taylor and Mr. Pavlov were right—people and animals were easily programmable and every stimulus would eventually be met with a response. Creating pig-iron workers became easy.

Of course there was the occasional David blazing trails here and there and everywhere in the hallways of the schoolhouse, but he was a special cause of variation—an outlier—and could be accommodated in a more controlled environment. That was where he was sent.

It's hard to debug the program after so many years, but one day Dina felt that she had to, even if Superintendent Avelli objected.

She had learned from the great voices sitting on the shelves in the library that by knowing oneself, she could look with deeper scrutiny at the motives of others. She had learned that she needed theory to guide her if she wanted to model democracy in the schoolhouse; she had learned that the parts in a system interact with other parts and affect the system in some way.

She had learned that it was the interaction of the parts that was more important than the parts themselves. She had learned from Democritus, Descartes, and Newton about separating parts out to understand their whole. She had learned from Will Kane that it was really the whole thing that mattered. So what was missing?

Back to the campus litter problem. She didn't trust the individuals at the school to help her solve the problem. She also didn't realize that the problem of litter on campus had many parts: it had a people part, a data part, a mandate part, a morale part, and an academic part.

The parts were not as important as the interacting effects of the parts. She didn't have the foresight to see what interactions would occur once she mandated change because she never thought that there were more than two parts to the problem—the problem and the solution.

The problem was too much litter, and the solution was to have everybody pick it up. What could be easier? The principal's new idea was a good one, and besides, in a democracy, doesn't everybody work together for the common good? But when she sent out the memo dictating what each person would do to solve the problem, a morale problem called resentment developed in both teachers and students.

Her solution also took time away from achieving higher test scores and produced more work for the custodian, who had to remove from the school walls expletives about her mother.

The different parts in the system reacted to her mandate and, like the stuff in a bomb, exploded. She had no theory of management to help explain what happened. Understanding this now was moving her ahead. The more she thought about it, the more she realized that democracy was about people talking to each other face to face instead of back to back. It was being informed enough to debate and weigh issues before coming to decisions.

She also learned that, in order to debate an issue, you had to provide evidence that a problem existed. And it had something to do with the word *variation* that Adam Smith was whispering in her ear.

Then along came a guy named W. Edwards Deming (Deming, 1986). He jumped off the bookshelves—part of him had come from the physics library and the other from the business library. "Why doesn't this library make me whole and include me in the theory stacks," he was overheard muttering.

"You never stopped to think that maybe there was no problem," he said to Dina. "Maybe the amount of litter deposited on the ground by the students was normal. Maybe it was not. If it were normal, what did normal mean? How much litter could be tolerated?

"Maybe there were special causes for the trash on the day you observed it. Maybe the cafeteria food was fouler than usual. Maybe you were in a bad mood. Because you were angry about the problem, you aggregated the problem of litter to the whole problem of uncaring students and teachers. In a flurry of rage, you shared that anger about the paper with the faculty and students, faulting them for the litter problem.

"Did you know what an acceptable level of litter was?" asked Deming. "If you didn't, how could you say there was too much?

"Let me tell you a story," Deming said, his tall, gaunt body sliding down on a chair that just seemed to appear at a table (Deming, 1986). "I call it the parable of the beads. And wait until the end before you declare that what happens in business has no application to the school organization. After all, as Mr. Weber and Mr. Taylor have demonstrated, you base your organization on a factory model.

"In my story of the parable of the beads, I use volunteers in the audience to role-play the typical work environment, which is composed of workers, managers, and inspectors. The managers want the workers to produce white beads. But inspectors are finding defective red beads being produced as well.

"Customers won't pay for red beads,' warns the manager. 'The company loses money each time the workers produce the red beads. So do your job right!'

"There are six people from the audience who play the role of workers," Deming goes on to explain, "who each stir a mixture of red beads and white beads. There are four thousand beads that they will stir and eight hundred are red.

"Each worker, using a paddle, draws a sample of fifty beads." Deming reminds them that the company does not want red beads. "The workers use the same tools. The design of the paddle used to produce the beads, the size and weight of the beads, and the size of the container are the same.

"After the workers complete bead production, an inspector records the defects produced by them. The work performed by individuals varies. . . . Terry has produced the most defects and Jack the least."

Deming says parts theory would suggest that Terry should be fired. He produced too many red beads. Jack surpassed expectations. He should be given merit pay.

There are many sources of variation in business and educational systems, but managers and administrators are not trained to work with this fact. They think that someone or something has to be blamed when things go awry.

Deming suggested that the existence of chance is present in everyday life, but it is assumed that chance is not responsible for differences in individual performance. When the system is not stable, people must be considered as a source or variation, but it should not be concluded that they *are* the source of the problem. We keep on blaming them, and still have the same results.

Dina was beginning to catch on. When there is a problem in her educational system she must ask herself how much of what the workers are producing is caused by random variation and how much is caused by special causes.

The system is composed of far more than each individual person doing his job. It is represented by the tools that the employees are given
to work with, the materials used to make the tools, the tools that are
selected for use, the procedures used to produce the outcomes, political
and social climates, and so on and so forth.

Deming emphasizes that the red beads are defects that exist within
the system. The workers are merely exposed to these defects. It is not
Terry who is defective. He is doing his best. His variation can only be
attributed to something going on within the system.

As the demonstration continues, Deming asks that the inspector conduct another evaluation. Now another person is at the top and another
at the bottom. Should the new person at the bottom be fired?

Dina began thinking about a really good teacher she had back in high
school. Was she a good teacher because she was teaching to a test, or
was she a good teacher because she educated me, she asked herself?
Would the teacher she most remembered survive in a political climate
that demands that students learn only what is on the state test? Would
she still be a good teacher?

Sometimes our systems produce something out of the ordinary, and
this occurrence in some way changes the system. How would we know
this? That's where data become important.

If you wanted to find what was causing the problem, you have to have
ways to explore the problem. The pointed finger had to be left out of
the equation.

The parable demonstrates how blaming the part—the employee—for
something the employee may have no control over does little to improve
the whole—the system. It also teaches us that breaking the system down
into parts does nothing to find the root causes of the problem.

Deming is not suggesting that teachers could not be a cause of, say,
low math scores in the school. He is just saying that they work in a
system of reactive parts, and the interaction of these parts is what is
producing the results.

"Pointing fingers," Deming continued, "is a false strategy that per-
petuates the problem. We use it because we don't know how to access
all the data that contribute to the variation in the system. We focus on
the input we best understand, aggregate that input to the cause, and

assign blame. Inputs come from a multitude of sources of variation, people being just one source."

Dina began thinking about the parable of the beads as the parable of teaching. There was a speaker she remembered in the library, a man with a very sad eyes brimming with tears. His nametag identified his as Jonathan Kozol, educator.

Kozol lamented, "I wrote a book called *Amazing Grace*.

"It told the story of Taft High School in the Bronx. In the early 1960s, the student population was mostly white and known for its academic achievement. In the 1990s, the school had become one of the grimmest schools in the United States, the self-esteem of children being crushed to the degree that students ridiculed themselves . . . by making a bitter joke out of the letters of the school's name.

"They say Taft stands for *Training Animals for Tomorrow*. The area around the school is heavily patrolled so that students can get from the subway to the school unharmed. But the greatest harm that faces the 4,000 boys and girls who went there may be what is done to them inside the building after they arrive" (Kozol, 1995, p. 152).

Dina was thinking about this and the interactions of the people in the system, the system as a whole, and how we measure what it produces. She thought about a theory, that people want to do their best. The system is more than the components of its parts, that we have to measure what the system produces, and how all of this applied to Taft High School in the 1990s at the classroom level.

Let's say that Mr. David is a teacher at the school. With his paddle of knowledge, he tries to scoop his overcrowded classrooms of students into his world of literature. He wants to show his students, who are plagued by asthma, AIDS, and alienation, that there is a better world. And they all have the potential to live in it—they can still dream. But dreaming is a hard sell when loose wires hang from the classroom ceiling, the rooms are filthy, and Mr. David does not have enough textbooks for each student.

Mr. David expects all his students to do well. He has examined their individual files and knows that each of his students is intellectually able to learn the content. But when he assesses them, he knows that each of them come to school with baggage that can't be left outside his classroom.

There is variation between each student depending upon the particular crisis in the student's life: whether she has a textbook from which to study, the fear she experiences going from the subway, crossing the gang-infested streets to school, the effect of the wires hanging from the ceilings, the temperature in the room, her health problems, her family support structure, and a multitude of other social, economic, emotional, cultural, and environmental factors.

Mr. David cannot control the environment in which he is teaching and in which his students live. He cannot control the spread of AIDS and violence caused by poverty. He cannot control the building conditions. He is stuck in a system, doing the very best he can.

Mr. David can do little to change the number of defects he will produce under the current system. The system of poverty that interacts with the system of schooling is like a crap shoot; the odds will favor some shooters sometimes and other shooters other times.

The parts—the teachers—cannot change the system alone. They have a limited effect on the poverty of the neighborhood and the way the school is run. They too are its victims.

So why do we blame the teachers when test scores at Taft High School are low? Do we conclude that the teachers need to be reeducated? Do we infer that the teachers are not doing their jobs? Can we fix the part—teachers who produce low-test scores—in isolation of the whole problem?

She was beginning to suspect that the reason her school had returned to the same conditions three years after winning the big award was because she was practicing a theory of organizational management based on a theory that had only limited application.

That was Ms. Margaret Wheatley's message to those who were listening to her. Dina had improved the parts, but she had done it in the absence of understanding how the parts related to each other and to the goals. The template designed by Mr. Weber and Mr. Taylor might have helped to increase production in the factory, but did little to increase the achievement of students over time in the schoolhouse.

As a principal, Dina clung to the thought that if each person did his or her job, student achievement would improve. Her district allocated huge sums of money to teacher improvement. If teachers practice their new skills, their students would be successful. Reading scores would look good in the newspapers. If a teacher were delinquent in his or her duties, that teacher would receive the appropriate consequences.

It was a punishing game. Teachers punished students, the principal punished teachers. As she became more entrenched in the game, absenteeism and dropout rates started climbing again. Student achievement began to take a dive.

As a result, she played the blame game even harder as the snake under the carpet popped up here and there and everywhere, and she kept running after it, stomping her foot down each time the curve in its sinewy body reared up.

But now she was learning something that Principal Nick Chez found hard to digest; the school could not be operated as if its people were machines. How could you blame teachers for the flaws in the educational system when they were given no control over the machine?

The apparent differences between people come entirely from the action of the system in which they work, not always from the people themselves. They had no access to the feedback loops that organize systems. Only the administrators had this access. And they were capable of predicting system performance, but principals had not been schooled to do this.

How does a principal use knowledge of people, data, systems, and theory to affect school governance, student performance, and the preservation of democracy? How does a principal transcend the Newtonian organization? How does a principal acknowledge that her theory of mechanistic and materialistic determinism is antithetical to human values?

Quantum mechanics revealed the validity of Kant's thesis that the nature described by physics was not nature in itself but man's relationship to nature. Plato's truth was not truth in an ideal world but truth in relationship to us trying to build an ideal world. That is, there were no absolutes in the schoolhouse. There was only what we brought with us, what others brought with them, and the art of the acquisition of knowledge that mattered to nurture the nature of democracy.

The physics of connections was beginning to trump the physics of absolutes. Could her schoolhouse accept the challenge, knowing that Superintendent Avelli controlled her school and principals like Nick Chez still supported governance by fiat?

We know that we would rather live in a free world than a controlling world. It is just part of our nature. The social contract theorists brought this to our attention. But how do principals make the new principles operational?

"The world is a complex network of interactive parts, all operating to accomplish the system's aim," Ms. Wheatley said. "Each part is limited in its ability to perform without all other parts. Individual activities are necessary in a system, but not sufficient in themselves to accomplish the aim of the system" (Wheatley, 1992).

Dina now had a theory of school governance. Could she embed this theory in practice so that democracy would survive and she could save the Republic?

REFLECTION

How does a principal use knowledge of people, data, systems, and theory to affect school governance, student performance, and the preservation of democracy? How does a principal transcend the Newtonian organization, where there are no connections between parts, to an organization filled with connections? Do you play the blame game even harder as the snake under the carpet pops up here and there and everywhere and you keep running after it, stomping your foot down each time the curve in its sinewy body reared up?

Now that you have completed Part I of this saga, which path will you choose to follow? Will you choose the path less traveled and begin to blaze your way toward Quantumland, or will you respond like Alice in Wonderland:

"Cheshire-Puss," said Alice, "which way ought I go from here?"
    "It depends on where you want to get to," said the Cat.
    "I don't much care where, as long as I get somewhere," said Alice.
    "You're sure to do that if only you walk long enough," said the Cat.
(Fior, 2000, p. 22)

II

TAKING THE
QUANTUM LEAP

Philosophy is about how we look at things—our beliefs. We have to understand those beliefs, where they come from, why we have them, why we find them meaningful, and how they hold up against other beliefs. We have to test our beliefs so that they are consistent with facts, our experience, and the consequences of our experience.

Plato frowned upon philosophies based on the uninformed opinions of the marketplace. Principal Dina Macksy concurred. She reasoned that her expeditions up and down hills were due to the movers and shakers in the marketplace. Every time they came her way, she bought into what they were selling. What made one school look good would certainly make her school do the same.

She brought program after program about effective teaching models, learning styles, quality management, effective school research, brain-based teaching and learning, and so many more of the latest fads and trends to the school, but the classrooms still looked the same and standardized scores still stagnated.

It was not that these new ideas were bad. They were very good—but put into place without considering the bigger picture. They were like the ribs on an umbrella—all the ribs were held together by something at the top, but no one knew what to name the top, although she heard the word *vision* all the time. And rarely were data used to demonstrate a connection between programs, the schoolhouse, and the students.

As principals, we just make pronouncements like the one that said that students would do better if the teachers knew more about effective schools. The idea of doing better was good, but Dina questioned what the students should do better. Was the latest bandwagon that had come down rallying higher test scores really the bandwagon on which she should climb as students dropped out of school, got pregnant, and stole prescription drugs from their parents' medicine cabinets?

Was there a connection between the fads and our test results that were displayed in the newspaper? Rarely. And we all knew that after the latest fad was introduced, it would stay around a while and then leave through the schoolhouse's revolving door as another fad pushed its way in. What she learned from all this was that fads come in as fast as they go out, but nobody was looking at the students as the doors revolved.

As principals, our philosophical beliefs have to be tested over time in the context of not only our experiences and their consequences, but also the experiences of others and their consequences. We have to have a deep understanding that evolves from these interactions. Of course, one has a philosophy, but one must also find the conduits that will put beliefs to work so that they can continue to be tested.

Dina believes, for example, that having freedom is better than not having freedom. She knows this because when her superintendent tells her to do something, like enforce his time clock mandate, it is not consistent with her deeply held beliefs and experiences. She expresses outrage, internally of course, because she still wants to keep her job.

Her internal rebellion occurs as a result of the deeply held conviction taught to her by the social contractors. When we come together as a people, they said, we have to give up something to get something. She had to give up her objections to *clocking in* in order to keep her job. You see, she bought into what Aristotle said about the ultimate result of democracy being happiness.

Dina learned from the many voices at the library that people need to work together to pursue her belief that people should be happy. Happy people are educated people who need to make sense of why teachers have to clock into work.

She also learned from the library voices that the classical way in which many view the world—where things are fixed and determined, where cause follows effect, and where parts were examined separate from the whole—was not a model of school governance that aligned itself with democracy.

On the other hand, she was beginning to think that the quantum world of interconnectivity lends itself more readily to organizations based on human relations. Even though she wasn't quite certain what democracy looked like in the schoolhouse, she knew that it was based on voices that were not afraid to speak out, where people debated, dialogued, and created mutual agreements from diverse thinking, where people had common goals, and where problem solving was based on perceived needs underscored by hard evidence to support those needs.

There were many voices from many speakers in the library. At this point, Dina may have not shared all her conversations, but they may pop up here and there later. The point is they said so many things that made sense to her and to her belief that being born a free person was better than being born a widget.

With her new beliefs, she felt confident that she could change the way things happened in the schoolhouse, giving people the opportunity not only to be more committed to school goals, but to be happy. It was a change that evolved slowly within her, delayed for a long time because she had done what had always been done in terms of organizational leadership.

With the use of the following vignettes or series of events, Dina now will illustrate the lessons learned from the library discussions and how her thinking about school organization changed. She didn't create any miracles, but she did create an environment where people talked to each other about our most important resource—our children.

However, she forgot one thing. When you start climbing a new mountain, you have to realize that there are still larger mountains surrounding you, and sometimes avalanches just happen.

Vignette

DRIVE FEAR FROM
THE WORKPLACE

How does Principal Dina Macksy move from thinking about the people in the schoolhouse as interchangeable parts to thinking about them as trusted and valued resources in the leadership of the school? Application of the theory appeared so easy to envision in the pristine environment of the library. It became very nebulous in the messy affairs of a workplace held together rather tenuously by the complexity of human relations.

One day, as she walked through the school corridors contemplating how to stand on the shoulders of the great thinkers, her secretary, Mrs. Hogarth phoned her. "Five of the tenured members of the faculty, the movers and shakers, are waiting in your office," she said stoically.

"It's probably about all the time I've spent off campus learning how to exit Mr. Newton's world and create a democracy in the schoolhouse," Dina said, sanguine expectations underlying her ebullient tone of voice.

"I can hardly wait to share my knowledge with them. It's hard to change one's thinking about living in a world where everything is fixed and determined and then dive into one where everything is connected and sometimes can go astray in the night."

Mrs. Hogarth, always skeptical that anything in school really changes, said, "They're here on an exploration mission, all right, but not the kind you're thinking about." Dina couldn't help but notice a bit of cynicism in her voice.

She was right. As Dina walked into her office and greeted them—Mr. Newt Owen, social studies; Mrs. Edna Lightment, business education; Mr. Quintin Waver, science; Mr. Henry Berg, English; and Mrs. Desiree Cartes, math.

She could immediately tell by the grim look on their faces that they were not on the same glorious page as she. Mr. Waver and Mr. Owen stared at the clock on the wall. Mrs. Lightment scanned through a book called *New Ideas for the Classroom*, while Mr. Berg looked over her shoulder. Mrs. Cartes was scribbling random numbers on her yellow tablet.

Could it be that Dina had been away from the schoolhouse too long, and they were about to call her on it? No, they would never do that. She was the principal, the person on top of the hierarchical chart for the high school.

Dina wished she knew them better. But then again, all she was interested in was their classroom performance and their dedication to teaching to the state tests. But it didn't matter. Once they understood her new knowledge, they would be in a more forgiving and favorable mood.

They sat down on the five hard-backed chairs that ran in a straight line in front of her desk. She realized then that the seating arrangement in her office seemed to create a powerful boundary, suggestive of her power over them. She needed a round table to equalize things, one that would create a less deterministic and fixed universe. She made a mental note to order one.

Mr. Owen began the meeting. For some reason his white, starched shirt, red tie, and the carefully ironed crease that ran down the center of his blue trousers attracted her attention. He's always so neat, she thought.

"Well, we are glad that you are finally back from your workshops," Mr. Owen began, the murky smile suddenly daunting Dina.

"While you were away, however, the faculty held a meeting and appointed the five of us to share with you something that concerns them."

There was a silence, that uncomfortable silence that follows the preface to a communication that you know is going to sting.

"Some members of the faculty are concerned that interpersonal relations between them and the administration are becoming negative." *She knew that administration was the code word for principal.*

"They think that your negative, unconstructive criticism during evaluations caused them to feel demoralized and angry. The general emotional environ . . . environment (*he was stammering as if he were apprehensively parroting what the faculty had decided that he should say*) should be one of encouragement and collegial support." *Are teachers supposed to reproach principals in this manner?*

"Instead, what has developed is an atmosphere of disapproval and fear. You are using intimidation and personal attack to motivate improvement."

Dina was mortified to be chastised by a faculty member. She thought that the rating system she developed to evaluate teachers was fair. After all, they rated their students with grades for performance, and she had decided to do the same.

Her belief was that grading them as they did their students would provide the motivation they needed to improve. You see, she deplored what she saw every time she entered some of the classrooms.

Teachers stood in front of the room and talked while students didn't listen. Although they had all been Taylorized via Hunter, the soporific teaching continued. Maybe if Mr. Owen and company saw this, they would feel as avenging as she did. *Did she say avenging?*

But Dina didn't understand why these teachers abjured her new rating system. Their marks were among the highest.

"So what is it that the faculty perceives they need?" Dina asked him, as her voice got temporarily stuck deep in her throat. She was thinking about what Mr. Hopkins had said about the quality of learning of any individual being a function of the quality of his total psychological field at the time that learning takes place (Hopkins, 1941). If she were to allow the seething anger she felt bursting inside onto this scene, she would only create negatives from what could be potential positives.

But, at the time, Dina thought it was so unfair that they didn't see what she saw in the classroom. However, it wasn't their fault, she reasoned, that Mr. Weber had developed a division of labor in the workplace, separating out those who worked on the processes from those who worked in them, separating the planning from the doing stages. She had to be rational and not react reflexively to their allegations.

Principal Nick Chez of Berlin High School would have invited these faculty recalcitrants out of his office. Not Dina.

Ms. Wheatley said she had to look at the organization in a new light. Mr. Sarason and others had suggested she had to look inside herself, to her own motivations, to understand the motives of others. And Mr. Einstein had said that she could not separate herself from that at which she was looking. They were looking at her, she was looking at them, and, instead of breaking the connection, she had to build upon it. This was going to be tough.

"They want you to be more understanding," Mr. Owen said, his facial muscles tightening as he spoke. *Didn't Mr. Deming say that workers were not satisfied if the organization shows no interest in them, she asked herself.*

Mr. Owen looked up at Dina. "You know this faculty respects you as a leader. But something's happened. They don't think you are listening to their concerns in a genuine way anymore. They want to feel respected by you. They want to feel that we all have a shared purpose and we are pursuing it together. They suggested we begin a dialogue to deal with these concerns. We have to rebuild trust. We can't affect student achievement if we are suspect of each other all the time."

The faculty was right. Over time, beliefs had become divergent and trust had been lost. More and more, Dina had come to believe that teachers lived in a comfort zone from which they were reluctant to retreat. She became critical of them, blaming them for not engaging students in their classrooms, especially in lieu of all the training they received.

Each time Dina observed bright students passing notes, clowning around in class, or doodling on the desk while the teacher practiced elocution in front of the room, she felt frustration and indignation. Democratic principles were not being practiced, and the cause of democracy was being lost on students who were enduring endless tedium. After one classroom visit, she recorded this journal entry about what she termed first period teachers—teachers who didn't understand that the teaching-learning process included students.

> I observed a first period teacher today. "Today," he starts, "our objective is to discuss the meaning of Goethe's masterpiece, *Dr. Faustus*, which as

we all know is an allegory about man's quest for knowledge at any cost and for those of you who are really into this . . . there is going to be an extra credit assignment where you can apply this allegory to a more universal theme by turning in a paper on something you might have recently read or seen . . ."

"Universal!" shouts the enthusiastic interruption from the young man sitting in row three seat four. "I just saw *Star Trek*. Can I apply that?"

The room turns silent. The student is connecting to an idea the teacher has advanced. But instead of reacting, perhaps advancing knowledge to include what the student brought to class with him, the first year teacher says something feeble like he does not expect students to call out in his class.

"We must preserve order in the classroom," he states with some asperity.

His statement has belligerent overtones . . . indeed, even cushioned in arrogance. Why doesn't he take the opportunity to connect what the student is suggesting to what he is teaching? Couldn't there be more than one muse in the classroom?

Tic . . . toc . . . tic . . . toc . . . goes the mouse up the clock. The quest for knowledge at any cost continues.

". . . and so ladies and gentlemen that is the allegory of Dr. Faustus."

The lecture ends but one wonders what knowledge was shared. Did the students learn anything that might have occurred before they were born? We live in a new world where communication is more apt to have meaning if it allows others into the conversation.

How long will it take for this first period teacher to move into second period . . . even after all the workshops to which Superintendent Mac Avelli has sent him and all the individual help I give him? Sometimes it takes so long, and sometimes it doesn't happen at all. It's all so depressing that kids, who bring so much natural energy with them to the schoolhouse, have to put it on hold and wait for the football or volleyball practice to begin.

Dina was bored like the kids; a thousand workshops over the years hadn't changed the teaching styles of so many teachers. They were still first period teachers. And their excuses for the perennial, insipid lesson plan were always the same.

"I don't have enough time to work on lesson plans or call parents. I stopped giving homework, because nobody hands it in . . . the only reason kids come to school is to be with their friends and because it's the law.

"Anyway, the only thing their parents want from us is to babysit their little darlings. I don't let my students take home their textbooks because they don't bring them back . . . the kids here are lazy. They only come to school because the law says they have too."

Dina was as indignant as the teachers. But she hadn't overtly shared that anger with them. Instead, she had stored it up, simultaneously and furtively losing respect for those who were doing the job. She aggregated the weak teaching skills of some teachers to the teaching skills of the entire faculty and pointed fingers at them all. And now her anger had built into rage. And her rage had become their fear.

She recalled the moment she had decided to do their evaluations by numbers. Here is the journal entry she recorded.

I wanted to do evaluations this year that meant something and could correct the deficiencies I see in the teaching staff. Instead of building morale through the evaluation system by telling everyone how great a job they are doing, I decided to rate them by category.

For each of the four categories . . . preparing for instruction, instruction, management of instruction, and professional relationships . . . I would assign a number. I would average the numbers and group together those who needed help by categories.

This is an objective idea. Descartes would applaud me for my efforts because numbers are truth—the only truth—and they define the teacher. Finally, evaluations will have some meaning and connect in some way to the achievement of students.

As I break down the areas in which they need to improve, perhaps they will do this individually for their students . . . instead of the usual giving out grades without much explanation other that the student needs to study harder or is just not doing the assigned work.

Dina didn't share the new idea with the teachers. She just did the evaluations unaware that the chatty nature of conversation in the teacher's lounge had taken a vitriolic turn. She—and her mother—became the target of the rancor. While she added and subtracted numbers on each teacher's evaluation form, they questioned how their teaching performance could be quantified.

Dina responded that it could be quantified in the same manner as they quantified their students' grades on a report card. This explanation only served to heighten the new strand of fear that she had developed.

Dina was beginning to understand that when fear is placed on the agenda, we began to lose our direction and miss our goals. That's what her rating system had produced.

A family is a group of people who are together much of the day. A school of people is like a family. They share so many different emotions during the working hours when they are compressed into tiny cell-like structures.

Dina had taken those teachers who live in cells and stripped them of their human qualities by assigning a grade to their work. Her intent at objectifying the evaluation process resulted in treating them like widgets. She was quantifying what teachers did. But she still couldn't understand what was different about their assessments of their students and her assessment of them.

Did rating systems divide their students as it was dividing them? Dina remembered a time when she had received a low grade in a high school English class. She felt ashamed.

Is this what she was making them feel? Perhaps rating systems divided people between the have's and have not's. Perhaps the reason why only some of the faculty objected to being given a grade was because Dina was making them compete with one another.

She could hear them in the teacher's lounge, asking each other what grade they received. Those who did not receive the high grades must have felt the same shame she felt in that English class. Dina was teaching them to compete against one another instead of fostering cooperation.

Mr. Owen was right. If teachers and principals could not trust each other, students would be affected—but not in the ways she thought. Teams win when they work together. Because of her anger with the lack of change in teachers, she had pointed fingers without inviting them into a process where they could understand why the necessary changes were not occurring.

Perhaps some of them needed more training, more mentoring, and perhaps fewer students in their already overpopulated classes.

Dina had not been able to find the true causes of the problems that were occurring at the high school. She had fallen into the traditional trap of approaching organizational problems by assigning blame.

In a democracy, we have to learn how to work as a team, eliminating control by threats, coercion, and rating systems. Teachers needed her support and she needed theirs. With mutual support, more effective work processes could be produced and processes more closely aligned with student learning.

Dina was no longer a classical mechanic, looking for the part that caused the problem and fixing it. That was Newton's Flaw. Teachers who lectured all period were a problem. But maybe she had to look for another way to approach the problem rather than instilling fear.

She was now a quantum mechanic, looking at the interrelationships that guide the system toward accomplishing its aim. This was going to be a messy process. There was no point A, B, or C from which to start. But if she wanted to continue improving the high school using democratic processes, Dina would have to start on this journey now.

Vignette

②

CONVERSATION LEADS
TO DIALOGUE

"The world of relationships is rich and complex," Ms. Margaret Wheatley (Wheatley, 1992, p. 34) told the audience at the San Diego conference. She went on to say that if nothing exists independently of its relationship with something else, we can move away from our need to think of things as polar opposites; what is critical is the relationship between the person and the setting. The relationship will always be different, will always evoke different potentialities. It all depends on the players and the moment.

Principal Dina Mackey thought profoundly about Ms. Wheatley's ideas throughout the summer and again as the new school year began. Times were changing in her district. Remember that story that Jonathon Kozol told about Taft High School in the Bronx? Well, she couldn't help but think that what had happened at Taft was spreading like an incipient cancer to her school, even though they were thousands of miles apart.

The neat and tidy universe that Mr. Newton extolled was not the one in which she was now living. She readily identified the part in the external system that was creating the problem. She was able to connect the part to the other parts. She saw that outside her school was a system that was in self-destruct mode.

She wasn't sure how her system could surmount the encroaching problems, although the monitoring committee that was created after her visit with Mr. Newt Owen and company made her suddenly aware that she did not have to work alone on this problem. Because of the monthly meetings, trust was slowly being rebuilt.

She could always detect the elevation of the fear barometer in the workplace, but now Dina had a conduit for lowering it. She had met with the movers, shakers, and others who rotated into their slots. Although some individuals were still apprehensive about coming directly to her with their professional concerns, at least now they went to their representatives.

But a new fear entered the neighborhoods surrounding the school. The fear wafted into the schoolhouse.

At the outset of the school year, Dina began to perceive that the hopes, dreams, and joys of a new beginning were eclipsed by the violence that had spread throughout schoolhouses all over America.

Classrooms were becoming darker, and students were changing. Gangs and violence had entered the schoolhouse gate. Teachers were becoming more entrenched in their classrooms as students challenged their authority. This entry in her journal bookmarks the time.

Monday, August 21

I watch the teachers as they return on this first day back to school. Their faces are so pale that you would think that formaldehyde fills their blood vessels. I think they are afraid.

They have seen the newspaper headlines about terror overtaking the schoolhouse and share qualms about what the new school year will produce. There was a time when they worried about students coming to school drunk or drugged. Now they worry about students coming to school drunk, drugged, and with guns and knives . . . external weapons added to the internal arsenal.

When you think about the situation that society has created for principals, teachers, and students, you realize that schooling is a war game and the trenches do exist. Each year those trenches extend a little farther and we dig in a little deeper.

I used to take offense when Superintendent Mac Avelli said he was taking the principals out to lunch because the principals work in the trenches all day. My first thought was, with whom are we at war? Fact is, he was right.

First, principals are at war with superintendents who declare, "Get me the test results at whatever cost . . . just as long as it looks good in the newspaper."

Second, principals are at war with the teachers who don't get the results, even if they are good teachers.

Third, principals are at war with the students who would rather do drugs and bring weapons to school than learn how to prepare themselves for their roles in a democratic society.

Fourth, principals are at war with the parents who abandoned childrearing responsibilities years before their children reached hormonal age.

Fifth, principals are at war with politicians who demand that the schools be fixed part by part, proclaiming broken the part that will get them the most votes.

Sixth, principals are at war with big business that caters to the undeveloped mind . . . there's money in it . . . while teachers feebly attempt carrying on the social institution called schooling. . . the only institution that still stands to perpetuate our democracy.

She was depressed, but she knew that the wan, strained expression she wore had to be replaced by a more sanguine one. Grimness had to be put aside. Her meetings at the library were going to be the way out of the darkness.

She had to do something about the new population of students who had been forgotten by their parents and the churches and reared by the tens of millions of pixels shaped into sound and form on a screen. The reality was that something had to be done to save the Republic from the abyss into which it was dropping. Democracy could not survive with children being raised not to care about one another.

And then one day the process of renewal began. Just as you never know which radium atom was going to disintegrate first on any one day, you could never predict exactly what was going to happen in the schoolhouse. Newton's world was only a partial reality, sharing stage front with packets of energy that were oblivious to cause and effect, sometimes going boom in the night or even in the day.

She was listening to Mr. Owen talk to his students about the nature of democracy. One of his students, Jon Deway, asked why the mechanics of democracy were taught in the classroom, but not practiced in the schoolhouse.

"Society assumes that when we leave school, we'll know how to be-have in a democratic manner and that when we receive information, we'll know how to weigh in on it, but in my classes we don't even talk to each other.

"I hate to say it because I like and respect my teachers, but the con-versation in most of my classes is one sided. Information goes in and out of my head because I have no experience with what the teacher is saying."

What insight, Dina thought. He saw what she saw in the classrooms. This kid was on to something even though Principal Nick Chez and Superintendent Mac Avelli would have said that bureaucracy and de-mocracy were antithetical to each other.

But the kid was indeed insightful. How do you align school bureau-cracy with democracy? Democracy was about people talking together, and bureaucracy was about separating them so that the conversation never begins.

A picture of democracy would show people sitting at a round table, and a picture of bureaucracy would look like the five chairs in a straight line in front of her desk. Jon Deway's statement made her suddenly aware of how students receive conflicting signals in the classroom where democracy is taught but rarely practiced.

After class, she asked Jon to stay and spoke with both him and his teacher.

"What would you think if we formed a Democratic Council?" she asked. "I know the name sounds hokey but it describes what I would like to see happen . . . and invite representatives from the entire school to work on making our school a happy place to be as a result of having a common dialogue about our problems?"

Mr. Weber's factory and Mr. Bobbit's teachers were not designed to work democratically in the schoolhouse, she thought, but maybe its design could be changed by realigning the seating arrangements.

They liked the idea. At the next faculty meeting, she asked for volun-teers to work with her on the Democratic Council.

Our goal, she explained, is to look at our problems and find solu-tions that would be more than just another bandage attempt to fix what doesn't work. In addition, she announced, any teacher, staff member, or student who wanted to participate, but couldn't be at every meeting, was invited to attend and share their input, as long as their input was a continuation of the ongoing discussions. That meant they had to read the minutes of the meetings. She did not want the meetings to become gripe sessions.

At the faculty meeting, a staff member, Mr. Evan Mann, asked why aides weren't invited on the council. "School improvement is about all of us," he pointed out with some asperity.

Dina immediately invited him to represent them. Jon volunteered to be their first student representative. His job was to report back to the Student Council. The meetings were to be held once a week in the library, one hour before school officially began.

The first teachers to serve on the council were Mr. Owen, Mr. Henry Berg, Mrs. Edna Lightment, Mr. Quintin Waver, and Mrs. Desiree Cartes, the movers and shakers of the faculty.

Why were they classified as such, she asked herself? What made them different from the rest of the faculty? What did she perceive as their beliefs regarding the mechanical universe?

Mr. Owen believed in a neat and orderly world, a world where once you found the answer to the algorithm, the problem was solved. Mrs. Lightment, too, lived in this world, but lately she was changing and moving into the world in which Mr. Berg lived, a world where cause did not always precede effect, where the part did not always explain the whole.

Mrs. Cartes believed in the truth found in numbers. "What do the data say?" was her mantra.

Mr. Waver lived in Newton's world, but lately he was talking about how humanity had inherited a world in which we don't always live. "The quantum mechanics are lurking in the shadows," he was known to say. The faculty looked at him as usual with dubious eyes, although somewhat impressed by his scientific understandings, even if mechanics meant to them something under the car hood.

Could a committee of people with such different worldviews work to enact change that would promulgate democracy? Democracy was about including the views of diverse thinking people into the conversation. It had to work, she concluded.

One day, as Dina sat in the rear of Mr. Berg's humanities class, pondering how all the pieces could be put together into one big whole, the dialogue in the classroom suddenly jerked her away from her private thoughts. She listened as students discussed the oriental symbol of wholeness—the yin-yang.

"So you mean, Mr. Berg," said Jon Deway, "that in the West we have been taught to believe that all living things are essentially unconnected and their relationship is competitive in nature? Doesn't that idea go back to Aristotle?"

"That's right, Jon," Mr. Berg said. "However, the concept of wholeness . . . the yin-yang . . . is also divided into two parts but the parts are not at war with each other. They are mutually inclusive, each half depending upon the other for its existence.

"Neither has meaning without the other. Nothing can exist without its opposite. Knowing good is impossible without knowing evil. Each part enriches and enhances meaning to the other. It's a total system, not divisible."

"It sounds like the opposite of the basketball team," Jon countered, contemplating the information he had just received. "We keep losing because we don't play as a connected group of players who have to depend upon each other's skills to win. Instead, each player does his own grandstanding. We actually compete against each other, yet we're on the same team."

At the first meeting of the Democratic Council, which Mrs. Lightment volunteered to chair, Dina reviewed the volunteers' role on the Democratic Council. Their job, she explained, was to involve the faculty and staff in developing and implementing a school improvement plan that would affect student achievement in a meaningful way.

"As you know, every year each principal has to submit a school improvement plan to Superintendent Mac Avelli. This year, I told him I would like to create a plan that had meaning . . . *and wasn't written just to satisfy the superintendent.*" She didn't voice the last part of her sentence to them. "I told him I also wanted to work with the faculty, staff, and students on developing this plan. If we showed progress, I would also invite the parents into the process.

"As you all know, the plan usually says that we will improve our reading, writing, and math scores by such and such a percentage. To do this, we have workshops for you designed to improve your teaching skills. We all know that this plan is a fiasco . . . sometimes the scores go up and sometimes they go down."

She showed them a graph she had created that demonstrated this fact. "It's all a big joke because as you can see some years we are one percentage point better than the previous year. Sometimes just the opposite occurs. In effect, we accomplish little for our students but make ourselves look competitive in the newspapers with all the other high schools that are fluctuating in the same manner as we are. So where's the improvement?

"Lately," Dina continued, "I have been asking myself what this school is about. Why do we keep on doing the same thing over and over again and literally go nowhere?" Dina had never shown this degree of candor with faculty members.

"It seems to me that anytime a principal says we're going to improve things around here," Mr. Berg said, "we get a plan . . . a plan we file in our desk drawer and take out only when the principal is in our classroom." His remarks should have flayed Dina, but he was showing the same candor that she had just shown. They were both taking risks, checking the other's attempt at trust building.

"Not this time," she said. "All people working within the processes of education at our school will be invited to work on them by developing plans of action to counter problems. Together, we will study the inputs and outputs of our planning processes. If outputs are successful, we will continue refining plans, while looking for other windows of opportunity in terms of improvement."

Mrs. Lightment slowly rotated her head, seeing if everyone was on the same page. Satisfied that they were, she said, "Well, then, let's just jump right into this change process.

"Before we can change anything we have to have an aim . . . a purpose for what we are doing . . . and we have to come to some consensus about the purpose.

"I would lay odds that everyone at this table feels differently about what the aim of education is at this school. That's one way in maintaining the status quo. For example, I think the purpose of our school is to facilitate human growth through both individual and group socialization."

"Wait," Dina abruptly blurted out. "I think that somewhere in the school there is a vision statement for the school district. Does anyone know what it says?"

The room was silent until Mr. Berg suggested that they forgo this needless task of locating it. If nobody knew what the district vision for education was, it couldn't be very relevant, at least for now. "I think the purpose of education is to take the student from where he is and build upon his knowledge so that he can make an informed decision in the voting booth."

"I think the school should give students what will help them with their lives after they leave here," said Mr. Mann.

"I believe in self-discovery," Mr. Waver said. "Knowledge is a tool we give kids, and with that knowledge they can unlock the secrets to the universe."

"I certainly agree with that," Mrs. Cartes said. "I share my love of numbers with students because it's my philosophy, that in life, numbers are the only things that never lie to you." Turning to Dina, she asked, "And what does the principal believe is our purpose?"

"I believe," Dina said, without any hesitation, "that it is everyone's job in a free society to shape democracy toward nobler ends as we create thoughtful, caring citizens. Therefore, our purpose should be to guide students as they learn how to acquire knowledge toward that end."

"After we establish a school purpose," Mrs. Lightment continued, after the principal finished speaking, "as to why we come to school every day . . . why the kids come to school every day . . . why the parents send their children to school every day . . . we would then define our school system. How much were we willing to take on in terms of changing our school for the better? What would be our startup parameters?"

Mr. Owen looked bewildered. "Huh . . . say that again . . . define . . . startup parameters?"

Mrs. Lightment responded: "We use these terms in my consumer affairs class when we discuss how to improve the teaching-learning process so that achievement levels increase. Before we can take on any project, we have to explain fully what the project is, why we are taking it on, what we hope to accomplish so that we don't bite off more than we can chew.

"How often do we take on the whole world in education and wind up only working on a single part . . . like the teacher part, or the principal part, the curriculum part, the testing part, and then proclaim that singular part is the cause for all our problems? So we fix the part . . . or at least we think we are fixing the part . . . and after a while things return to their original condition."

"Yes, like our first improvement plan!" Dina sulked. "It started and it stopped. It had nowhere to go."

"But the cave dwellers are now ambulating out of their caves," Mr. Berg chortled, making light of her self-reproach.

"To continue with my previous thought," Mrs. Lightment said, ignoring his metaphor, "once we decide upon the system we will be changing, we will assess its current capability. Then we analyze the system looking for challenges in our processes that hinder student achievement."

"You mean like what was causing the problem?" asked Mr. Mann.

"Right," Mrs. Lightment said. "Our goal would be to find the real causes of the problems. For example, I started coughing about two months ago. Every day, in class, at certain intervals of time, I would cough. The kids began to notice and asked me if I had a cold. Everybody else did. So I thought I probably had what everybody else had.

"But when everybody else got well, I was still coughing. I went to my doctor. I told him that I didn't feel sick, but this cough was very persistent. He asked me if I was taking a certain drug for my blood pressure. I said I was. He wrote me a new prescription. The coughing stopped. A side effect to the drug I had been taking is coughing. We have to find the real causes of our problems. We have to go beyond what seems obvious."

"I remember last year," Mrs. Cartes interjected, "the middle school principal, Mr. Van Waggoner was giving out certificates from Burger King and Blockbuster's for students who came to school every day for a month. I was amused when I saw the students who were receiving the certificates."

"Yeah, I was too," Mr. Mann offered. "They were the same kids who would normally come to school anyway. I see what you mean about finding real causes. My son loved getting the certificates for doing what he was already doing. You have to dig deeper to find out what causes kids not to come to school."

"Right, and as we analyze why things were really happening," Mrs. Lightment said, "we'll brainstorm ways to address the problem and theorize about how we can change the system . . . and not change for change sake but for enhancing the education of our students.

"Once an improvement plan is generated based on our theories, we'll study the results. If the results show improvement, we'll continue to monitor them, planning for further improvement, while actively reviewing at appropriate intervals the data we are obtaining from the processes. If the results show that there was not an improvement, we will reassess and reanalyze our work, looking for where we made mistakes in our explorations."

"But the most important thing," Mr. Waver added, "is for us to look at the problem's relationship to the other parts in the system and the whole system. In effect, we'll use our knowledge of our school to improve education for our students instead of shopping around for a plan from another school, which doesn't have a clue about our problems."

"I like this plan," Mr. Owen said. "It's systematic. One thing follows another, and it looks like we'll stop blaming each other when a problem occurs. We'll use data instead. We can do it but we're going to need a great deal of guidance and time." He looked at Dina. "Will Superintendent Avelli wait that long?"

"I don't know," she answered, "but real change takes time and work. It will be my job to explain this to him." Underscoring her thinking was that he would again call her indecisive . . . and ask her who was running the school. But, Dina reflected, one giant step leads to another.

By coming to terms with fear in the workplace, teachers now trusted her enough to work together on a shared commitment to school improvement. She wasn't certain where all this would lead, but for once she felt she was wearing the proper mountain climbing equipment.

Vignette

BUILD CULTURE THROUGH SHARED BELIEFS

$\mathbf{Q}$uantumland is all about relationships, Principal Dina Macksy had heard Ms. Margaret Wheatley say at the meeting in San Diego. Particles come into being and are observed only in relationship to something else (Wheatley, 1992). Dina was starting to understand what she meant.

People in the workplace were beginning to come in contact with one another and share their beliefs. Dina was beginning to learn that her voice was one among many, and the voices she heard were those of informed people. She was glad that Mrs. Edna Lightment volunteered to chair the Democratic Council. It was important that a teacher do this so that the faculty would see it as their council, not the principal's.

"So now what shall we do," Mrs. Lightment asked, "now that we know that problem solving involves always looking at the parts, their interaction with the system, and their relation to other parts?" All faces turned toward Dina.

"Well, I don't think that we can change anything unless we all share similar beliefs about education as our founding fathers did about democracy," Dina began. "They were diverse in their ideas about what freedom and liberty should look like, but they all believed that King George's version did not fit theirs. I know it sounds like we're starting backward, but each school culture is different, and we can't fix anything until we have an idea about what our culture looks like.

"As you know from our past experience, we were rewarded for climbing a steep hill, only to fall off it again. Why? Maybe because I was the only one who believed in what we . . . at least I thought we . . . were doing. I never thought of what you might be thinking, only what I thought was best for all of us.

"If we can talk about our picture of the classroom culture, it might tell us a lot about what we believe. No matter how many mandates I memo to the faculty, unless they believe in change, it won't happen."

"I would like to say something," Jon Deway said, his fingers intertwined and pointed upward as if he was about to begin a prayer. "I don't know what teachers believe . . . maybe I do . . . but I can definitely state that teachers and students don't share a common culture in the classrooms.

"It's the teacher's culture we walk into, and it's the teacher's culture that dominates the scene. The teacher has no understanding of who we are and what goes on inside us. It's like the teacher says to park whatever we have outside the door and open our minds to what she is about to give us." He paused, rested his chin on his laced fingers and looked down at the table as if giving himself permission to continue.

"Most of my teachers do all the talking and a lot of the work. I don't mean to be disrespectful, but the teacher is most of the time doing the doing. The students try to listen, but let's face it, we need to be involved as well. So what do we do? We pass notes or cause trouble because human beings have got to be doing something. It's up to the teachers to involve us in their dialogue.

"Like right now, you have involved me. I'm not sitting like a vegetable. I'm talking and listening and reacting as a full partner in this learning situation that you've created. You have accepted the fact that I have something to contribute to the dialogue. And why shouldn't you? You're talking about me."

The teachers were uneasy as Jon talked . . . Mrs. Desiree Cartes closed her eyes and rubbed the bridge of her nose, Mr. Henry Berg twirled his thumbs. The others stared at the student, their eyes moving in their orbits as if they were asking themselves if what he was saying applied to them.

"Well Jon," Mr. Berg said, "That took a lot of courage to say. I'm sorry you feel that we are monopolizing the classrooms . . . not involving you in the teaching-learning process. I always felt that I tried to be a good teacher."

Dina suspected that Mr. Berg felt chastened by the boy's words. She hoped that, as the hurt dissipated, he would look in the mirror, turning it inward. Maybe she could give him the book by Mr. Sarason . . . or send him to the library.

Tic toc went the handles of the clock until Mrs. Lightment broke the disquieting air that had shrouded the room. "So, what is the relationship between a teacher and student in the classroom?" she asked.

"Jon maintains that students are interacting with students and teachers are interacting with themselves. So who is using our work? Somebody has to use our work, or are we being paid for talking to ourselves?"

It was at this point that Dina could have talked about her one-minute classroom visits and confirmed Jon's statement, but she held back. It was no use telling them what she knew. They had to discover it for themselves.

"Well, it's not that we're not interested," Jon said, groping for the right words so that the group would not think he was assailing them. "We want to feel useful too."

"What you're saying Jon," Mrs. Lightment said, "is that students do not interact with teachers, and teachers do not interact with students. If there is no yin and yang in the classroom, how can learning be shared between teachers and students? If we think of the teaching and learning process as interactive, are we both sharing in the process? What do we do for students, and what do they do for us?"

Distributing sticky notes to the team, she asked them to list the services teachers supply students. Each person began attending to the task with a renewed intensity.

Jon, his face bright red, stated, "Teachers share with us their knowledge and skills . . . or at least try."

"But I sense you are inferring, Jon, that the sharing is not two-sided," Mr. Newt Owen said. The student didn't respond . . . just rolled his tongue from the corner of his mouth and hunched his shoulders.

The social studies teacher, chagrined at Jon's words, removed his eyes from the boy and continued. "We supply students with a delivery service for knowledge, skills, and information."

"We provide them with assessment services as they learn," Mr. Berg added. "For example, we provide them feedback through exams as to whether they are learning the material."

"We also model appropriate behaviors for conducting oneself as an adult," Mrs. Cartes noted.

Mr. Evan Mann finished, "And we support them with encouragement as they attempt to learn."

Mrs. Lightment summarized: "So we supply our students with knowledge, skills, information, and strategies for teaching the information. Also, guidance, feedback, modeling, and encouragement. Okay. Then what do students supply us with?"

"Just a minute," Dina interrupted. "Mr. Owen, I'm not certain what a delivery service for information means." She didn't like the term *delivery service*. It was too business oriented. Was she forgetting what she had learned in the library . . . that knowledge comes from various locations in the library?

"What I mean is that we attempt to ascertain the best way to deliver the knowledge, skills, and information to the thirty plus different kids in our classroom six times a day," Mr. Owen explained.

"If we're different," Jon suddenly erupted, rolling back his shoulders, "why do you all treat us as if we're all the same? We are not machines with on/off buttons. Really, I have never thought in terms of supplying teachers with anything. Students come to school to take home what teachers have to give them . . . although they rarely do anymore.

"You are supposed to provide us with knowledge. You get paid to do that. It's our job to assimilate that knowledge, but sometimes we don't because of the ways in which you deliver it. There are so many times when we can find no relationship to what you are providing. It seems to have no purpose, unity, or even relevance.

"Because I am a thinking individual, I can't always make sense of the barrage of audio sentences my seven periods of teachers run-on with. So much of the information that vibrates from all of you to me is lost because of my short-term memory failing to dump the audio sentences into my long-term file.

"Please excuse me for saying what I think, but I do hope my exercise in schooling means something. The fact is that I feel offended sometimes because I'm not allowed to say anything or bring my own experience to the table.

"I once had an English teacher who was telling us about Dr. Faustus. For some reason, all I could think about were the *Star Trek* reruns that I enjoyed watching on television. I wanted to share that the series was about man's search for knowledge, similar to Dr. Faustus, but when I tried to say something the teacher told me not to call out in class. It sounds crazy to me that the teacher thought he was the only one who had anything important to say."

"Maybe that's the point," Mr. Owen said in a fit of pique. "So many students are not like you, Jon. So many of you are not willing to do the student's job, which is learning. I can give you all the knowledge I have, but you have to be willing to take it. That's what makes it interactive. I can't do my job, if you don't do yours."

"But are you doing your job, Mr. Owen," Jon asked, "if I am willing to learn it, but don't?"

"It's like the yin-yang, Jon," Mr. Berg said. "Teaching and learning are part of the same system. One draws from the other. They are part of the same whole."

His condescending manner clearly irritated Jon, who sagged back in his chair, his lips spreading wide across his face, folding in and then falling out. "You said that teaching and learning are interconnected. But few teachers practice this belief. It should be like you said, Mr. Berg, but it's not . . . at least much of the time. Teachers separate teaching from learning."

"We'll not get anywhere if we attack each other," interrupted Mrs. Cartes. "Let's move on. With what do students provide us?

"I never thought in terms of what a student could provide for me. I guess he could provide me with good grades so that I know I am successful as a teacher. But when I think about it, unless I can tell a student why his mark on a test was low, I haven't really provided him any feedback other than shame.

"Think about it . . . what happens to the student emotionally each time we red letter a paper? This is the first time I have ever thought about the relational value between a red letter I mark on a paper and the student. If teaching and learning are part of the same system, why are we having a problem finding the interconnections between them?

"We say teaching and learning, but we view them as separate parts of the whole. There is no yin and yang between them. We tell the kids it's their job to learn the material and our job to teach it . . . separate entities. That's what Jon has been telling us."

"Thank you, Mrs. Cartes for trying to understand the student's position in the classroom," Jon said. "Would any of you be angry if I said something else?" Dina began to cringe. How much truth could the teachers absorb, she asked herself?

"We're a democracy. There's nothing stopping you!" Mr. Berg answered, still feeling that his profession had been sullied by a mere boy who was not even a senior.

Ignoring Mr. Berg's sarcastic comments, Jon continued. "Well, you said, Mr. Owen, that you provide us with an instructional delivery service. And you said, Mr. Berg, that teaching and learning are part of the same whole . . . system is the word you used. But I don't see it practiced that way. I could give you feedback on the way you are providing that service.

"What I mean is, I could let you know, if I were real brave, if I'm having trouble learning the content. High school students could tell you what's running interference with their learning in the classroom. Then learning would be more interactive and closer to working as a system.

"Of course, so many of us don't even know how to ask questions . . . or are afraid . . . or simply don't care. But I think the latter is an exception, not the rule.

"My school is not like the automobile plant that my father goes to every morning. He tells me that it's his job to work on the part . . . he does windows . . . of the car that the company is producing. All day he interacts with that part trying to make it the best part possible. But teachers don't interact with parts. They interact with real people.

"The part my father works on doesn't have any way to tell him about what he is doing. Students do. We are people who have minds and like to use them. But so many of my teachers don't know how to invite our minds into the conversation, and we don't know how to start the conversation.

"My father cannot speak to his part because if he could, it could tell him that the screw he is tightening may require fewer revolutions . . . or maybe more. Teachers can ask, but never do. All they ask after lecturing us is the usual . . . 'any questions?' Have teachers ever thought about the fact that maybe kids don't know how to ask questions? I know, the thought sounds remote, but maybe they don't.

"So many teachers just want to keep all the kids on the same page even though so many of them are not. They say things like we have to cover the curriculum. And you are right, Mrs. Cartes. A red mark on a paper doesn't make us feel good about ourselves."

Dina waited for reaction to what Jon had just stated. But there was none. There was no learning in this teaching, just more silence, as if they had been hit over the head with a blunt object, temporarily stunning their minds.

"Students provide us with natural highs when they learn the intended curriculum. It makes us feel successful," Mr. Owen announced as if Jon had never spoken. "They provide us with feedback in this way. Students show us how they are making use of the new knowledge when they perform well on tests."

Jon slumped back in his seat. What's the use, he mumbled.

But Mrs. Lightment was listening to what he had to say. She asked, "If teaching and learning are part of the same system, what is their relationship?" She seemed to be asking the question in a different way. Again silence fell upon the group.

Mr. Mann sensed the group's discomfort. "I think I know what's wrong," he said, breaking the silence. "As teachers, you don't ask kids for feedback about the classroom. You avoided what Jon said. You provide all the controls. Maybe if teachers asked kids about the learning process and did something with the information, providing it was useful information . . . maybe the feedback could help kids learn better."

Student feedback became a topic of teacher lounge dialogue. Oprah Myden, a young, upbeat special education teacher, said that there was not much feedback from students in terms of the way teachers delivered services in the classroom.

"Perhaps two-way communication could help deliver lessons in a way that would prove more satisfactory to the student," she said, "and get beyond a stimulus-response atmosphere. Maybe, if we asked students how they learned, the classroom would become less of a battlefield."

"What's that got to do with anything?" Mrs. Indika Trench, one of Mr. Berg's counterparts in the English department, was overheard saying. "Why doesn't the principal just leave us alone to do our job?"

Some of the faculty approached Dina—Mrs. Trench was not among them. They wanted to take on the project of developing a way of objectively gathering student feedback about the classroom. Others feared such a step. Mr. Berg, who was always open to new ideas, suggested they not pursue this course of action immediately.

"This kind of a question," he said, "at this point in time, might create more tension in the ranks than we want. Some teachers are already thinking that we are going to ask students to evaluate them. I think we need to take this one off the burner until we know how to cook it better."

His response probably was fallout from the rating system Dina had devised earlier. Teachers didn't trust evaluations because she didn't trust them. If her evaluation system had been more helpful to them, maybe they might not have feared the project. She had learned from that experience to always examine all the effects of something new being attempted in other parts of the system.

"I suggest we prepare a history lesson for the faculty on the way we traditionally solve school problems," Dina suggested. "Let's do this in order to begin building a faculty dialogue about improving what happens at our school. Using this strategy might calm some folks down." All members of the Democratic Council concurred.

At a faculty meeting in September, the Democratic Committee facilitated the history lesson as Dina reviewed why high schools solve problems the way they do.

"Where did our current thinking about the structure, function, and form of schools come from?" she began. Using a PowerPoint presentation she developed, she outlined the centuries of thought controlling our mindset about the process of education. She said that the flaw in her own thinking was a result of not updating the worldview of Newton and Descartes.

"Solving problems by trying to fix the part did not help solve them. It just kept us doing the same thing over and over again. We have to look at problems from the context of the world in which we live."

She presented her messy model on how she conceptualized the work of schools as interactive, interdependent activity. "This messy model is based on the relational value of four elements," she explained.

"First, the way people in the system view their work in relationship to themselves and others; second, the concept of a school system as being indivisible; third, the use of data to assess and analyze what the school system is doing; and last, theories of knowledge to flesh out and work on problem solving.

"What all this means is that you can't blame a person for doing a poor job without exploring the whole system and its relational parts, using data and theory." To make the point, she reviewed with them the red bead experiment.

The counselor, Mr. Carlton Rodgers, who usually snoozed through all faculty meetings, became energized. "So for years we have been blaming the teachers for the inability of the students to read, but it has really been a management problem."

Mr. Owen chuckled. "Don't forget who you blame," he cautioned, "when you get fed up with the way things are going in your office."

"Touché," Mr. Rodgers replied. "I blame the parents for not caring enough about their children. If they'd spend more time with them, their children wouldn't have to spend hours in my office because I'm the only one who listens to them. We really are into the blame game, aren't we?"

Mrs. Trench stood up, putting aside the stack of papers she had been grading. "Teachers come to school every day wanting to do their best job. But how can they? What with the overcrowded classrooms, poor equipment, poor parent and administrative support . . . you all know what I mean . . . how we can possibly do our best even though every day we try?

"But the dropout rates climb anyway and those kids will earn a lot less during their lifetime than will the high school graduate. We will probably have to support the dropouts. So it's nice to know we are not the blame . . . for now anyway."

As she sat down, she glared in Dina's direction. She was not smiling.

"Mrs. Trench makes a point," Mrs. Cartes said. "The public blames us for doing a poor job, when in fact the schools are doing what they can with what they are given. If only we were handed less deficient equipment . . . students who want to learn.

"I hate to say it because I'm a parent too, but the truth is I myself forgot that my first responsibility was my son. It's hard to raise a kid on your own.

"I know I'm blaming, but that's where I am right now. It would be easier to do it right the first time, which means that society has to take more time with its children. But as a single parent I have to earn a living. And when we get these deficient kids in high school, the resources aren't there to do the job right the second time.

"The public says to us, 'We give you more resources and you still don't do the job.' If they would send us kids ready to be educated, instead of retreads, we wouldn't need all the extra resources. I sometimes think of my own kid as a retread, because I didn't do my job right the first time."

Her comments were a natural lead in to the next part of Dina's presentation. "There are several reasons why I think that, as a school principal, I have to change the way I think about school culture and governance so that we are all on the same page."

For some reason her eyes were fixed on Mrs. Trench as she spoke. She was a principal's worst nightmare, the malevolent teacher who would go into the teacher's lounge and disparage anything the principal proposed, whether she agreed with it or not.

"We have to understand how our school processes work in conjunction with one another. What I mean is, when we change one thing, we change another. Every process has a relational value to something else.

"You will recall that I solved the litter problem through mandate, but by doing this new problems arouse . . . problems that I didn't see coming because I failed to look at the relational value of what I was mandating to other parts of the system. Instead of synergizing potential, I continue to divide it. I make the decisions and you carry them out so that I can keep my fingers on what is happening and what is going to happen next.

"A few minutes ago, Mrs. Trench made a significant comment. I sometimes think that more of my taxes are poured into the construction of new prisons than the creation of new minds. We keep on mass creating widgets and when the widgets are deficient, we build prisons for them to live in . . . instead of doing it right the first time, as Mrs. Cartes suggested.

"Now, at this juncture what should happen? The failure rate is escalating, the number of kids coming to school on a daily basis is declining. From this, we can predict more students will drop out. We are adhering to standards and failing students who don't make the grade, so whom do we blame for the problem?

"As teachers, you blame the parents or me for not giving you the resources you say you need. As parents, you blame the school for not doing more to help your children. We have to look at our own system in a new way.

"I think this can best be accomplished by the school community acting together through inquiry and reflection. We must communicate about how to lead children forward. And the children have to be part of the process. We have to put a halt to warehousing kids and moving them along an assembly line. We must understand that we are a social institution."

Dina hadn't realized until this juncture how absurd those people were who were writing books on the importance of collaboration in education. It was a given—democracy could not survive without this given—yet we had to be reminded about it all the time.

"So what you are saying," Mr. Owen summarized, "is that we can't accomplish the goal of educating children unless we are able to work together. And we can't work together unless we revisit how we communicate in this organization."

"Sort of . . ." she responded, admiring how he had summarized what she had said in one concise sentence. "Additionally, the system can only accomplish its aim if people worked from a theory, not just experience," she added.

"Experience tells us where we have been," Dina said thinking of what Mr. Deming had taught her in the library, "but unless it produces further questions, it is limiting in its value. Only questioning leads to theories. And to make changes in the system, we need evidence supporting our theories."

"We have to do a lot of rethinking about our professional commitment," Mr. Rodgers added. "It's hard to change. Let's face it, our first priority is our own classroom. It's where our students go . . . it's our empire. We feel safe behind these closed doors. I know many of you are asking yourselves why should you exit your comfort zones and enter a place filled with uncertainty?"

Mrs. Lightment seemed discouraged. Not wanting the faculty to morph into *poor me* mode, she went off into what appeared to be a non sequitur.

"Let me ask this question," she said. "From where does that classroom constitution come? How do we explain rules in the classroom? What are the assumptions that govern the constitution?"[1]

Without hesitation, Mrs. Trench responded. "I believe that the teacher knows best, adult rules are better than student rules, students want the teacher to determine the rules, and students want the teacher to tell them what to do. Above all else, my classroom is my kingdom!"

"Do you realize that all of these assumptions focus on control?" Mrs. Lightment said, pausing momentarily so that her words were absorbed by her audience.

"If we as adults refuse to give up total control, how do we produce a thinking individual who sees himself as a part of a community of people? We are so used to thinking that we know best . . . and only we.

"As a result, we no longer see how control influences us and puts us in conflict with our students. Instead of an integrative whole in the classroom, we have parts at war with each other. What I mean is, we should be learning from one another. Instead, the influence of control puts us in competition."

"I teach kids about democracy," Mr. Owen said, "but I don't do it very democratically. I don't really practice what I'm preaching because I believe that I have to control the classroom."

As the dialogue continued, Dina knew that the Democratic Council and the faculty were on the right track. People were talking to one another. It wasn't neat and orderly and at times went off on tangents, but it was the first time many of the faculty had exposed their ideas about education publicly. They were talking to one another, and they were talking to her, just like the students and university professors did during the time of the French riots of 1968.

When the dismissal bell rang, some teachers remained in their seats and continued to meet.

"So you are saying that the children have to be in control. No students are going to control my class!" she heard Mrs. Trench roar at Mr. Owen. A sour chord had been struck. But that was okay. People were talking, and as in a quantum world, new relationships were being formed. It was a starting point.

NOTE

1. This question is also posed by Sarason (1971).

Vignette

LISTEN TO THE SHAREHOLDERS

"**A**re you naive?" Superintendent Mac Avelli scoffed, when Principal Dina Macksy suggested to him that children are the most important people in the world. "Don't read too much into the posters you make your teachers hang in their classrooms. They're slogans . . . slogans are just that . . . inspirational twit . . . platitudes without any underbelly.

"What you are suggesting is that we serve children . . . that we get to know them, integrating what they bring into the classroom with what the state and school districts demand they know.

"Children are not part of a social order yet. They haven't earned their keep. We're here to pry open their little heads in order to intravenously feed their minds with the cultural nutrients we deem worthy. We prepare them for their future.

"But are they happy with what we give them? No, they would rather foul their Facebook page with neurotic accountings of themselves, Twitter their twaddle, download to their iPod's annoying music, and paraphrase their history reports from Google . . . for a price of course. Serving them would be easy, but would not preserve the democracy you go on and on about."

Trying to keep the dialogue as anodyne as possible, Dina said nothing. Sometimes she thought that maybe he was right. She was plowing through the corridors of never-never land, and he was forever lurking in the hallways. She once even observed him talking to Mrs. Indika Trench, watching his body language as it veered between listlessness and hysterical fanaticism. That was scary.

On the other hand, she also saw within the schoolhouse halls unique conversations occurring. "What use is Shakespeare if students can't find use for him in their lives?" Mr. Quintin Waver inquired of the English department. "What good is the brain if it does not have the mind to make manifest its behaviors? Without one there is no other." His questions succeeded in ingratiating himself with English teachers.

Mr. Newt Owen was articulating his own reflections. "I don't think I quite agree with you, Mr. Waver. Learning as a discipline strengthens the brain. It exercises the brain muscles. Even if we don't use the information right away, it is stored later for retrieval."

"When is the last time you used trigonometry?" Oprah Myden asked. The spunky, young special education teacher was intermittently attending the early hour meetings. "And if you learned trigonometry in the absence of a meaningful context, could you apply it today? I took trig and couldn't tell you a thing I learned. It was taught in a void of any meaning. I don't think my brain muscles were made stronger. I just think it was wasted on useless stuff that could have been made useful had the teacher made it so."

Mr. Waver took the offensive. "Wouldn't it be nice to learn something useful? Like useful math and science? Why can't we find useful connections that have meaning for our students? We are a species that thinks and acts in tandem. Yet our teaching runs contrary to this notion.

"We think that if we teach, students will learn. We treat teaching and learning as if they were two separate entities that never talk to each other. But these two elements are dependent on each other if meaningful change is to occur. It's as subtle as not understanding that the brain needs the mind to relate it to the world.

"My father-in-law had a stroke recently. He just lay in bed and stared. The family speculated on whether he was in or out of his mind. We knew his brain was there. We just didn't know if it was performing any meaningful communicative action with the mind."

"What does that have to do with anything?" Mr. Owen asked, seemingly frustrated.

"Mr. Waver, in his own unique way, is saying something," Mr. Henry Berg affirmed. "I suppose teaching Shakespeare is a waste of time because it doesn't communicate. I suppose we should eliminate all the classics from the curriculum."

"On the contrary," Mr. Waver quickly countered. "Literature contains the stories of the human tragedy. Students need to understand this drama as they experience the world. What better way to facilitate this learning than through the classics?"

The idea that knowledge should be taught in a way that students found relevant incurred wrath from some of the faculty members and staff. Mrs. Trench, like Mr. Owen, maintained that the brain was a tool that could be sharpened with the installation of knowledge. The more critical the knowledge, the sharper the brain.

The industrial technology teacher, Bob Boiler, argued that knowledge was only useful if it made sense to our construction of the world. Others thought they should not spend so much time asking dumb questions.

"We are teachers, not philosophers," they roared. "Our classrooms are overpopulated. We have gone through the usual fads about learning styles and how to integrate students with the classroom conversation. But we have not done it because it takes time. The school pushes us to cover the curriculum and, at the same time, says that we have to figure out the learning styles of each of our students.

"It's just too overwhelming when our classes are packed with limited-speaking English students, special education students, kids who don't care about learning, and the few we teach to who do. We don't have the preparation time it requires to do everything for everybody."

Negativity was beginning to surreptitiously meander throughout the schoolhouse.

Mrs. Edna Lightment was quick to extinguish the fire, though a few glowing embers remained. One day, as she exited the door of the teacher's lounge, she proclaimed, "Students today are different from students a decade or two ago. They are experiencing a different world from the one in which we grew up. We created them, and because we did, we have to give their world credibility.

"Teaching them about the Romantic period or the Civil War is important because literature and history are important. Nevertheless, it is equally important that students *learn* about the Romantic period and the Civil War. Students will not learn as long as we ignore the world in which they are growing."

At the faculty meeting that week, Dina asked the faculty to begin brainstorming what they perceived the students and parents expected from schools. She informed the Democratic Council that she wanted to take all the faculty lounge bark and banter and see where they were in terms of throwing their ideas into her imaginary collection bowl of thought.

"Are we truly becoming reflective about what we as professionals do or is it all a dog and pony show?" Dina asked the council members.

She used a group process to pursue this discussion because she desired that every person in the room have an opportunity to be heard. At first, attempting thinking from the students' and parents' perspective was not without its difficulties. Gradually a thought from one person prompted a thought from another. The faculty perceived that from the point of view of parents and students, their job fell within both cognitive and affective areas.

Affectively, they thought of themselves as having many roles—that of teacher, counselor, caretaker, and police officer. The parents saw them that way as well.

As a group, the faculty maintained that students and parents expected them to help students understand who they were. This meant they wanted teachers to help solve problems or enable students to solve their own problems. They wanted this achieved in a caring environment.

Cognitively, the faculty suggested that students and parents expected them to prepare students for the future through a quality education by developing, challenging, and improving their skills. Their individual statements included: they want us to get smart students into college, to help them obtain the skills necessary for success in a democratic country, and to teach them to become productive citizens in society.

There was additional discussion about the role of the school as a babysitting service and dumping ground for students with problems. A few staff members were very vocal about this.

Mrs. Trench said: "Some parents expect us to raise their kids, because they don't know how to deal with teenagers. And to make up for their guilt in abrogating their responsibility, they come to their child's rescue the moment the school calls and says those threatening words: 'I need to see you about Johnny.' But they are thinking . . . my baby could not possibly do anything wrong . . . after all, you're bringing him up."

Mr. Evan Mann, sensing that the blame game was about to be played by the faculty, quickly stood up, voicing a summary statement, which reflected what many had been thinking.

"Let's face it, parents want their students to be prepared for the future. Our students expressed a similar need. They want to be prepared for their postsecondary world, whether it is college or jobs. And they want it done in a way where students will see it as fun . . . stimulating or engaging would be a better word . . . and under conditions that are safe."

"We wouldn't need the security guards," Mrs. Trench blared contemptuously, reluctant to refrain from the blame game, "if the parents had done their jobs in the first place."

As teachers left, Dina paid attention to the mumbled gripes: I'm tired of that word "fun." I wasn't trained to be a counselor, that's Rodgers' job. If I wanted to be a police officer, I would have applied for the police academy. I'm tired of bringing up everybody else's kid but my own.

At the next faculty meeting, Mrs. Lightment asked the group to respond to the ensuing question, "What do we expect of ourselves as educators?" The group, now used to brainstorming techniques, responded with little hesitation.

"I expect that I will teach and find a way to teach every student so that each student feels successful."

"I expect to grow as a professional, learn new techniques, ways of thinking and facilitating learning, while continually working to improve myself."

"I expect to have the equipment and class choices available to give students a good, complete education."

"I expect that I will have opportunities to prepare students for the future in a safe environment."

"I expect that the students will have the necessary attitudes toward learning."

"I expect that I will stop being blamed when the test scores printed in the newspapers are down."

As Dina listened to their comments, she perceived that as the brainstorming progressed, the answers abruptly jumped track. Mrs. Lightment, sensing this as well, revisited her question. She asked the group,

"What do you expect of yourself as an educator? For example, one of you said that you expected to learn new techniques to improve your teaching."

"Well, I guess," Mr. Owen offered, " I expect to continue to improve and get better at meeting the needs of my students as we learn more and more about how much it takes to preserve democracy."

Everybody nodded as Mr. Berg provided closure for the meeting. "Although it has been directly voiced, I know this faculty well enough to suggest that, as educators we expect a lot from our students even while having to play the additional roles of caregiver and policeman.

"We don't mind assuming these roles, but it gets so frustrating when the public doesn't understand that they . . . the public . . . the parents . . . the business community . . . are necessary in this effort to educate society's children. Hillary is right . . . it does take a village to raise kids today."

Over the course of time, the dialogues continued. They now extended to the entire staff of secretaries, security, and maintenance employees. Ideas were being thrown into the bowl. People were beginning to hear one another and, at times, the pot boiled over.

They continued to discuss the purpose of education. Would the responses be similar to the ones Dina had heard in the Costco line? Even the maintenance people entered into this dialogue. Mr. Owen led the discussion. "We spoke about what as professionals we expect from ourselves and what the students and parents expect from us.

"Now let's throw our thoughts together in order to define a purpose for the work of our schoolhouse. Let's brainstorm. Circle your chairs and write your ideas on the flip chart.

"What is the purpose of education at this school?" Mr. Owen wrote. The list was quite extensive, each person contributing his own ideas. Mr. Mann summed up what had been said. "So I guess we are all saying that the purpose of education is to work as a team to educate, socialize, and prepare students for their future, offering them as many horizons as they can dream." Cousin Michael would have appreciated that response, Dina reflected.

While all the brainstorming was occurring, some of the faculty as well as Superintendent Mac Avelli were getting nervous about all the talk and no action in developing a school improvement plan.

"Matter is showing inertia," Mr. Waver euphemistically said, mimicking the superintendent. "You're spending too much time on obvious questions and obvious answers."

In the confines of his office, Superintendent Avelli continued to badger Dina. "Why all the discussion? What does it matter what teachers think? If they don't like it here, they can seek employment where they do. I want to see results."

He demanded that she accelerate the process and get on with the school improvement plan. "The teachers are getting annoyed at how much time it is taking to develop the purpose statement . . . although I don't know why you need that. The district wrote its mission statement years ago. Find it and use that."

He paused as if he had to frame his next words carefully. "But you know I never involve myself in how principals do things at their schools. Your evaluation will be the testimony to that."

Dina brought Superintendent Avelli's demand—that they accelerate the process—to the Democratic Council. They were annoyed.

"Doesn't Avelli know that for the first time people on this faculty are talking together about education?" Mr. Owen said, his arms crossed across his chest, his fingers tightly clinging to his elbows.

"We have produced a lot of lists, but it's not the lists that are important. It's the relationships that are being formed as a result of the lists. We need to continue what we are doing."

"I agree with Mr. Owen," said Mrs. Desiree Cartes. "If we want to develop a shared professional culture, we have to make sure that people feel free to put their thoughts on the table without threat or fear of retribution.

"We can't develop a plan that everyone will buy into until we are free to share our feelings openly. If we don't, we would be circling the wagons again and shooting inward."

"Well, I guess it's unanimous," Mrs. Lightment said with a hesitant grimace. "I guess you're going to have to stall him."

Stalling was going to be difficult. When your superintendent gives you a directive, you are expected to attend to it. But Dina didn't tell them this.

Shortly after the advisement from Superintendent Avelli, the faculty became curious as to parents' thoughts on the subject of expectations for their students. Were their perceptions aligned with parents' perceptions? A month later they held a meeting with them to figure this out.

As usual, not many parents attended. Those who did were the parents of the *good* students. Mr. Owen told the group that they were in the process of writing a new school improvement plan.

"We hope," he said, "that all the participants in the school system will support this plan so that the changes we make for our students will have meaning. To develop this plan, we need to begin by asking parents what their beliefs are about their children in regards to education. In other words, what do you expect this school to do for your child?"

After the scheduled hour was over and the parents left, the Democratic Council summed up the parents' views. Mrs. Lightment expressed it succinctly. "The parents wanted their children to be successful and have a quality education. They wanted them to attend schools that were safe, helpful, challenging, and motivating and where children would not be penalized for failure. They wanted their child to graduate and value continuing education by either attending college, technical school, or entering the job market.

"They considered good teachers those who have a sense of humor, challenge students with knowledge, understand the differences between children, cared and believed in them, showed compassion, were flexible, a role model, and lived in the community."

The faculty and staff had spent many weeks dialoging and sharing beliefs. This had put Dina at the top of Superintendent Avelli's *hit list* (sometimes spelled with an "s" . . . for principals who tested the authority of their superiors). She knew she was walking a razor's edge between keeping and losing her job.

For the first time the faculty, staff, and the principal had exchanged ideas about educational beliefs at morning meetings, in the teacher's lounge, at faculty meetings, on the way to and from school, and between class passing periods. They were beginning to view education from a perspective of relationships, each relational piece having value in creating the whole.

They had responded to questions, which delved into their own beliefs and the beliefs of the community they served. They were now ready to move toward developing a purpose for education at their school that all members of their educational community could understand and in which they could play a relational part. They were developing unity within their diversity.

Vignette

IT'S ALL ABOUT THE
WHOLE THING

Mr. Deming believes that when people work together, everyone wins (Deming, 1986). Superintendent Mac Avelli didn't know this. Principal Dina Macksy was hoping to show him that the statement was true, even though most principals that she knew thought that the statement should have been *when we compete, we all win.* These are the principals who favor merit pay and believe that competition made people better at their job.

It was October. Dina was beginning to feel like she was swimming in murky ocean water where her ability to sight land oscillated between rapture and apprehension. All these meetings took so much time.

She had nothing to share with the superintendent regarding a high school improvement plan. The other school principals in the district had outlined their goals and objectives. They submitted them in triplicate with the appropriate percentage points by which they would increase their student state test scores.

Each received the standard chilled smile from Superintendent Avelli. She wasn't certain about what she was doing. There were times when she didn't really know in which direction to turn.

Nevertheless, there was something energizing about educators probing their relationship to their profession and to themselves. There was something productive about exchanging insights about their own understandings of their jobs. There was something momentous about exploring the way in which the workplace was structured.

Questions were being asked and answers discussed. Educators at her school were involved in education, the growing and learning part. They were taking time to think.

George Counts (1931) had once said that educators liked shaking the baby rattle, merely content with the vigorous movement and noise. He was wrong. The educators with whom she worked were beginning to reason through what they were doing.

"The last school improvement plan that won the school all the accolades was never constructed from an exchange of ideas from the participants," Dina told Superintendent Avelli. "We never pursued a common inquiry. We never reflected. We used a model that was used by many other schools, fired, and then aimed."

But her words fell on deaf ears. The man at the top of the hierarchal chart demanded a plan *now*. "People will do what they are told to do. Just replicate the model you used before. You are becoming an aimless leader," he avowed, making her feel chastened and abashed as she left his office.

He just didn't understand, she thought late at night. First, he did not understand that using a pill based on someone else's prescription did not always provide the palliative necessary to solve the ailment.

If the people working in the schoolhouse didn't think the pill would work, they would slide it under their tongues, throwing it in the litter basket as soon as the principal turned her back. That's simple human nature. A plan for improvement based on ideas that were foreign to a school system would not impact students over time. People could be force-fed, but did that really change anything?

Second, the changes that were made on the first go around were directed from the top. And the expectation was that it would trickle through the organization from the top down. She never asked the teachers about the philosophy underlying the process for improvement. Her thoughts and their thoughts didn't count for anything.

Somebody in Newton's mechanical universe had told her that the model she borrowed was the correct one to use if she wanted to change things at her school. Who was she to contradict what those in the know said about what she didn't know? It just seemed like a good idea. She thought the teachers would think the same. "It's the way things work," Mr. Tribus had cautioned her.

Further, Superintendent Avelli did not take the time to understand that using a one-size-fits-all model would not have long-term effects. But why should he? Few superintendents had a long tenure in a particular school district. They mostly lived in a political world disengaged from the schoolhouse workplace. At least that was her theory.

So while Dina was *piddling around* . . . Superintendent Avelli's words . . . the Democratic Council conducted an exercise to demonstrate how students could be a valuable asset in the feedback loop. They wanted teachers to think with more depth about the teacher–student relationship that existed in the classroom.

Earlier they had said that high school students could provide teachers with feedback. If a student was receiving poor grades in class, what were the variables that contributed to the student's negative performance? It was all in the relationship, and they had to begin to think in terms of that relationship.

Dina began the exercise by using herself as the subject. She knew that teachers feared receiving feedback from students.

"As a teacher," she told them, "I always looked forward to evaluation time because I wanted to know how I could improve my classroom. Evaluation, I thought, was a tool that would help me better serve my students. At least that's what I used to tell myself. However, because of time constraints, the principal was only able to spend forty-five minutes, once or twice a year, observing me interact with my students" (Walker, 1997).

She looked around. They all thought she was crazy.

"Well, it really is true," she affirmed. "When I became principal, I also looked forward to the superintendent sharing his evaluation with me. I believed evaluation was a tool . . . almost like a customer feedback form, which could better help me serve teachers. But the superintendent spent more time analyzing state testing scores and making the school board happy. The process being used to offer me feedback was not giving me information as to how I could strengthen the teaching-learning process.

"I felt that my primary job was to always enhance what occurs in the classroom by spending sufficient time interacting with teachers.

But, just as principals before me, I was saddled with a job description, which required me to do everything from monitoring the plumbing in the girls' and boys' bathrooms to dealing with gang violence on campus.

"I didn't have time to work directly with teachers on a consistent basis and offer them the feedback they require to further their daily interactions with students . . . no matter what the literature says about principals as instructional leaders.

"So I have a theory. If I could not support teachers directly by being in their classroom on a consistent basis, perhaps I could focus on their needs, indirectly. As the students noted in one of our surveys, they won't learn until they are noticed. I think that's true for many of us.

"But I didn't know what kinds of direct supports or qualities teachers required from the principal to enhance their classroom performance. That is, what do teachers need from principals in order to enhance the job they do?" She looked around at the faces completely engrossed in listening to her. "Can you help me with this? Think of it as a customer feedback form."

And help they did, so she thought. After completing the brainstorming process, their list of needs included a principal who was *honest, fair, experienced, cooperative, child-centered, decisive, empowering, dependable, flexible, thorough, touchy-feely, even tempered, supportive, a natural born leader who had vision and direction, represented the school well, a good conversationalist, receptive and responsive to teacher needs, had high energy levels, could take constructive criticism, knew the different parts of education, was an educator first, had a sense of humor,* and *had a firm knowledge base of the curriculum.*

In all, there was a list of over fifty qualities! She was getting a little nervous as each person took his or her turn listing the character expectations for the principal. She then began to realize that asking the teachers the qualities they desired in a principal was a little like asking them to reveal what a principal who walked on water looked like.

She then asked them if they could brainstorm with their students the qualities or supports their students required from a teacher in order to enhance the teaching-learning process. She watched the teachers at the table purse their lips and suck in their cheeks, sagging back into their chairs. They were still not at all comfortable with the question.

Mrs. Edna Lightment took the disquieting air to mean it was time to plan for their next meeting with the faculty and staff. For now, this dialogue ended.

At their faculty meeting that week, they discussed the writing of their statement of purpose. What was the purpose of their work? Again, they divided into groups. The work seemed easier now. People had discussed what they valued. They had listened to what the students and parents valued in education.

The district vision, which someone found in the back of a file cabinet, informed them that a graduate from their district was one who had an independent, inquiring mind. In addition, that graduate was to be a productive, contributing member of society. Dina secretly wished that the statement had included somewhere in it the word *democracy.*

"How were we," Mrs. Lightment asked, "as educators, based on what we knew about our clientele and ourselves, going to support this idea?"

Their educational values rested on respect, trust, honesty, open mindedness, community, justice, and love. How could they facilitate the educational process incorporating these values so that students acquired the knowledge, skills, and learnings necessary to support themselves when they exited formal education?

The students had told them that they valued "teachers who respected them, who listened, were organized, could explain things so that the student understood it, were willing to help solve problems, made work fun, got to the point quickly, helped them out, had a sense of humor, didn't get mad, gave rewards besides grades, knew where a student was in the class . . . both physically and mentally . . . and had more activities such as field trips." If the teachers perceived value in this list, how were they to support it?

In terms of their educational expectations, the faculty agreed that they had to prepare students for the world they would enter. The parents had said, "Help our kids be successful." And the teachers had confirmed this belief. All those involved in the system wanted the very same thing. They wanted to be and feel successful.

"But as an educator, it is difficult to make 150 kids a day feel successful," Mrs. Indira Trench, said warily. "The overall flavor of schools is that of a machine. We are like cogs in it, programmed to perform certain tasks at certain times. But the fact is we can't provide that many kids with all the things kids today need."

Of course Dina thought Mrs. Trench was right. But she didn't say any-thing. Maybe at a later date they could assess and analyze the problem of a teacher having too many students to see if that was really a problem.

She knew that they could realign the schedule so that teachers had fewer students per day. There were many schools doing block schedul-ing but, because they hadn't analyzed the research to see if it was right for them and because they needed to know more about themselves as a family of people living much of their day in the schoolhouse, she was reluctant to go for quick fixes.

The faculty suggested that they align their values with their profes-sional workplace beliefs. What professional beliefs would guide them as they continually improved their workplace? From there, they would generate a statement of educational beliefs.

Once again, in round robin fashion, Mrs. Lightment wrote the profes-sional beliefs on the flip chart. They poured out of each person's mouth in quick succession because of the continual dialogue that had perme-ated the campus.

"When something goes wrong in the schoolhouse, don't point fingers. Problems are generally due to something in the way the school system and its processes are working."

"Look for the relationships in the schoolhouse that will produce en-lightened students able to acquire and use knowledge."

"We have to look for the real causes of problems if we want to find long lasting solutions."

"We all try to do our best."

"The educator performing the job is the most knowledgeable about the job, just as the secretary is the most knowledgeable about her job. But we can always improve, especially if we work together."

"People who work in the school have input to offer."

"All educators need to be involved in the change process in order for change to occur."

"We have to stop fighting with each other. We accomplish more when we work together. Divisiveness takes us nowhere, being on the same page does."

"For kids to learn democracy, the people populating the school need to practice it."

"Diversity of opinion has to be respected."

Mrs. Lightment, summarizing their educational beliefs as a group, wrote on the flip chart: *We believe that all students and staff need an environment where they feel secure, have a sense of belonging, feel free, empowered, engaged, and emulate the democratic process. We believe that all students and staff must constantly prepare for a changing world. We believe that we are committed to preparing our students to thrive in the community of their choice by providing them with diverse educational opportunities. We are committed to working with the community as a partner in producing varied forms of educational delivery based on the needs of our students.*

Dina liked the notion about varied forms of educational opportunities. The faculty discussed this. The general feeling was that the district wanted them to prepare a student with the necessary knowledge, skills, and learning to be successful. It was their job to prepare that student according to how that student learned and what that student brought with him or her to the schoolhouse. One size did not fit all.

The curriculum was in place and shared in common what other high schools taught. But delivery of the curriculum was a problem under the current structure of seven, forty-five-minute periods a day. There was not much time to teach content, much less pay attention to student needs. They left it at that for now. One dilemma had produced another.

Back in her office, Dina was still attempting to find out what teachers needed from a principal. She knew she had asked the wrong question of them on the first go around. What she really needed to know was what they needed from her to satisfy or exceed their classroom expectations. Mrs. Lightment suggested she use a climate survey.

There were many climate surveys out there. Instead of reinventing the wheel, she adapted one of them to fit their needs. She then asked an ad hoc committee of three people if they would review the form and provide suggestions.

The questions in which they showed the most interest were centered on principal support of teachers in terms of treating them fairly, helping them problem solve and seeking new ideas, respecting subject matter, showing pride in the school, and welcoming parents.

When the climate survey was completed, Dina asked the teachers to rate her performance. She also asked them to rate their perception about the importance of these qualities related to all principals. She wondered, would a principal possessing these qualities help enhance student performance in the classroom?

She administered the survey . . . her customer feedback form. The Democratic Council suggested that individuals not sign their names to it. The trust was still not completely there. Her heart sank as she plodded through the results.

The teachers perceived each item as important and perceived her as meeting their needs. Once again, she knew she had a false start. The survey failed to discriminate what supports teachers needed from the principal in order to enhance their classroom performance. How could she ask them to ask their students to give them feedback if she did not have a successful model to present to them?

As she pondered the results, the Democratic Council discussed the basics of an organization. "What are the parts in the systems that interact with one another to create the system?" Mrs. Lightment asked.

"Well, an organization has people. The people do something. The organization has an aim in which the people doing something, accomplish," Mrs. Desiree Cartes said.

"And all personnel have to have a common belief about the organization's values or forward movement would halt and inertia would result," Mr. Quintin Waver offered. "And it's not primarily the parts we are interested in. It's the relationships between the parts and how they emerge and energize to create a system aimed at the purpose, almost like an ant colony. They don't write anything down. It all comes naturally."

"I suppose you can't separate out each of these parts," said Mr. Newt Owen, still contemplating Mr. Waver's last sentence, "because if you do, you miss the interactions.

"Geez. Mr. Waver, I think I'm beginning to think like you. I am beginning to perceive a system that is indivisible . . . is organic. You can say it has these parts, but these parts can't stand alone. They can only stand together. Like the eye . . . without the brain, it can't see . . . that is, if the purpose of the eye is to see."

"And I would like to add," Mr. Henry Berg said, "that the interaction between and among the people and the processes is the key to accomplishing the aim. But there also has to be interaction between the community and us. Does the community like what we are doing? They are part of the organic process."

Finally, they thought it important to review the components of an organization so that when they were ready to develop a plan of action, they had an understanding of an integrated system.

Oprah Myden said: "Hey, let me do that. Our school organization is composed of a structure, which divides up the work to be done. It has a plan for delivering the learning, skills, and knowledge. It uses a staff of people who possess certain knowledge and abilities and who apply these skills using a specific style. And it has a purpose for existing. Everything is connected."

Or is it, Dina thought? What she had described was a bureaucracy. But it didn't matter. They were talking about connections now and could eventually erase the bureaucratic lines between them, something that had not happened before.

The first school improvement plan had not included any notions about how each of these organizational elements interacted to create change. Strategies for improvement had been developed but never probed in terms of the interactions between what teachers did and what students did, their skill levels, their common commitment, their different voices.

November was fast approaching. All this time, they had been focused on understanding the relational values inherent in organizations whose focus was on people. They were at the fringe of understanding how the elements of an organization integrate to produce a purpose. They had jumped from one question to another, sometimes not knowing which question would be probed at a particular time. But they were now speaking about their professional purpose using a common voice.

Vignette

THE YIN IN THE YANG

By November, faculty and staff were still talking about purpose statements. But at this point, it was important to Principal Dina Macksy that they not become sloganeers. Once they did that, the conversation would come to a squeaky halt. People would think, okay we've done that, now it's time to get back to our jobs.

No, they couldn't stop the conversation. They just had to keep the dialogue going, knowing that they were gradually throwing into the bowl common beliefs that would guide students while focusing on how to make teaching and learning one entity.

Of course, Mrs. Indika Trench still insisted that it was her job to teach and the students' job to learn, and a great many other teachers thought that as well. You couldn't change this deeply embedded belief without dialogue. It had lingered in their educational history far too long. Unless they could change this conception, they were doomed and democracy would fall prey to the barbarians at the gate.

Dina was most happy that many on the faculty and staff bought into the concept of a school where democracy was practiced. It was not that any of them were practicing democratic concepts on an ongoing basis, but an open dialogue was a beginning.

She was still working with them on how she could best serve them, and they were as a group working on how they could best serve their students. They were becoming more aware about the concept of relational values as they probed their organization. She was hopeful that, as they spoke about it, the practice of democracy would *quantumly* appear.

But things were happening in a democratic way. Because of Jon Deway and other students who had been on the Democratic Council, she could hear the student body leaders talking. How could they make their organization more than a popularity contest by amending the requirements for running for office?

While they were doing this, Mrs. Edna Lightment was developing a student feedback survey. She thought it would give her information about her communication with her students. The idea about students providing classroom feedback to teachers raised the fear barometer among the teachers. They didn't mind Dina fumbling about with her own survey, as long as they, the teachers, were providing the input.

As the faculty continued to talk among themselves about their statement of professional purpose, the Democratic Council suggested that they take an insightful look at the way their school functioned.

At first Dina became paranoid at this suggestion because she thought they would throw daggers at her. However, Jeb Plowfield, a new member to the team and a progressive thinker (he had a long tenure at the school as an agriculture teacher), suggested that they needed to modify the system to fit the student instead of modifying the student to fit the system. "We need to focus on meeting the diverse needs of students and put in place organizational patterns to support them."

There were nods of approval when Mr. Plowfield spoke.

"You do have a point, Mr. Plowfield," she heard Mrs. Desiree Cartes say. "Maybe the way the workplace is organized is not the most effective way in which to educate kids."

Dina could hear in the background, Mr. Weber, Mr. Taylor, and Mr. Bobbitt saying, "If it's good enough for the adults, it's good enough for children. It's the way environments have to be organized in order to produce the product."

Mr. Carlton Rodgers, who sporadically began attending the early morning meetings, agreed. "The faculty has been suggesting that the purpose of our teaching-learning process is to provide students with diverse delivery systems. One size didn't fit all. Students have different cognitive and affective needs.

"We have to change something that happens in the classroom and in the schoolhouse if we want the students to interact actively with learning. It would be so wonderful if we could do what Mr. Plowfield suggests . . . tailor the system to fit student needs."

"I think if we want to tailor the system to fit the student," Mrs. Lightment said, "we have to know what the current situation in the classroom is. What I mean is, if our primary relationship is with students, what kinds of interaction do we now have with them as we deliver the curriculum? What value does that relationship have in terms of our purpose? How are we going to ascertain this?

"The parents had said that they wanted their students challenged at all levels. They wanted their children prepared for the postsecondary world of work by quality teachers. Teachers wanted students who valued education."

"The classes that the students enroll in," Jon added, "play a huge role in defining their future."

"Why not flow-chart the teaching learning process?" Mrs. Lightment suggested. "A flow chart would allow us to capture the work of our school where it was happening . . . in the classrooms. It would show us how elements relate to each other . . . within the social warehouse . . . and play themselves out. Let's flow chart the process in order to see what it really looks like."

"Is this a useful project?" Mrs. Trench asked. She also was intermittently attending Democratic Council meetings. Dina didn't know if this was value added or value subtracted from the discussions. On the other hand, it was always good to know what the enemy was thinking, and maybe even telling Superintendent Mac Avelli.

"Is it a necessary thing for the teachers to do?" Mrs. Trench inquired. "Would this be viewed as an intimidating ultimatum? Do this or get written up?"

Mr. Henry Berg nodded his head in agreement. "Some teachers might not accept this as its true intent, which is to create a generic model of what happens in the classroom regarding teacher-learning processes. It would make a great deal of difference how it was presented to the staff."

Mr. Plowfield was visibly annoyed with the opinions just expressed. "We can't make anyone change. But we are committed as a school to continuous improvement regarding what we do and, as a result, what our students do. This is one method we can use in achieving this goal. The faculty must ask themselves how they each perceive their own classroom processes. Unless we do this, how can we improve instruction? The purpose is to scrutinize our teaching in relationship to our students' learning."

Mr. Newt Owen, attempting to mediate the heated debate, said, "All pedagogy aside, what doing a flow chart of our classroom activities boils down to is a matter of trust between faculty and administration."

Dina couldn't help thinking when she heard the word administration that for every one step forward, we go two steps backward. Maybe that was just the way the change process worked.

Mrs. Lightment chimed in: "What we have to do as a faculty is decide how we are going to improve instruction for students. But we can't do this unless we know what exists now. And since we don't get much of a chance to visit each other, I suggest we ask the faculty to come up with a flow-chart model of how the classroom delivers instruction. Let's leave it up to the teachers as to who does or doesn't do it."

And so they did just that. They received input from about a third of the faculty. Some, who chose not to accept the assignment did so because of fear, or because Mrs. Trench had talked to them. Others simply did not want to take the time or didn't understand the voluntary assignment.

In truth, the old trust issue was at work. Furtively, the Mrs. Trenches of the schoolhouse asked themselves *how will the administration use a flow chart of my activities in the classroom to get at us?*

The teachers who took on the voluntary assignment flow charted the activities involved in a forty-five-minute period. The Democratic Council drew up a composite of the results by creating a generic model. The flow chart was linear and began with the 8:20 bell ringing.

- The 8:20 bell announced that all students should be in their seats, minds ready to learn.
- The teacher took attendance and made the necessary announcements to the class.

- She put on the board an opening activity, which kept the students busy while she did the housekeeping work.
- The teacher collected the opening activity and then reviewed it with the students.
- The teacher reviewed the day's activity while collecting homework.
- The teacher directed instruction.
- Students would then do work individually or in pairs or groups.
- The teacher walked around the room to help students with the assignment. The students who completed their assignment would begin their homework.
- The teacher closed the session, reviewing what the students had learned.
- The teacher reviewed the homework assignment. The bell rang.

Dina was shaken by this model of education, but it was the one she had observed repeatedly during her classroom visits.

"Were students succeeding using this teaching-learning process?" Mrs. Lightment asked. "Was this process developed for the student or the teacher? How could we further assess this situation in order to complete a picture of the teaching-learning process that we're attempting to define?"

"Why not ask the students to draw up their flow chart of the teaching-learning process?" Mr. Plowfield suggested. The group decided that this might be productive. After all, they were talking about the teaching-learning process and feedback loops. They voted for the principal to come up with a way to pursue this activity.

After this meeting, Dina continued to think about how students thought the teachers were delivering the curriculum. The teachers' view was very structured and contained limited interaction among students, between students and teachers, and about subject matter. Models of teaching that teachers utilized were very structured—so inauthentic, in terms of the way learning occurred in natural settings. Of course you could say that schooling did not occur in a natural setting, but why couldn't it?

How many of us learned anything if we were not actively engaged in the learning process? It seemed from the flow chart that Jon was right in his assessment of the teaching-learning process—the teacher did most of the work in the classroom. Did educators really believe that students today were going to come to a classroom and wait for knowledge to be installed inside their heads?

As she was pondering these thoughts, she passed Mr. Berg's humanities classroom. There was a substitute there and a great many off-task students. It was a small class of perhaps fifteen students.

Suddenly Dina entered the quantum world as the idea jumped out at her. She asked them if they would come to her office and help her define the teaching-learning process. They didn't understand what she was talking about, but she knew they would do anything to escape the boredom of their current situation, even if it meant going to the principal's office.

She asked the students to use the floor to flow chart their perceptions of their school day. What do students do? "What happens to you from 8:20 in the morning when the first bell rings to 3:20 in the afternoon when the last bell dismisses you?"

They divided themselves into groups of five. Writing on butcher paper, they produced this composite list:

- The bell rings and while the students are still dragging themselves to their seats, the teacher reads the announcements.
- Those students who are already seated socialize while the teacher takes attendance. "It was important to be on top of the social events seven periods a day," a student said. "In fact, the events changed radically by the time you got to seventh period."
- The teacher finishes reading the announcements, takes attendance, and tries to get order in the classrooms. "This is sometimes difficult," one of the students admitted "if it is a Monday and lots of partying occurred over the weekend."
- The teacher then collects the homework. "The collection does not take long because there is little to collect," a student noted. "The lecture about the lack of homework takes longer. Then valuable class time is taken up while the majority of students, who have not done their homework, do it instead of doing what the teacher planned that day. The students who did their homework end up repeating what they already know."
- Then the teacher gives the objective for the day's work. She gives lecture notes.

- While the teacher does this, some students continue to socialize and some take the notes. The students organize their class material and the teacher walks around checking student work. Students ask questions about what was just explained because they were not paying attention. Some or most of the students don't finish, and the work gets carried on the next day. Students who do finish must wait until the rest of the class finishes the assignment. "These students lose out," a freshman affirmed.
- The bell rings but everybody is already up by the door five minutes before it rings, waiting to leave.

This was their school day.

Dina was flabbergasted when she saw their perception. She showed it to her secretary, Mrs. Hogarth. "It looks like the students know how to manipulate the classroom quite well," she said.

She shared the results with the faculty. Mrs. Minsey Well looked like she was on the verge of crying. "Are we wasting our time? After all my years of teaching English, I feel devalued as a teacher!"

At first, there were the excuses. Who were the students who did this? She told them they were from Mr. Berg's humanities class. "There are no slugs in my class," Mr. Berg said. "Most of my students are extremely intuitive."

"Looks like the teaching-learning process is relational but is producing insignificant energy that is antithetical to our purpose," Mr. Plowfield said pedantically. "The teacher thinks she is supplying students with instruction, guidance, feedback, modeling, and support. The student, we perceive, was providing feedback, personal growth, and showing work satisfaction.

"Seems like something is missing from this picture. Shouldn't work satisfaction mean that the students in some way demonstrate that what they are learning is meaningful to them? The only thing that appears meaningful is the opportunity we provide for them to personally socialize."

Mrs. Lightment concluded the distressing dialogue. "What gets accomplished during a forty-five-minute period from a student perspective? Ten minutes is wasted on getting ready. Another five minutes is wasted *getting ready to leave*. That leaves thirty minutes. These kids sure have busy weekends. No wonder they don't have time to learn anything!"

They were all depressed and needed time to see their way through the dust storm that had just clouded their vision.

As they drifted through the storm, Dina continued to ponder the results of the customer feedback form she had administered to teachers. Mrs. Lightment took it upon herself to perform a similar task. She instructed her students on how to design a survey that would let the teacher know how she could better meet their classroom needs. She chose one class as a pilot group. The students developed the survey, administered it, and interpreted the results. They then prepared what they appropriately called her report card.

"My next step is to review it," she announced to the faculty who were clearly not comfortable with what she was doing. "I am going to try to keep an open mind as I look at the results. If I view the data as being valid, I will work on changing some of my behaviors, as a service to my students. In that way, they will also modify their performance and we can begin interacting as a team, building trust between us.

"I really believe that once the trust is there, my curriculum will be learned with more ease. At least that's the theory I'm working on."

Indeed, what Mrs. Lightment was doing frightened a great many teachers. They perceived that she was asking her students to rate her. This could be intimidating because students had not yet learned the nuances of critical review. They could be Leviathans unleashed from their harness when asked their opinion. They didn't hide behind subtleties as adults did. They didn't parse words.

Dina thought of something Mr. Quintin Waver had shared with her. It reminded her of the courage it took for Mrs. Lightment to conduct her pilot survey. "Our problem," he explained, "is that we have to look at the world differently as we do school improvement. The world is not so simple. It's far more complex.

"We're used to perceiving that something is there or it is not there. The fact is, it is there and it is not there all at the same time. It just depends on who the viewer is. What I mean is that Plato was totally wrong. We are not prisoners locked into our bodies. There is no reason to escape from our prison in order to find some world outside us. We are that world we are hoping to discover."

His statements recounted for her something that Mrs. Lightment had shared with her. "I want more of a relational position to the teaching-learning process in my classroom.

"Teaching is not about them and us. It's a cooperative effort among all of us. I want my students to truly know, understand, and use my curriculum. The knowledge they glean from it will help them succeed in life. If they don't glean anything, I'm wasting my time. So I need to know how to increase our connections to each other so that the learning value will increase."

Was she attempting to replace competition in the form of her control of the classroom with cooperation in the form of building student confidence, Dina asked herself?

It was Mrs. Lightment who provided Dina the incentive to continue with her own survey. She needed a new approach to determine teachers' needs. She designed a new instrument. She threw away all her climate surveys. If she wanted to know what teachers needed, she would ask them, knowing that one size didn't fit all.

During one week in November, she walked around the schoolhouse asking teachers her questions. "Tell me what services you need from me so that you can enhance your performance within the teaching-learning process. How important is this service to you?"

By informing Dina of the services they required, they would be sharing with her what they valued in a principal. She needed to know less about what the principal who walked on water looked like and more about what perceived needs teachers valued. She was beginning to accommodate herself to the term *service* that Mrs. Lightment always used. In a democracy, we serve ourselves while serving the common good.

As she did this, the faculty and staff wrote the purpose statement. It was easy. The yin and yang of continuous introspection had produced the results. In forty minutes, they knew what they were about as a professional organization of educators. It was their job to ensure that their students learned the curriculum in a matter conducive with democratic processes. They knew that they couldn't do this as yet. Other parts of the system needed work in conjunction with this purpose. But everything they did fell under this umbrella.

They didn't write down the purpose or produce huge posters. They just knew what they had to do. Dina also knew that Superintendent Mac Avelli would not accept this.

"Of course we expect the students to learn the curriculum," he would declare, "that is a given. And this thing about democratic practices," he would rant, "do you mean that there will be more discussions going on in the classroom or that the teacher will attend to the learning needs of all her students . . . are you out of your mind?

"The state tests are coming. Teachers don't have time to do anything more than prepare the students for the tests. You must continue to use the model of teaching that has always been used . . . the teacher teaches and the students learn. You are walking a fine line, Principal Macksy!"

But she knew that one size did not fit all. She didn't say this to him because . . . well . . . what was the use?

Vignette

UNBUNDLING STRUCTURES
TO FIT STUDENTS

It was now late November when the school began assessing what their current teaching-learning process was producing. They didn't really know what they were going to find because they had never asked themselves this question before. Additionally, they were less than sure about what assessing a system populated by people and about people was going to tell them. Were they going to learn something that they didn't already know?

The truth is, some thought, why go through all this trouble especially in the eleventh month of the year? November's are difficult for schools. As you are trying to move forward with the school year, you have to remind yourself that you still have to work with where the school presently is—or isn't.

Principal Dina Macksy made this journal entry.

School has now been in session for almost a semester and teacher–student interactions are beginning to combust. In the peaceful atmosphere of the library, we talk about how we can change our educational practices. When the meeting is over, we all return to the classroom and office trenches.

The discipline referral I received today stated that a freshman boy, Cal Surgeon, had screamed at his teacher identifying her as a f_____ white bitch. Security removed him from the classroom. I was perplexed as to why the freshman added "white" to his descriptor of his teacher since his origin as well as hers are steeped in Caucasian roots.

Years ago, Cal Surgeon would have been removed from school. But kids now grow up with the expectation that they can say what they want, how they want, and to whomever they want.

How can you remove a student from school when he is simply doing what society gives him permission to do? Students are brought up in environments where the FU expletive is evidenced on an ongoing basis. The parents use it at home, and it is rare to see a movie that does not contain this word. I heard a board member say . . . at a public meeting . . . that the use of profanity was the way kids today assert themselves. Her complacency unraveled me.

I read in the newspaper that one of our students was found dead by a transient in a dumpster near a Pizza Hut. The kid who died . . . Tab Bader . . . was only seventeen. He wasn't a bad kid. He attended the school, off and on for two years. He had no parents and lived in a home for boys who were no longer wanted by their parents. His parents couldn't control him so they gave him away. They too had learned the FU expletive, only this time the words were put into practice.

The Democratic Council met at its usual time and all members brought their November blues with them. Mrs. Edna Lightment began the meeting. "Coming to work this morning, I heard on the radio about Tab Bader's murder. I didn't really know him."

"He was in my English 11 class for a while," Mr. Henry Berg said dimly. "He was a bright kid. No family, always neatly dressed. It's a pity. He was probably involved in a drug deal gone bad. I'm sure he dealt drugs."

The group was silent until Mrs. Lightment smiled wanly and started them up again. "I also heard that 30,000 new kids will be entering the juvenile justice system. The state is not prepared to meet the challenge. We have got to do something about this situation. But every time we try, something new comes up and runs interference."

"Like discipline problems," Mr. Berg offered, attempting to quell the spell that November casts on school people. "There's so much going on right now. It's as if all the students were on drugs, and we are all in reactive mode. Sometimes I wish some of my students would stay home."

"Can you divorce the child from his problems?" Dina asked.

"I guess not, but we see more than a hundred kids every day. How can we deal with more than the manifestations of what they are bringing with them to class? A kid screams an obscenity . . . we throw him out of class. We don't have time to take the kid aside and deal with the fact that he found his girlfriend sleeping with another boy. If we do that, we ignore the other bodies in the class."

"Besides, we can't leave those bodies unattended," Mrs. Indika Trench added, sarcasm underlying her tone. "It's against school policy. We'll get written up even if we do it for a good purpose. Anyway, their baggage is just that . . . theirs . . . and their parents. It's not our problem that some of the students come to school with the attitudes they have. It's the parent's fault, not ours. If the parents can't handle their children, how do they expect us to?"

Mr. Berg shuddered. "With all these kids exploding, it gets increasingly difficult to teach. How can we talk about diversifying our instructional methods in order to form relationships with the different ways in which kids learn and the experiences they bring to school, when we're doing all we can to keep the pot from boiling over?"

"Let's change the subject and talk about the curriculum," Mr. Jeb Plowfield said, "because it's related to *those bodies* and discipline. Curriculum is the entire body of courses offered in the program of a school. It's what the state and we manufacture because we think that kids need a certain standard of knowledge in order to participate in a democratic society.

"It's important, society feels," he continued, "that our children learn how to read, write, and do math. With those skills they will acquire further knowledge in terms of history, science, English, and the other disciplines. I teach my students how to plow a field, but I also teach them that, without the other disciplines, they will never excel at anything that has to do with land management."

Mr. Plowfield paused, cleared his throat, and started up again. "In my class, they can practically apply what you have been teaching them in math, Mrs. Cartes. And what you are teaching them in science, Mr. Waver." He nodded to each teacher.

"They also have to know how to write, read, and critically think," he continued. "These are the skills they should be building upon when in English class they discuss and debate the meanings of the books they read and in history where the ideas of great men . . . and women . . . are explored.

"At least that is the way I think about our school and the work we do. We poll the students every year regarding their elective interests, and we do our best to build on those interests and the needs of society. What students need and what society needs are reciprocal. Democracy must have thinkers and workers who have the capability to adapt and work together."

He went on to say that as chairman of the vocational department, he felt it incumbent upon himself to research national trends and develop course offerings based on those trends. "When the curriculum offers something kids want," he explained, "they're more likely to integrate educational experiences into their schemes of meaning, which in turn broadens and deepens their understanding of themselves and the world."

He ended with the idea that teachers have to integrate across the board what students and teachers bring to the classroom. "The teaching-learning process is relational," he said. "It's about those yin-yang brothers. If done well for students, it would decrease the number of discipline referrals we are talking about."

"It's true," Mrs. Desiree Cartes said, "that what we are teaching is important. But do we ask ourselves when we prepare our lessons how we can make our lesson plans connect in some way to the student's experience?"

"Education is a social process," Mr. Plowfield continued. "Why is the interest of the school preferred over the interest of the student?"

"I know that some of my students ask themselves how the information in their history text is connected to them," Mr. Newt Owen said. "They tell me that they are tired of reading about all that old stuff. I know full well, after all our conversations, that my students are organic creatures who learn the material so much better when they can integrate knowledge with their own. The problem is not in the curriculum. The problem is the way in which my students and I relate to it.

"If only I had more time to plan," he explained, "I would work with Mr. Berg over there on integrating periods of history with periods of literature. Instead all I do is cover the curriculum so that the students will do their best on the state tests. Imagine having the opportunity to uncover the curriculum, going deep rather than wide?"

"What you are all saying," Mrs. Trench erupted, "is that knowledge for knowledge sake should not be the primary purpose of school. I don't see how that is unimportant."

Jon Deway would not allow her comment to pass without retort. "Real learning takes place when I feel a need for it or can find a connection with it, Mrs. Trench. When you pronounce statements like this you encourage docility, obedience, dependency. Knowledge is what separates one person from another, but the knowledge must be more than spouted . . . that isn't knowledge, its regurgitation."

"He's right," Mr. Quintin Waver said. "We experience, we elaborate on the experience, we differentiate the experience, and we integrate it. That's real learning."

"We don't remember so many things," Jon said, "because the remembrance is not part of our data bank. I feel sometimes that what happens in the classroom is not how people really learn."

There was a long pause, broken by Mr. Berg. "Let's go on. While this is a difficult task, it's nonetheless more and more essential that we ask ourselves: if I present the lesson in this way, will all my students learn it? It's a difficult task, but I don't think it's an impossible one. We just need time to put our heads together.

"We all know that kids learn differently. We know all the buzzwords about learning styles, integrated curriculum, thematic teaching. But they're just that . . . buzz words. Maybe we should be talking about why we don't take any of these ideas seriously."

"In the traditional classroom," Mrs. Lightment said, "the entire group moves as a whole toward some predetermined goal. Our students come to school with such a variety of behaviors that it is very hard for the classroom teacher to anticipate and meet all their needs and expectations on a fully individualized basis. I have tools in the classroom that my students love, but it is still difficult. I imagine it is harder in the classes where every student does not have a computer."

"Well, let's look at the efforts we are now making," Mr. Berg said. "I always try changing my way of delivery in order that all my students get it. I can tell by the grades on tests if I have been successful or not.

"And I am starting to do what you suggested Mrs. Lightment. I'm analyzing the responses the kids give to certain questions, especially if many of them got the same one wrong. While many of my attempts have been failures, some have worked surprisingly well. I introduced the idea of the yin-yang when students were having difficulty understanding Milton's *Paradise Lost.*"

"And that really got me thinking," Jon said. "What I understood from this lesson was that heaven could not be understood without a hell. Some of the kids started talking about how one element gives way to another . . . like loyalty to a gang becomes more important than loyalty to the family. And then the kid from Africa in our class, Mohammed Jallon, started talking about why tribalism has to give way to nationalism if African countries are to become stable."

"That's exactly what we want to happen, Jon," Mr. Berg continued. "But I told myself as I took time to do this that I couldn't detour from the curriculum too much or we would fall behind Mrs. Trench's classes. But I did because the students were so interested in what we were doing.

"Sometimes I say the heck with it and spend the time trying out new methods which will engage all the students. I began teaching my students how to work in groups. We practiced and practiced the roles each of them had until they got it right.

"As a result of teaching and practicing the rules, the students remain on task for a longer duration and actually have meaningful discussions. What I called grouping prior to teaching them the theory and practice of grouping was ludicrous. Most of their time was spent off-task and that was my fault. They didn't know how to work together because nobody took the time to teach them.

"And it's not enough to say these are the rules . . . they have to be practiced and reinforced until they all get it . . . by doing it over and over."

"But how long did it take you to do this?" Mrs. Trench asked. She didn't wait for an answer. "We don't have a minute to spare for nonessentials."

"Well, I think that sounds great, Mr. Berg," Mr. Owen said with obvious ebullience. "Even Congress has rules for engagement, even though they never seem to move forward on anything. I believe that our students don't see the light at the end of the tunnel soon enough. Graduation seems too far off as a goal. I believe that if students could experience some incremental success that was meaningful to them, they might see graduation as more achievable.

"Maybe we need to go to a quarterly system of credits. Or maybe blocking off our schedule would give us more time to do the things we need to do."

"We're not ready for solutions to problems," Mrs. Lightment cautioned, "until we find out where we currently are and why we are there, Mr. Owen. Remember we all agreed that any changes we made had to be based on evidence that the change was necessary. We also said that we would have to analyze the effect of any change on other parts of the school."

Mrs. Trench broke in again, notably disturbed by the direction the dialogue had taken. "The students who come to school, but not to class, say that we are boring. Well, I'm not in the entertainment business! It's up to the parents to make their students right when they come to school. Then we can do our job of teaching.

"I don't have the discipline problems in my class that Mr. Berg does. That's because I know how to control my students by providing them with structure. They do as I direct them to do.

"I didn't have it easy when I went to school. I had to struggle, too. Let's face it . . . school is tough work. I always tell my students that learning is a job. You get out of it what you put into it."

As she talked, Dina asked herself how students learn responsibility if teachers do all the work for them?

The dialogue turned to what teachers wanted the classroom to look like. Mr. Berg said, "It would be nice to find a way to move from the conventional classroom where the teacher does all the work to where the student could be part of the work and we would become facilitators of instruction."

"Yeah, it would be nice," said Mr. Owen advancing the wouldn't-it-be-nice theme, "to teach in an environment where the teacher could say to the students, 'I don't know all the answers but I can lead the way in helping you find them.' In this day and age, there is more than one solution to an existing problem . . . too bad each student doesn't have a computer."

"It would be nice if we could work together as a team with our students and colleagues," said Mrs. Cartes. "For example, I really admire what Mrs. Lightment is doing with her student feedback form.

"I did something similar with my students. I said to them, 'This is the content we have to cover and that you have to learn. What is the best way for you to learn it?' And they told me.

"Some said they liked when they worked together with others, others said they would rather work alone, others said that they needed more visuals. I couldn't believe it. So it would be great if there was a cooperative spirit with teachers, parents, and even community members."

Mrs. Lightment added, "The business community says they need people who know how to work together. So we would be preparing them for the future."

They talked about a vision of a school where information was not organized, evaluated, interpreted, and communicated to students solely by the teacher. They envisioned a classroom where information was organized, interpreted, and evaluated by students. They talked about students acquiring learning and sharing it with appropriate audiences.

Ms. Oprah Myden, who believed that education in the classroom should be "instilled" in students, not "installed" and who believed that her role was that of a facilitator of education, said, "Currently, educational delivery systems are for one audience. One size fits all. All students receive the content in the same way no matter what their learning style. We know this and have discussed it a great deal.

"However, being aware of something and actually putting it into practice is different. It's easier for us to stick with the old than experiment with the new. But it looks like some of us are beginning to diversify the way in which we present content. I am not a lecturer and I don't like to listen to people who prattle, thinking that only what they say is important.

"I also feel we have to go beyond learning styles. We have to look at the curriculum . . . the way subjects are taught in isolation of each other. For example, Mr. Waver tells his students . . . I know because his students tell me . . . that they can't do physics without math. But then we teach math in one room and physics in another. That doesn't make sense.

"Problem solving is part of everyday life. The most ludicrous thing I have heard, and I have heard it from teachers on our staff, is that thinking needs to be taught apart from content. I've even heard teachers prescribing teaching thinking skills as a hierarchy. Thinking can't be put on a stepladder and isolated from context. In the end it's all integrated. It's a whole that is more than the sum of its parts."

"Amen to that," Mr. Berg said laughing. "I can see it now in the curriculum. Thinking 9 . . . Thinking 10 and so on."

Ms. Myden chuckled and then continued. "In the conventional classroom students are expected to follow teacher rules. How can students learn to be responsible, socially able, self-managing, and even resourceful if we make all the rules?

"I view my classroom as an organic body where we all monitor one another. That's why the students generate the rules in my classes as I guide them in terms of acceptable social norms."

As the group contemplated what Ms. Myden said, talk about the student flow chart again surfaced. Being cognizant of the way in which the students viewed their day at school had dampened teacher morale.

"We shouldn't get too depressed about it," Mr. Waver said. "In a quantum world, there is always the possibility that other worlds, besides the one we observe, exist. The students were sharing their world with us. We see it differently. So maybe we have to collapse both worlds and make them better . . . more productive in terms of learning."

"Maybe if students were given more responsibility," Mr. Evan Mann said, "teachers would not be so tired at the end of the day. Empowering kids means teaching them the responsibility that comes with it. And that's hard because they are not taught responsibility at home.

"They have been super exposed to media that cares less about them and more about the dollars they spend. Their parents are working all the time, giving them less attention. My next door neighbor works nights so she sleeps most of the day. She rarely has time to see her children. That's why so many of our kids have turned to gangs. It's where the family is."

His remarks gave Mrs. Lightment the lead-in she needed to redirect the group. "Well, I think that we have to probe our system and see how the one-size-fits-all mentality has influenced the teaching-learning process," she said, ending the dialogue for now.

Vignette

UNDERSTAND INTERACTIONS: PEOPLE, DATA, SYSTEMS, AND THEORY

In the next discussion group, Mrs. Edna Lightment started, "We need data to assess what the current system is producing. For example, last semester we had a lot of kids who failed one or more subjects . . . 40 percent. I have the actual numbers broken down by subject area, teacher, gender, and ethnicity, which I will distribute later. How many of you have ever looked at your failure rates compared to other teachers? It's revealing. I sometimes ask myself what an *F* means to a kid. I never received one."

"My brother did," Principal Dina Macksy said. "There were so many that after a while he didn't care. Finally he dropped out of school."

"Well, that's what happens when kids get discouraged," Mr. Carlton Rodgers said. "Forty percent . . . that's a lot of self-esteem . . . and democracy . . . going down the tubes."

"I wonder which teacher fails the most kids?" Mr. Evan Mann muttered.

Mrs. Lightment changed the subject but they all thought they knew who it was.

"In order to assess the system, we should create a statistical picture of our educational community," she suggested. "To do this, we need data on enrollment, attendance, dropout, failure, retention, honor roll, discipline referral, and graduation rates.

"We need to discern what happens to our students after they graduate in terms of postsecondary education or employment. We need more data on how students and teachers perceive each other's work. We need to know more about the teacher–principal relationship. In other words, we require baseline information from which we can view our system's operating capabilities. Once we are able to discern the areas that signal trouble, we could probe for real causes of problems."

"Why do all this work?" Mr. Mann asked. "We know where we're at."

"Actually, we don't know, Mr. Mann," Dina said. "We have data here and there but they have not been drawn together to show us what the teaching-learning process is really accomplishing. We can guess, but if our guess is wrong, we will be barking up the wrong tree when we begin to problem solve.

"The data are a tool that can show us what we look like, undressed. If we don't like our appearance, we can begin theorizing about what we need to do to make us look better . . . do we begin to exercise or keep the look we now have?"

The consensus was that they needed to strengthen their schoolhouse. Ms. Oprah Myden volunteered to begin the research. Mr. Jeb Plowfield, Mrs. Desiree Cartes, and other members of the faculty said they would work with her on this.

During the next few weeks, data collection began. They were doing what so few schools did—they were measuring the current capability of their teaching-learning process.

They began with a picture of enrollment, observing that the number of registered students shifted during the year because of the number of students who transferred out and in. Grade nine had three times the number of students than grade twelve had. In grade nine there was an almost equal distribution of males and females. This equal distribution became skewed in favor of boys as the students moved up in grade level.

"It's strange," Mrs. Cartes remarked. "We had a lot of students who were in ninth grade and fewer students who were in twelfth grade. Why? When did this pattern begin? Did they all move out of the district . . . or drop out?"

They searched for more data that might provide an answer to her question. First, they discovered that four years ago there had been a slight increase in enrollment. Second, many students were being socially promoted to ninth grade from the junior high school. Third, many more students were being retained in ninth grade than in other grades.

The state instituted new tests. Many students were being retained because they were not passing those tests. A holding pattern of students had developed at this grade level, which eventually led to students dropping out.

They reviewed attendance reports. In their state, high schools are required to remain open for a minimum number of days each year.

"Students who are absent and miss instruction," Dina informed the committee, "increase the need for teachers to spend precious class time reviewing and reteaching. In addition, because state funding is based on attendance, students who miss school reduce school revenues.

"Superintendent Mac Avelli decreed that he wanted no more than an average of 6 percent of the students absent on a particular day. 'If this could happen, our district would receive more revenue dollars,' he told me. Therefore, our attendance rate has to be at 94 percent. Our attendance had never been higher than 90 percent."

"Last year, I remember Mr. Van Waggner, the middle school principal, suspending students who missed too much school," recounted Mr. Mann, "His method of handling low attendance did not make sense to me. I'm sure that suspending kids only meant that more students were absent. And while he did reward students who came to school, he was rewarding the kids, like my son, who came anyway."

He was right. Treating the chronic problem with a system of rewards and punishment was applying window dressing to a deeper-seated problem. That is, they were treating the problem superficially when they failed to search for the reasons why the problem was happening. A cure for what ailed their system could only be found by first probing for the root causes, something that many of the voices in the library had suggested.

Participants on the ad hoc research committee asked several students, parents, and community members to help them interpret the attendance data. Looking at the numbers only told them that they had a problem. It didn't tell them why they had the problem. They needed people who worked in the process to help theorize about the causes of the problems.

The task force began with a macro question to guide the project. Why isn't the attendance rate at our school at 94 percent? What influences a student's decision not to come to school?

To answer this question, they created a picture of the variables that could affect student absenteeism. Five categories emerged: instruction and curriculum, the economic environment, adversarial relationships, the social environment, and outside agency influences.

They then brainstormed further details for each category: under outside agencies, students sometimes miss school because they have to wait all day to see a doctor at the local clinic; under curriculum and instruction, because they hadn't studied for a test; under social environment, because they had been out all night; and under adversarial relationships, because of gang-related problems.

Their next activity was to identify periods where high numbers of students were absent. They asked two questions. First, what is the mean attendance rate for grades nine through twelve on a monthly basis? Second, is the variation in attendance from year to year stable? The data were gathered from the past six years.

The data indicated the potential number of days students could be in school each school month and the actual number of days they were in school. They used the first eight school months of each year. The data output was the mean attendance rate each day that students were in attendance.

Using a line graph, they plotted the data over time. The graph informed them that attendance was at its highest point at the beginning of the school year, steadily declined until the second semester, where it spiked . . . although at a lower level than the beginning of the year . . . and declined again, spiking at increasingly lower levels.

This roller coaster pattern of attendance perplexed the team. Parents and community members hypothesized that the consistent roller coaster pattern might indicate that there were common elements among students that caused them to miss school. They speculated that the nonrandom nature of the pattern might be a result of events that occurred in the community.

The team split into two groups. The first team formed the hypothesis that the nonrandom causes were due to planned community events. They compared the attendance patterns of the school with two other feeder schools in the district. These schools drew from similar populations.

The second team disaggregated the data to determine if certain grade levels contributed more to the attendance problem than others.

The comparison with other schools showed higher attendance at the start of school and then a general decline with small spikes in similar months as the high school. Although the mean averages of students attending school were higher at the two other schools, the patterns were the same.

The team probed deeper. They found that on Mondays, students were most likely to be absent, followed by Fridays and Tuesdays, then Thursdays and Wednesdays. The team brainstormed reasons why Mondays, Fridays, and Tuesdays would have lower attendance rates. Then they listed the events that were occurring in the community to verify their findings. They found that on some of these days, important events occurred in the community, which took a higher number of children out of school.

The first team wanted to determine the influence of certain months on attendance rates. During what months do students have the highest absentee rates? The diagram they drew depicted that February and March had the highest absentee rates. The August and September period had the lowest.

Attendance spiked during the January period when finals were administered and a new semester began. Similar patterns existed at the other two schools. This indicated to the team that the time of year and the day of the week influenced student attendance. Knowing when students would be out would help predict future attendance rates.

The second team, using monthly attendance rates over a six-year period, found that grade nine had the lowest attendance rates. In addition, the roller coaster patterns generally appeared to repeat themselves over time. The ninth grade revealed a general pattern of instability, but the pattern shifted slightly upward during the last year they reviewed. The team speculated that this might have resulted from a new at-risk program, which had been piloted during the school year.

The teams then regrouped. They had identified which months and days of the weeks contained points indicating special events. They had disaggregated the data and found certain grade levels contributed most to the problem.

The team wanted one more piece of information before determining root causes of nonattendance. They wanted to be able to predict the characteristics of the student most likely to be absent.

They decided to draw up a profile of a truant student. They defined a truant as a student who missed half the semester or more. The input was individual student attendance records.

The team found that a high percentage of students fit into this category. They collected data on the grade level, gender, average age, address, and working status of truant students.

By analyzing student attendance data, they discovered that a typical truant student at their school was in the ninth grade, male, 16.1 years of age, and lived close to the school. His parents did not work.

Data on retention informed the group that it was the ninth grade that had the highest level of students who remained at that grade level for more than a year. They eventually dropped out of school.

The attendance ad hoc committee had accumulated a great deal of information on student attendance. Though they could predict when students missed school from the profile, they did not know why students were missing school. What reasons do students give for being absent?

They developed a simple survey that asked students to check reasons they were absent on a particular day. They did this for a three-week period. The output showed that the primary reason students gave for being absent was illness, followed by death in the family, oversleeping, sick children, no babysitter, transportation problems, medical appointments, ditching, suspensions, incarceration, hospital treatment for substance abuse, and pregnancy-related illnesses.

Some absences appeared to be factors that were outside the school's locus of control, such as death in the family. Their data indicated that sick children, babysitting, medical appointments, and pregnancy-related events accounted for 24 percent of absences. Disciplinary infractions comprised almost 13 percent.

The team decided to investigate this further because these were areas that presented opportunities for improvement.

In order to determine the influence of suspensions on attendance, the team asked Dina for data on the percentage of students at each grade level who were suspended for discipline infractions.

The resultant data indicated that the greatest majority of suspensions occurred in grade nine. This was the grade that had the highest rate of nonattendance. The team probed further to determine if there were certain times during the day when the greatest number of infractions occurred. They found that most students committed disciplinary infractions during class changes and at lunch.

The team also wanted to determine the influence of student-parent status on attendance. They defined student-parents as students who had children or were in the process of having children.

As they looked at attendance records of the representative groups, a simple check sheet indicated that student-parents were absent at four times the rates of students who were not parents. Being a parent directly influenced a student's ability to attend school. Further disaggregation of the data on student-parents found that these students seldom had unverified absences, were ill infrequently, and had no suspensions. But a high percentage of these students dropped out of school.

They then moved on and examined last year's statistics on retention. They knew that students who did not move from grade to grade were more likely to drop out. An average of 24 percent of the students were retained at the ninth-grade level.

The four-year graduation rates were low, although during the prior year the rates were higher. Could it be due to the introduction of a new alternative program? Were alternative programs helping to reduce the dropout rates? Why?

Honor roll percentages were equally low when the committee compared them to other schools.

They reviewed discipline referral rates, focusing on suspensions from schools. That accounted for a high percentage of days missed. They also noticed that a number of discipline referrals were for drugs and gang-related activities, which usually resulted in suspensions.

Each year, seniors were administered a survey about their high school experience and their postsecondary plans. Almost 67 percent of the students said that they planned to go to college. Of that percentage, less than 40 percent actually went but dropped out within the first few months.

A small number of graduating students said they thought they would attend technical school or join the military. Many were unsure of their plans. Those students went directly into the job market or remained at home unemployed.

Dina asked the team if they were happy with what the school system was producing. If the answer was no . . . and it was November . . . could they begin analyzing the root causes of the problem?[1]

NOTE

1. For additional information on data collection in schools, see Walker and Walker (1993) and Walker (1995).

Vignette

USE DATA TO UNCOVER DEEP-SEATED DILEMMAS

"**E**verything in Newton's universe is ultimately reducible to so many individual parts and the forces acting between them. Atomism encourages a model of relationship based on conflict and confrontation, on part against part" (Zohar & Marshall, 1994, p. 26). Little did the authors know that they were providing a descriptor in their book for what the beginning of December was bringing to Principal Dina Macksy's school.

While Dina was beginning to understand intellectually the concept of an indivisible schoolhouse, the students at school were reminding her that the parameters of that indivisibility existed beyond the wrought iron fences that surrounded them.

Mr. Evan Mann accurately assessed the situation. "Students are entering the schoolhouse gate carrying emotional baggage far beyond their capacity to bear," he said, patting Jon Deway's shoulder. "It's kids in blue clothing facing off with kids in red clothing. After school, they guard their streets, like male dogs, urinating over and over again on what they declare is their territory. It's all so crazy. It's getting so bad that I make sure my kids are home before dark."

"I know what you mean," Mr. Henry Berg said, sympathetically. "They act one way in front of us and another way after school. If only we could help them unlock their baggage."

"We're not locksmiths," Mrs. Indika Trench affirmed. "It's my job to teach. It's Mr. Rodgers job to counsel."

"And there is little incoming help," Mr. Carlton Rodgers rued, ignoring her comment. "It is as if the entire country has in tandem declared that childrearing after age five is the school's job. We just don't seem to know how to care about our children anymore!" He shot a quick look at Mrs. Trench before continuing. The unflappable Mrs. Trench stared right back.

"What students carry to school each day is different for different students. There are those students who don't attend school on a regular basis because they have their own children at home. Others don't attend because they are in the ninth grade for the second or third time. Their contact with the world has been diminished by the phantoms inherent in their drug-induced wasteland.

"Some don't attend school because they were told by their report cards one time too many, they haven't met their teachers' standards. Others don't attend because the toxins of weekend clubbing and drinking have poisoned their young bodies. Some students don't attend because they had to spend all day waiting to see a doctor at the hospital only to be told that without health insurance they can't be serviced.

"Finally, there are those students who don't attend school because they have decided to unconsciously replicate their grown-up society and follow the gene pool to jail.

"The students coming to school have indeed changed over the years. A new student population has contributed to new dilemmas and challenges. Maybe Mrs. Trench is right after all. We're not their parents! We're their teachers and counselors!"

It was a struggle all right. It was tempting to think that there was an absence of dedicated students at the school. The fact is the school had many good kids . . . like Jon, who did well, who smiled, who participated in afterschool programs. But these so-called normal kids were eclipsed by those who brought their entire set of baggage inside the schoolhouse gate.

Dina suggested to the Democratic Council that they invite all students who had dropped out of school to join them in a public forum. If they wanted to know why students dropped out of school, why not ask them? This is just what they did.

"School was boring," said one young man. A creative string of vile expletives cascaded down the epidermal covering of his right arm. Dina wondered why he chose not to cover that arm. "Nothing exciting was happening like it was on the street," he said pensively.

A young woman with empty eyes decried the teachers. "What teachers do should have interested us. We should have been involved doing things that made sense to us, not what the teacher told us to do all the time."

Another young woman, who was now attending a junior college, said, "High school was always the same . . . talk, talk, and more talk. Teachers always in telling mode. Do you know how monotonous it is listening to teachers talk at you all day? Learning should be about something you can relate to. People like to be in on the activity, not just sit in a plastic cutout all day and be treated as if they were an attachment. We just didn't want to listen. We wanted to be part of the experience the teacher was having."

Two of the dropouts remembered school as being fun. "I feel that most of my teachers encouraged me. I remember students sometimes working on their own, or being in drama, music, or shop classes. These teachers made school fun. It was not only learning from a book.

"Math was fun, too. Math was taught so that we could see the connection between it and the world. I remember my teacher showing us how geometry related to building houses. She even had us build a model home. I got an A on that project and still have it. But I had a lot of problems at home. That's why I left."

The dropout sitting next to her added, "I feel the same way. Teachers really cared about and encouraged me. School should be a fun place where students work at their own pace. Some students need more time and some students need less time to learn something. I was given the time, but then I got pregnant."

Sid Munn, a tall, brawny man with a bald head that added to his striking appearance, was a trained psychologist and teacher whom Dina had invited to facilitate this dropout forum. He was piloting the school's first dropout prevention program. While the program succeeded in eliminating from the general school population some recalcitrant kids, it did little to keep them in school, or at least that's what she thought. Until recently, she never checked the data to ascertain the current capabilities of the program.

A year ago, Mr. Munn had begun a resiliency study with students who had a potential of dropping out of school. He and Mr. Rodgers wanted to know why some students graduated and others did not. They were looking for characteristics that would help create a profile of students who graduated from high school.

"What could the school do to prevent students from dropping out?" Mr. Munn asked the former students. There was a long quiet period in which everybody stared into space or fidgeted with the paper or pencil on the table or just stared down at the floor.

Then Orville, a slight boy with two rings in both nostrils and attired in red and black gang regalia, cryptically admonished, "What the hands do must be connected with what the mind does. The two must act in concert. We were either given mind things to do, like in chemistry, which made no sense to me, or given hand things to do like in autoshop, which made sense to me. But nothing ever totally connected for me after a day at school, except my homies.

"I knew there was a connection between chemistry," he said, "and the project I was working on in autoshop, but I couldn't figure out what it was. I got real frustrated. I needed guidance and didn't get it. Isn't that what you teachers were paid to do . . . guide us?"

Dina stared at the boy ruefully, reflecting about the time when Orville attended school dressed in a manner that did not make a statement . . . and with an unadorned nose. She remembered him as a poet, meeting with her in her office in the morning before the first bell rang and reading the lyrical phrases he had created overnight.

However, he wasn't there every morning. Orville was tardy a great deal of the time because he had to mop up the muck his mother left on the living room floor after partying all night and falling down drunk.

After he wiped her up and put her to bed, he still had to feed his younger sisters and brothers. When he arrived at school, he was assigned a detention for being late. If she only knew at that time how lucky they were to even have him at school. If only the school had had a plan that could accommodate this young man and his talent.

He was a poet and they were blinded to his beautiful words and ideas. And his mother . . . well, she slept right through it all.

After Orville spoke, the former students became more reflective. The room was somber. She could hear the students nearest her taking deep breaths.

"We need a jump start in life," reflected a nineteen-year-old who had a tattoo of a crossbone and skull etched into his upper arm. "Being able to have goals would help. At the juvenile detention center, where I spend a lot of time, people would come in and talk to me about careers. They just didn't do it once a year, either." Dina glanced at Mr. Rodgers. His cheeks flushed as the boy echoed his thoughts.

Other former students shared with the group that they saw no sense in an education. An eighteen-year-old student declared that she was living on welfare. There was frustration in her voice as she spoke. "Why bother with school. It's not going to get me anywhere. Nobody in my family finished school. No big deal. They're doing okay. Many people where I live sit home all day. They're making it. And besides, I have my own children to take care of so I can't go to school."

After the dropout forum ended, Mr. Munn shared his impressions with the faculty. "They drop out for a lot of reasons; because school failed to engage them, they had limited family support, or they got pregnant."

He shrugged his shoulders as if in despair. "Hell, they didn't make this world . . . we did. I want you all to listen to a tape I made with one of your students, Lester Thanfund. It's the first data I've collected for the resiliency study I'm conducting.

"I think a common characteristic that dropouts have is their lack of a family and school support structure. What's revealing about Lester is that he was searching for someone stable in his life. It's only when he finds that someone, does he turn around and begin to come to school on a more regular basis."

He then ran the tape. "Listen for yourself," he urged, "forming your own conclusions about how we can help the Lester's stay in school, that is, once we know that a problem exists. The tape is long, so I'll play only part of it."

Mr. Munn: Tell me about yourself? What do you do when you are not in school?

Lester: Most of the time I like to do art work like drawing and dirt bike riding . . . and take care of my little brother. He's about three years old now. His name is Lloyd, so nowadays he keeps me busy and my mom keeps me busy.

Mr. Munn: You like taking care of him?

Lester: Yeah, I like taking care of him; I like it 'cause he likes to play around.

Mr. Munn: Is it just the one brother?

Lester: No, there are three brothers and me. He's the youngest one. The others go to the middle school. On my mother's side, I'm the oldest. I got little brothers and sisters on my dad's side.

Mr. Munn: You live with both your mom and dad?

Lester: No, I never lived with my father. I don't know him very well.

Mr. Munn: Tell me a little about where you live. How many people live in your house?

Lester: In my family? There are five of us . . . me and my brothers. Sometimes my half-brothers and half-sisters come to live with us. They go back when my father sobers up.

Mr. Munn: Have you lived in your house for a long time or have you moved around a lot?

Lester: I moved around a lot. Throughout junior high, I have been having problems with my family. One day I woke up and I was in trouble. My mom just kind of turned against me for a couple of years . . . for about two years and then I finally came back.

Mr. Munn: When did it happen?

Lester: I believe in sixth or seventh grade. I was living in a room on my grandmother's property and my aunt was paying for the electricity. I was living by myself then. My grandma had custody and my aunt lived across the road. They were watching over me in a way.

Mr. Munn: Were you taking care of your own meals and everything?

Lester: Nah . . . they would buy everything for me, whatever I needed. They were mainly there. But then Grandma passed away. That's about the time my mom said I could come back home. Now I kind of look toward my future. I'm nineteen and I took the armed forces test. Hopefully, I'll get my results soon. I plan to enter the service when I graduate . . . join the Marines and try to pick up on my artwork.

Mr. Munn: How did you make that decision?

Lester: I guess going into the service was something I always wanted to do. My grandfather talked to me about it. He was a Marine. Since I was young, I looked up to him because I didn't have no one to look up to.

Mr. Munn: I see. Are you close to anyone, a teacher or a family member, someone you could talk to about things?

Lester: I can talk to Mr. Rodgers . . . like he understands what I go through. When people don't understand what I go through, when people don't take time to sit down and listen, when they're all mad and everything and not wanting to talk, he would want me to sit down and be calm and ask if I was ready to talk now. Other people would just wave their arms and say get out of here and go.

Mr. Munn: Did you get interested in art through school?

Lester: Yes and no. The program in school is a reason for coming because my art reflects how I am feeling. I really admire my artwork. I do a lot of it because it helps me to escape reality for a while because reality sometimes is a bit too hard . . . I feel like I'm in prison sometimes.

Mr. Munn: Is there anyone outside of school with whom you relate?

Lester: Just some of my friends. I'm trying to talk them into getting help because they go crazy doing drugs. They don't do it all the time, but I know now that it's bad for you.

Mr. Munn: What's it like going to school? Are there any teachers you like best?

Lester: I like Mrs. Minsey Well and Mr. Quintin Waver . . . although he says weird things sometimes. I like Mrs. Well. We have our little fights here and there but overall when it comes down to it we're there for each other. She reminds me of my grandmother. She shows me that she cares about me because when I go crazy in class . . .

Mr. Munn: Go crazy . . .

Lester: You know . . . use words I shouldn't because I get frustrated. She tells me to go outside and sit by the door instead of writing me up. In the past, when I came to school and something terrible happened, like someone passed away in my family, I would try to avoid being angry and having it come out the wrong way. But I would wind up getting in trouble anyway because I didn't know how to control what I was feeling. Now I try to talk things over or ask teachers if I can sit outside by the door. Mr. Rodgers said I should do this.

Mr. Munn: Is there anything in particular that gets you in trouble in school?

Lester: Mainly just my attitude sometimes. When I come to school and I don't feel too good because of something that has happened at home I might get into an argument for some little reason. You know it carries on till school is over and that's all you're thinking about throughout the whole day and say you have a sub and don't want to work with her and everything just messes up and you end getting into trouble.

Mr. Munn: Sounds like you have a lot of stress in your life.

Lester: Yeah, I got a lot of stress. It would take a long time for you to hear what I got. The counselor helps me with it. And my mom . . . she has been really helpful. She shows that she cares for me now. She didn't before.

Mr. Munn: So you are pretty comfortable with the way things are going right now in school? There are other students who are not having so much success or are not happy. Why do you think other students don't do so well in school?

Lester: Maybe because they get caught up in what's going on around them. They get caught up in other problems like drugs or alcohol and that prevents them from wanting to come to school. They see their parents and families going wild, so they go wild too. And then there's the gangs. I stay clear of them.

Mr. Munn: If the schools wanted to help some of the kids out there, what do you think are some of the things the school should do to help them do better?

Lester: You know you can give them everything they need but you can't do it for them. I guess just support them the best way you know. You can really strive for them and tell them that you know that they can really make it. Like you kind of help them along and talk to them. You know, make sure that they are doing their best at whatever they are doing. School is important for your future. It took me a long time to realize that.

Mr. Munn: Who do you think should do that?

Lester: Teachers should really try to give them the attention. It seems like that's what most of the kids ask them for . . . the attention . . . because they aren't getting it somewhere else. The only way they get attention is when they act up in school. I know all of the things I did and a lot of things happened here. It's kind of hard to say. I tried too many things and people weren't there.

They could hear the click as Mr. Munn shut off the tape recorder.

"Wow, that's heavy," Mr. Mann stated, shuddering. "That kid carries an awful lot of baggage with him to school."

Mr. Munn nodded in agreement. "He does. He lived alone as a junior high student. His grandmother and aunt helped him out and then his main support, his grandmother, died. He had to learn to deal with and then cope with stress. He relieved his stress through weight training, art, writing, some kind teachers, and the counselor. He needed a great deal of support from his family, but that wasn't there for a long time. The bridge to his mother took more than half his young lifetime to build and he turned to drugs for his support systems. He also turned to the adults at school. Some gave it to him and others didn't. What also kept him going was that he had a goal. He wanted to be a Marine."

Mr. Newt Owen listened reflectively. "What are you going to do with the information?" he asked Dina.

"With the information we now have, Mr. Munn and Mr. Rodgers are suggesting that we change the thrust of the alternative learning center . . . the ALC," she responded. "After hearing Lester's story, and the stories of the others who were interviewed by Mr. Munn, we all think the orientation of that program needs some tweaking.

"It was designed to be a mini high school for students," she continued, "who were nearing expulsion . . . a holding pen almost. But now I think we need to collect more data and see how we can provide an alternative program with a strong support system and goal orientation because kids like Lester need to see the light at the end of the tunnel. One size does not fit all."

Vignette

SKETCH A HUMAN FACE OVER THE DATA

Based on their dropout students' memories of school, their reasons for leaving, and their high failure rates, the Democratic Council began using surveys and forums to gather information from their current students about their perceptions of learning in the schoolhouse. Their task seemed quantum in nature, lacking in order, going here and there and everywhere, producing questions that beget more questions and further surveys.

Plato would have been proud—that is, if they were asking the right questions.

They administered surveys to the entire student body, to graduating seniors, and to the faculty about their perceptions of school.

Mrs. Edna Lightment surveyed her students to ascertain how she could become a more informed teacher regarding student learning. Principal Dina Macksy surveyed the faculty and staff about how she could better meet their needs. They held various forums to validate the conclusions they were beginning to reach about the schoolhouse.

In the background, Dina heard Mr. Sarason reminding her that they had to know more about the various groups in the schoolhouse if they wanted to create a new kind of teacher and learner . . . a democratic one . . . one who saw the relational value of others.

The Democratic Council, with its ad hoc groups, sifted through the data they received. They shared the information with the entire faculty, staff, and parent groups. Some teachers were apprehensive about asking students their opinions about school.

"I have other things to do with my students' time rather than interrupt it with wasteful surveys," someone overheard Mrs. Indika Trench say. "Why should we care about what students think?" For some reason her comments stung Dina, especially after hearing Lester Thanfund's tape and the statements made by former students at the dropout forum.

The results of the surveys surprised the faculty. Generally, students reported that they wanted to go to school, but were not always happy. They felt that teachers only did things their own way and thought that they were always right. The students didn't think that teachers always listened to their concerns. Most students stated they wouldn't go to them if they had something on their mind.

Although they perceived schoolwork as being important, they did a lot of daydreaming because they felt that the work they did was busy work and a waste of time. About half the students felt that topics in class couldn't end soon enough. They didn't think that teachers wanted them to answer a lot of questions.

Overall, they liked their teachers even though they didn't think that their teachers showed any interest in them as individuals, much like Lester felt about most of his teachers. These were the students' opinion about school.

Having students speak out about their school created a curiosity about the faculty's collective feeling regarding the schoolhouse. So they surveyed themselves. The results showed that teachers were satisfied with the quality of relationships they had with their students. They believed that they were able to assess satisfactorily their students' strengths and weaknesses.

However, they were uncertain about whether the students remembered the most important elements of the subjects they were teaching. Most were not independent thinkers, they agreed. Dina couldn't help but wonder whose fault that might be. It was hard not playing the blame game, but at least now she was cognizant when she was playing it.

As a group, the teachers felt that students would learn more if they applied themselves and did their homework. They were not sure whether students were gaining a good understanding of the subject matter. They were dissatisfied with their level of intellectual involvement. For example, they said that most of their students never initiated discussion or took responsibility for learning.

Teachers, on the average, slightly agreed that they carried a fair workload and that the subject matter they taught was respected. They did not think that their experience as educators was satisfactory.

They believed that the structure of the school did not permit them to adjust to individual student needs or interact with their colleagues. The time provided for planning and meeting with colleagues was unsatisfactory. Dina could not help but think about what Mr. Jeb Plowfield had said, that the structure of the school should fit the student, not the structure.

As the faculty distilled and analyzed these data, they talked about what their school system should look like. They had done this exercise earlier. Dina was beginning to see the picture the teachers had was evolving from the previous one, the one that Mrs. Indika Trench, Mr. Nick Chez, and Superintendent Mac Avelli held.

"Our school system is composed of people working within and on processes to accomplish something," one faculty member said.

"Our system is based on teaching and learning," another said. "One does not exist without the other."

"The aim of this system is to produce an interdependent graduate with the skills, knowledge, and learning necessary to benefit a democratic society," Mr. Newt Owen offered.

"To do this, to transform a student from one who does not have the skills, knowledge, and dispositions to one who does, we have to deliver a curriculum where everybody in the schoolhouse has the opportunity to learn," said Mr. Henry Berg. "And we have to support our students."

At another faculty meeting, Dina shared their responses from the interviews she conducted regarding what they needed from a principal. "What you have said you need is an instructional leader who can teach teachers new instructional strategies, one who says positive things about teachers to the community, someone who can offer teachers new ideas about the teaching-learning process. You need a principal who is trustworthy . . . one with whom you can share your thoughts, a principal who can help you find the resources with which to do your job, a principal who shares new ideas with the faculty." They needed an educational leader.

"What pops out at me," she explained, "is that some of the things that you want are the same things that the students want. It is in the nature of an organization that people want to be heard and respected."

She informed them that she would commit herself to these needs. "Next year, I will ask all of you to tell me how I'm doing, especially in the area of trust. As a group, you gave me only an average rating in this area and I want to improve this. If we don't have trust, we don't have a system that can work," she said.

Mrs. Lightment also shared her student–teacher feedback system with the faculty. Her student report card, as she called it, had resulted in an enhanced working partnership with her students. The purpose of her project was to change the teaching-learning process in order to make learning more engaging—her translation of what students called *fun*—and interesting for everyone, including the teacher.

The students analyzed their classroom as a system. They said that, to improve it, teachers needed to let them offer ideas. They felt that teachers did not always hear them. They lectured too much. They wanted to do less work from a textbook and more thoughtful work using computers. They requested a variety of activities, which would make the subject fun, educational, and relate to the world around them. They wanted Mrs. Lightment to be more encouraging and understand that not all students work at the same pace.

Mrs. Lightment assessed her report card. After a great deal of reflection, she decided that the students were right. As a result, she said, "If I agree to change some of my behaviors in class, like talking too much, what will you agree to do?"

In a democracy, we negotiate the social contract. Mrs. Lightment was doing just that. The students said they would all agree to earn A's and B's. To do this, they had to decide on the things that affected their learning in the classroom. They developed a chart of the variables that affected whether they were happy in class. They then divided these variables into categories.

First, they needed the necessary materials such as texts, writing materials, and appropriate homework. Second, teaching strategies were important—lecture, hands-on activities, showing a DVD, or taking a field trip. Third, there was a need to lessen people who might disturb them—office messengers, disruptive students, or intercom interruptions. Fourth, there were external forces such as being able to do homework after school, problems at home, special events, or holidays. Fifth, they needed the proper resources—tables, whiteboards, chairs.

They suggested that by knowing what influenced their inability to do well, they could possibly change things. And if they could change things, they would be happy and get higher grades.

"Now we will look at the relationships among these influences and see how we can best control the negative ones that interfere with their learning," Mrs. Lightment told the faculty.

At another forum—a joint faculty meeting with students—the question was asked, "What are the problems facing young people today?" About fifty students sat side by side with the faculty.

In rapid fire, the students banged out their answers: Drugs, alcohol . . . gangs, guns trying to intrude into our communities and schools . . . teen pregnancy . . . peer pressure . . . lack of motivation for going to school . . . not getting an education that will qualify teens for jobs . . . no computers at home and not enough in school . . . graffiti . . . .lack of respect for others and from others . . . breakdown of respect for elders . . . youth who are not students causing problems . . . poor role models in our community.

Mrs. Trench asked the students, "What do you think the solutions are?"

The students were just as quick to reply: We need peers who help each other. We need to have parents more involved. Kids start with what they learn at home. We need activities that will keep us busy after school. There's never anything to do except hang out at the mall. We need counseling groups for students who have alcohol and drug problems. We need more counselors in school. Violence should be addressed through student groups.

Mrs. Lightment asked the students, "If you could wave a magic wand, what would you change in your life or the world around you?"

Again in rapid fire the students provided answers: I would change the problems that are going on such as alcohol, drugs, guns, and violence. I would have every person feel and understand her purpose in life. I would have everyone find themselves by looking inside. I would want to erase all forms of hate, violence, prejudice, and the negative feelings behind the soul. I would change problem people, their frame of mind. I would want them to develop respect for their elders and others.

Dina asked them if they could talk about areas they felt were positive about their family, school, and community. The consensus from all the students was that everyone was aware of the problems and was trying to deal with them. But it always seemed that *nothing was really being resolved.*

Students also said that their problems need to be addressed and not put aside. "They are real. The youth of today act violently to get noticed. But they are concerned about their future. The difference between today and yesterday is that some of our parents had a job with the same company for life. They retired with the gold watch.

"Today there is no guaranteed employment. We will have at least five different jobs in our lifetime. We need to be prepared with the skills to meet this new challenge."

This joint faculty meeting with students was one more piece of information to consider as they mused about school improvement theories. They realized that disaggregating the data provided them with significant information, but hearing students talk about the numbers put a human face on them, despite what Descartes might have thought.

Another source of information was the annual senior survey. They delved into this instrument, something not done in the past. The instrument once again confirmed that their students were taking longer to graduate and that contributed to higher retention rates. Students were graduating in five, sometimes six years, because of child-related difficulties: (pregnancy or childcare), lack of respect for school, suspensions, gang-related activities, failing grades, and personal problems. Again, what emerged as the most significant factor was teenage pregnancy.

Their alternative learning center, the ALC, helped a great many students stay in school. One student said that program was different from regular school. With this program he was "beginning to see a connection between school and the real world. There weren't as many people there and I could work at my own pace."

Maybe, Dina thought, she didn't have to tweak the program after all.

Many students commented on their parents and members of their extended families who kept on encouraging them to graduate and did not give up on them.

She thought of what Lester had shared about his grandmother.

Teachers were also a significant factor to some students. They encouraged students to stay in school and didn't let them get away with things.

They were also interested in the challenges that prevented graduation from high school. Students listed alcohol and drugs, gang involvement, lack of support from adult groups, and pregnancy as obstacles.

In January, the Democratic Council led the faculty in a brainstorming session to validate the information they already had about the schoolhouse. Students, faculty, and staff were again invited to attend. The question written on the flip chart was: *What are the root causes of our teaching-learning process that are producing unacceptable deficiencies in terms of attendance, failure rates, and dropouts?*

Mr. Berg listed the group response in the minutes of this meeting. "In general," he stated, "what our students reported was that having seven bosses a day is difficult for some kids . . . . four years was sometimes too long for them to achieve goals . . . they would like their teachers to know them better . . . not say negative things about them because it makes them feel that they are not respected. They also want their teachers to realize that kids don't always see what the light at the end of the tunnel looks like . . . or even see the light.

"On the other hand," he continued, "the teachers thought that curriculum and instruction might not always be relevant to students. Class periods were not long enough. The system was set up for educators, not students. In addition, teachers were expected to do too many things during the day not related to teaching and learning, such as bus duty and class sponsorships. Finally, the gap was too wide between learners in some classes.

"Each student is different. Yet the assumption is all the kids are the same and will be taught in the same way. We've been applying bandages for too long. The faculty thought that, with the existing structure, we were not able to meet student needs."

At the next Democratic Council meeting, the discussion focused on changing the structure.

Mr. Quintin Waver thought it meant that instructional strategies should be adapted to a structural environment, which could support them. "It is hard to teach a science lab in thirty minutes," he stated.

"Best we can do now," offered Mr. Newt Owen, "is to meet as many needs as possible. We can only pick up the defects when necessary.

Wait! I can't believe what I just said . . . I called some kids defects like they had been spit out of a factory machine."

"Well, that's the way we treat them sometimes . . . as a school I mean," Mr. Bale Sistem, the space science teacher offered. He was new to the committee, sporadically attending committee meetings. "It's all we can do. But what bothers me is if we are talking about making structural changes in our school system, we have to also think about the implications of such a change.

"We have to be careful that we don't tinker with the system. What I mean is, if we change the structure, we also need to examine the relationships between the parts and the change. For example, what relation would changing the structure have to teacher skills, student motivation, parent involvement?

"When we make a change, we have to be careful that we connect the dots. We also need to get everybody involved in a paradigm shift so we will all be on the same page . . . and that includes the students and their parents."

"We might start with the amount of time we allow for each class," Mrs. Desiree Cartes said. "We do need a place to start. There are four months of school left. We need a starting point. We need a plan of action."

"Well," Mr. Berg said, speaking with conviction and deliberation, "we can't be expected to make an overnight change or to implement our proposed changes in one year. And we still haven't come up with improvement theories, although we're close.

"But let's not forget, we are developing a long-range, continuous improvement plan. What we do has to be manageable. Changing the time schedule is a starting point but should not be relegated to a quick fix. I am voicing my opinion and the fears of some faculty."

The dread of change was permeating the group. Mr. Sistem advised, "We need to look at the magnitude of restructuring. Maybe we can restructure part of the school. Is there something in place elsewhere? Can we adapt it?"

Mrs. Lightment, aware of the faculty's new apprehensions about change insidiously meandering its way throughout the faculty and staff declared, "It's time to find out how we are going to improve this school."

Vignette

TRANSFORM POSSIBILITIES INTO ACTUALITIES

Mr. Quintin Waver was sitting at the table. "I want to read something to you," he told the Democratic Council. "A man named Fred Wolf (Wolfe, 1989), who writes books on quantum mechanics so that a troglodyte like me can understand it, said this:"

> If the world exists and is not objectively solid and preexisting before I come on the scene, then what is it? The best answer seems to be that the world is only a potential and not present without me or you to observe it. It is, in essence, a ghost world that pops into solid existence each time one of us observes it. All of the world's many events are potentially present, able to be but not actually seen or felt until one of us sees or feels it. (cited in Wheatley, 1992, p. 58)

He stopped and looked up from the book. "The reason I find this comforting," he said, "is because before we start on improving anything, we must understand that there is a world of potentialities out there, and we won't know which the right one is. We can come as close as we can to knowing by theorizing based on our data and reaching some conclusions. It is only when we pop open the quantum box . . . full of so many potentialities, that we will know truth, which will change because of different relational values that occur from time to time."

"I think what you are saying," Mrs. Edna Lightment said, "is there are so many things that can happen in terms of how our processes will act once we modify them. The quantum box moves us from a multifaceted potentiality to actualities."

"You're beginning to understand," Mr. Waver responded, quite pleased with himself.

"Well maybe what Mr. Waver means," Dina said, "is that in the past we did not look at the potential problems in our schoolhouse as a group. I popped the quantum box open without even thinking of all the potentialities that could be in the box.

"I did that because I was in control and didn't think that any of you could help me solve organizational problems because your territory was your classroom and mine was the school.

"In the past I didn't know that looking at a collection of data would broaden my understanding of what our school really looked like. I didn't know that by looking at variation in the way the system operated, we could find deep-seated problems. I didn't look at the interconnection of processes in the system. It seems that I focused on the input I best understood, aggregated that input to the cause, and assigned blame. I forgot . . . or didn't know that there was a world of potentialities."

"Well, now that we have that all cleared up," Mr. Henry Berg laughed, "let's review where we are so we can . . . eh . . . begin popping open the quantum box."

They were ready for theories but they were still having problems with words like process, system, variation, and even theory. These were terms they did not use very much in education, and when they did, they knew little of their practical value.

Dina suggested that the Democratic Council convene at her house for a Saturday meeting. This would be after her meeting with Superintendent Mac Avelli.

"Get on with it!" the superintendent bellowed at her. "It seems that what you are doing is redundant. You seem to be going around in circles with all your questions." Well, perhaps he was right. Where were all these questions . . . all these reviews . . . going anyway, she asked herself?

"So judging from where we are and what we have accomplished so far, process improvement involves the students and the entire faculty and staff," she said, ignoring her earlier skepticism. "The people who work in the processes have knowledge about how those processes work. Therefore, they should all be involved in any change."

"To change any process, we need buy-in from everyone about how the change is to be accomplished," Mrs. Desiree Cartes said. "It means that we understand the roles people have in the organization. It means we understand, or are at least aware of, the interaction and interdependence of our jobs.

"Everything we do relates in some way to what someone else is doing . . . all our actions in some way form a relationship with actions of others. If we don't work together for the common aim, we are not a system . . . we are just a bunch of independent teachers each doing her own thing. That's why we keep crashing into each other and producing the same thing over and over again. That's why the kids lose out."

"I sometimes think students live in parallel universes in the classrooms," Jon Deway said. "Students have their rules and the teacher has hers. Why don't we all pop open the quantum box and find one set of classroom rules that we all agree about? And why do all classes meet for the exact same amount of time? We all know, for example, that Mr. Waver needs more time for his experiments."

"We use data to assess and analyze the system in order to determine if there are problems," Mr. Newt Owen continued. "We don't shoot from the hip and say this is so, because somebody said so. The long and short of it is that we are not doing the old *this is the problem, this is the solution* routine.

"We are spending a lot of time determining if the problem really exists and if it does, finding its root cause and relationship to other problems. We know that we just can't fix our attendance problem without examining retention rates and discipline occurrences. We are viewing change as a process and not a one-time occurrence."

"I can't help thinking about what happened when we first all sat down as a council," Mrs. Lightment recounted. "We were a bit nervous, not knowing what Principal Macksy had in mind and not knowing if we could trust her and trust one another. We were nice to one another, but distant as we learned a little more about one another.

"We sometimes became irritable and tense because we did not always agree with what someone else did or said. For example, I remember how silly some of us thought the idea was that teachers would serve students. Our guard was raised but we talked. We decided that instead of our job being described as serving students we could better understand our roles in terms of relational value. The kids served us and we served them. There was an interdependence between us. It wasn't them and us.

"We then established ways to civilly approach and work with each other. Now we have developed some common professional values and ways of doing things . . . working together as a team, talking about ideas for change based on what we really know about our school."

"I agree," Mrs. Cartes said. "We've a team but I think some of the faculty is still fighting new ideas while we are just beginning to acquire a common understanding of what these ideas are."

"Ain't that the truth?" Mr. Berg said with a hesitant laugh. "There are other Mrs. Trenches on the faculty . . . with high failure rates . . . unwilling to do the work it requires to ascertain why so many of their students are failing. It's always the students' fault, they proclaim. They need to work harder.

"What I mean," he continued to explain, "is that we all need to bring our ideas to the table and discuss them. The Mrs. Trenches bring the same ideas and refuse to open up to any new ones. They are crippling their students. This country was not built upon the ideas of one person. If it were, we would be saying your majesty instead of Mr. President."

"Of course there are other variables in the system that cripple our students," Mrs. Lightment suggested

"Yes, there are," Mr. Bale Sistem retorted. "Fewer kids would fail if we could create a system where they had more time to do the work and we paid closer attention to them . . . a system without ciphers . . . kids getting lost in the system.

"I'm not suggesting we tear down the system. That would be unrealistic. But we do have to focus on the system that produces the unacceptable results we saw while we analyzed the data. And I noticed, other than failure rates, we didn't even look at those test scores that appear annually in the newspaper.

"Maybe we wouldn't have to, if we move the data we analyzed into more positive territory. We know, for example, that there is a relationship between kids attending school and their grades."

"We also know," Mr. Owen said, "that everyone has different needs or different uses for our school system. But how do we make our system such that it will increase student learning?"

He thought about his question, then continued: "First, we have to get the kids to school. At the same time we must figure out why so many of them are failing. We don't ever do this. How many of us ever analyze our exams after the papers are graded to see if there were any patterns that come from the results?

"Moreover, how do we philosophically understand it? I know our kids bring a lot of emotional baggage to school. We can't change what's out there, but we can set up the conditions for change right here in the school. We can short circuit the cycle of failure in the long term based on what they say they need to stay in school and what we see they need.

"We could work together on this. Why can't what we are doing on this council be taught to the students in the classroom? From Lester Thanfund's conversation I learned that the art program was keeping him in school, as well as a receptive counselor and an understanding teacher who was able to flex her class rules to accommodate his needs."

"Well, you're right. We can set up the conditions to foster change," Mr. Jeb Plowfield said. "If we had a child center for teens with children, we would at least have the teen and her child in school. And that's something that the vocational department can pursue. Mrs. Mo Hubbard, the home economics and consumer science teacher, has already started exploring this option.

"But something like this would also require community input. There are those people out there who think that having a child care center at school just encourages teenage pregnancy."

"I'm a bit frustrated," Mr. Owen said. "It seems that what goes on outside the parameters of our control affects what goes on inside the parameters of our control.

"For example, kids fail their exams but the reasons overlap systems. It's complex and we have to be cognizant that what is done in one system affects what happens in the other. Too bad we can't collapse the two systems into one, but we can only do what we can do."

"It's like quantum theory," Mr. Waver reminded them. "Systems cannot be made divisible. Everything is connected to everything else. We are all a set of relationships."

"So what you are saying Mr. Owen," said Mrs. Cartes, ignoring Mr. Waver, "is what was said earlier. We have to look at the system . . . both systems . . . in terms of how one thing affects another."

"That's what I said," Mr. Waver said, overjoyed that somebody had heard him.

"Right on!" Mr. Owen replied, pleasantly excited. "Working together, united by a common theme, bonds us and makes us indivisible. We can produce anything once we start working as a team. After all, nothing prevents us from doing something except the obstacles we place in the way."

Were they being idealistic? They were saying they could do the job if they all shared certain cultural values about education. Dina was now beginning to think that you couldn't be alone in an organization where people felt supported by each other. And she now realized why you sometimes have to say things over and over again in different ways. People listen differently and not all at once. Superintendent Avelli thought that saying something once was enough. He was wrong.

The Democratic Council continued the dialogue with the faculty. The tension barometer was on the rise. Some faculty members still resisted change. At one meeting, Mr. Berg said, "Everybody says if the system ain't broke, don't fix it. But when we are talking about process improvement, we are saying that if it ain't broken, you ain't looking deep enough at the system's variation.

"We have found that yelling at each other and pointing fingers is a waste of time. The stereotypical *us versus them* mentality doesn't work. All it does is keep us circling the wagons and shooting inward. It's important that we all realize that the idea of process improvement means that there are no hidden agendas or assumptions. It defines an attitude of professional growth and adaptability to the changing needs of our students.

"There is no predetermined goal we are moving toward. There is no secret agenda, unspoken assumptions, or canned pedagogical method that we are expected to follow. We are merely looking at the situation at our school as it really is. We are asking how it may be improved so that our graduates have the skills to question and become knowledgeable citizens in our democratic society. However good our school is now, it can always be better because we always have to raise the bar on potential."

Mrs. Lightment added: "We have to ask ourselves why we think the way we do? It is only then that we will discover why we don't know . . . what we don't know. It's then that we pop open the box Mr. Waver talked about earlier . . . as a team . . . and see that what's inside is what we hope it will be."

At their next faculty meeting, they attempted to establish a bridge between their last plan for improvement and what they were now doing. As Dina already suggested, she bought into a plan and the school had won a national award, becoming a model of school improvement for other schools.

The model was a good one. The only downside was that she didn't really spend time educating the faculty because she was in a hurry to send her plan to Superintendent Avelli, and she didn't really understand the theories underscoring the plan.

"The last plan we followed gave us a template to use," Mrs. Lightment announced. "We thought if we followed the guidelines and built on them, our students would improve. And they did."

"But after we did all the work," Dina added, "and reached the last dot on the page, we didn't follow through. I didn't know how to keep the momentum going because I didn't understand the theories underlying the plan. Without theory, we copy. And then we don't know where to go."

"Under the old plan, we worked together for a while, and then returned to the isolation of our classrooms," Mrs. Lightment said. "I have a theory for raising the potential of our students. It can only be accomplished by all of us working together. The people who work in the processes know something about them. If we pool our data on a continuing basis, improvement will be ongoing."

Mrs. Indika Trench muttered to all those around her who would listen, "If I didn't have thirty students, six times a day, I might believe that." And then she announced to the entire room, "Frankly, I don't buy into the fact that all students can learn."

"Would you buy into the fact that all students learn uniquely and it's our job to find what is unique about each child?" Mr. Owen asked.

"Only if I don't have 125 plus students each day!" she said firmly, shaking her finger at him.

"Do you think, Mrs. Trench," he continued, ignoring her gesture "that students should be actively involved in their own learning?"

"It takes too much time. We have to cover the curriculum."

Mr. Berg was visibly irked by Mrs. Trench's consistent commitment to control kids.

"How can we teach students responsibility," he shrieked. "How can we model democracy for them if we are always in total control? Can't they be involved in helping us determine how best they can learn the curriculum?

"Nobody is suggesting that students tell us what they should learn, although it might be a good idea to listen to them if they did . . . like Mrs. Lightment did with her students and Principal Macksy did with us. What is suggested is that we listen to what they are saying about the classroom environment! We are suggesting that some of the controls be lifted."

"Maybe, but I'm still the boss," Mrs. Trench replied curtly, her predatory eyes on guard for the next line of attack.

"Wouldn't it be nice if, as teachers, we could become educators and lead students to new knowledge?" Mrs. Lightment suggested in a feeble attempt to move the discussion along. "How many of us know how to lead students to new knowledge?"

"I still don't think kids should tell us what to teach," Mrs. Trench grumbled, ignoring the question. "I set the program and they follow it. My standards are very high."

"Well, you are right about one thing. We have too many students and too little time to work with them," Mrs. Lightment said. "I think a great many of our students become frustrated because they are operating at the system's pace instead of their own. One size does not fit all.

"Kids are different today," Mrs. Lightment rued. "They lack the institutional supports I had when I was their age. For many, school is their only real family . . . the family they see every day. Gone is the church, gone is a mother and father team . . . we are the only supports left. And we are not very effective either because there are so many of them.

"I'm not suggesting I can be successful with all my students. There are some kids who bring just too much baggage with them. But at least I would try not to create ciphers of them. If only we had more time. If only students had input, learned how to set goals, plan strategies to attain those goals, manage their plans, and review their progress toward attaining goals. Don't we really want a system where students learn how to locate information and use critical skills to synthesize and synergize concepts?"

"Most of us want all of that," Mr. Berg responded. "But we just can't do it because the scheduling of classes won't allow us to. It's the way we structure the learning in the schoolhouse that is handicapping us. To repeat what I heard someone say the other day, there's a flaw in the design of the system.

"We think that having six forty-five minutes classes allows us to control what occurs within them. If we can control what's in each class, we can predict the outcome. Well, the outcome is failure. Too many kids are failing and dropping out. Do we cherish control and prediction over student success? If we don't, why do we insist on working with Newton's Flaw?"

"I think it's about time we stopped all this chatter and talk about what we are going to do to improve this school," Mrs. Cartes said. "It's time to prepare ourselves for opening the quantum box."

Vignette

GET BUY-IN FROM
THE SHAREHOLDERS

It was now April. Superintendent Mac Avelli reminded Principal Dina Macksy that she was the only principal in the district who was absent goals and objectives. She kept him abreast of why this couldn't be done at this time, and presented monthly reports about where they were in understanding how their system's processes worked. To tell the truth, he was more interested in the sports section of the newspaper on his desk than in what she had to say.

She knew that she would not have a plan with goals and objectives for him this year. What she would have was a quantitative and qualitative report about what the school system was producing and a plan of action that they would put into effect the following school year.

As the Democratic Council continued reviewing the system, four needs began to emerge from the data they had accumulated: (1) they had to have more time to work with their students; (2) they had to allow students a voice in the teaching-learning process; (3) they had to tweak their alternative educational program; and (4) they had to provide services for teen parents.

You notice not one thing was said about test scores. This would be the first thing Superintendent Avelli would look for on her school improvement report. There would be a blank on the line that asked: *By what percentage will your students improve on the state tests over the previous year?* Dina knew she would be in trouble for this. But school was about educating students, not training them to take tests, she told herself.

The faculty and staff divided into four teams addressing one of the four needs. The job of team one was to write a plan for restructuring the bell schedule. Teachers wanted to spend more time with students. Students could then spend more time learning. The team made a list of what spending more time with students in the classroom meant. The list was long but they all agreed that they would have to diversify their learning strategies. One strategy didn't fit all. They would mentor one another and students. They would analyze, assess, and provide feedback to students regarding their performance on classroom assessments.

Team two wrote a plan for creating a culture in which students would become empowered. Their voice would be heard! This resulted in a plan for developing student leadership.

Team three reviewed the alternative learning program to determine if it was meeting student needs. If not, what could they add to the program?

Team four developed a plan to keep teen parents in school, teaching them the necessary parenting skills. All four teams were to look at how each change affected the system as a whole.

Teachers, staff, and students chose their team members, which included parent and administrative representatives. The Democratic Council insisted on an administrator on each team because, as Mrs. Edna Lightment said, "They held the larger view."

Mr. Newt Owen was team leader of the committee restructuring the bell schedule. A few years earlier, he had read a book by John Carrol called *The Copernican Plan* (Carrol, 1990).

"Mr. Carrol, a school superintendent," he informed his committee, "had suggested that the typical, traditional secondary teacher taught five or six periods each day with a total load of 125 students. Often they had more than one subject for which they prepared and had constant discipline problems.

"After reviewing the number of our discipline referrals, I knew Carrol was talking about us," Mr. Owen told the group. "So what he did was restructure the high school schedule so that classes were longer and teachers saw fewer students during the day. Just as Copernicus challenged the notion that the sun revolved around the earth, Carrol challenged the notion that high school learning had to happen in five-, six-, or seven-period blocks of time."

Mr. Owen's team decided to visit schools that had changed bell schedules. After their visits, the team shared their findings with the faculty.

"All of the schools we visited showed significant improvements in student performance. Failure rates, dropout rates, and discipline referrals declined. Students liked having four-period days. Their course of study was more focused. Attendance rates, however, had not significantly changed. Perhaps they had not done the extensive research that we had about why and when our students are absent."

"I asked students at the school we visited how they liked the schedule," Jon Deway said, sharing his observations with a student group. "Most said they were afraid that longer periods would be so boring. In fact, the time in blocks went faster. Teachers participated in professional development that focused on student engagement.

"Most of the students liked it this way. They said they could focus on studying a subject in depth. They also got to know their teachers better. Some even said that they had fewer teachers to hassle them."

One of the more salient findings of Mr. Owen's committee was that there was no research base for the traditional Carnegie unit where students attained credit based on attending a class for forty-five minutes a day during the school year. He was amazed by this finding (Walker, 1999).

Mr. Owen reported: "It's extraordinary. We have been doing this for over nine decades. Yet, there is nothing to support this structure. Students were scheduled this way because it was convenient. It has nothing to do with learning.

"The Carnegie unit traps teachers at the secondary level into teaching the same way to a large number of students using the same interval of time. The lecture style probably comes from the way college teachers teach. However, we are working with a different age group.

"Research shows that students learn better when they receive instruction that is differentiated. There is no connection between the way in which we deliver instruction and the time it takes for learning to occur."

Based on their visits to other schools and their research, team one became enthused about the possible implications of restructuring the bell schedule. They could reduce the total number of students with whom a teacher works each day, thereby increasing the amount of time spent with students.

From Sid Munn's interview with Lester Thanfund and students like him, the faculty had learned that students who come to school with lots of outside baggage cannot focus on learning. Teachers notice them when they become disruptive.

"They are just one more face in our classroom crowds," Mr. Owen remarked. Could this restructuring idea be a possible solution to some of their problems? Could the effect of reducing ciphers in our class increase attendance and reduce failure and dropout rates?

The team invited the community to talk about the restructuring of the bell schedule. They responded and filled the meeting place. During the meeting, parents asked relevant questions. Why should we change tradition? Could our kids graduate sooner because they could obtain the number of credits necessary to graduate faster? Do we want our kids to graduate at sixteen?

The committee responded:

- Forty percent of our students fail one or more subjects. That's not good for self-esteem. Maybe if they had fewer, but longer classes, they could be more focused.
- Teachers have too many students during the course of the day. We are teaching students we don't know. If we knew them better, maybe they would come to school more often.
- Having more time with students would also allow us to align our teaching style with the way different students learn.
- It is up to you as parents to decide if sixteen is too young to graduate.

Students on the committee commented:

- Too many of us are losing credit and finally dropout. That's what my brother did.
- All our teachers teach the same way. They are usually talking at us. When they do try to do something different, like have us work on a project in teams . . . just as things get going . . . the bell rings.

- It would sure be nice to have more time to do science labs. You just can't do an experiment in forty-five-minute blocks. Doesn't our country need more scientists?
- I am in the ninth grade. It's rare that I see a connection between what we learn and the real world. We don't even know what the connections are among subjects. Yet I read in the newspapers and magazines that companies are looking for people who can see the connections between things.

Parents on the committee spoke out:

- Taking a class for a year encourages students to give up faster if they are not doing well.
- We need to give them short-term goals so they can cope better and see the light at the end of the tunnel. Everything is changing so fast now . . . and our kids are caught up in the momentum. Our kids need to experience success.
- As a parent, I don't think the school is connected with the community. But with this new schedule, you might really get to know our children and have time to meet with us.

The parents were very positive about the change, especially after hearing from the students. It turns out that students are the school's best ambassadors.

Dina handed out feedback sheets at the end of the meeting to poll the parents. Ninety percent were in agreement with the change. Many noted that if their kids were happy, they were happy.

Following the community meeting, Mr. Owen led the Democratic Council in yet another dialogue about the downside of changing the bell schedule.

Mrs. Lightment discussed the problem inherent in attendance. "Attendance is a big problem. If we go to bigger blocks of time and students miss school, they will miss even more instructional time. Also, teachers would have to deliver the content in a different way because the classes would be longer. They will have the opportunity to put to work the skills they have, but don't use."

"The school would have to provide us with the resources to update our teaching strategies. This might be a good time to explore technological programs," Mr. Henry Berg said.

Mrs. Minsey Well commented: "We would have time for students to actually access computer technology and have quality time doing it. And speaking of time, we would have time to teach students classroom responsibility by allowing them in on the planning of activities. We are so worried all the time about trying to cover the curriculum that we don't do this. Of course, we would have a shorter amount of time to cover the curriculum."

After a pause, Mr. Owen proceeded. "There would be shorter semesters. What are the implications of this?"

Mr. Quintin Waver said: "Students would see the light at the end of the tunnel sooner . . . not becoming so readily frustrated. They would be attaining credits in half the time. They could graduate earlier. The down side may be that retention of material might suffer."

"Our committee reviewed the research on this," Mr. Owen explained. "So far, the research states that the retention does not suffer. Only time will tell regarding our students."

"Teachers prep periods will be longer. There would be fewer classes to prepare for. We all know the advantage of that in terms of preparing for student lessons," Ms. Oprah Myden said.

"There is a bigger problem," Dina warned, "in terms of the other schools in the district. The other principals are already calling me about it. They are appalled that our teachers would have a ninety-minute prep period. They don't think it is fair."

She didn't tell them that Superintendent Avelli had already called her on the carpet about this. "You're causing me problems, Principal Macksy!" he scowled. "Stick with tradition. I don't care that the students and parents like the new schedule. I run this district, not them. I know what's good for them."

Their concern about what the other principals and teachers were saying at the other schools concerned Mr. Owen's committee. "Instead of making a political football out of this," he declared," let's add a forty-five minute academic support class to the schedule. A kind of homeroom period where the teacher will work with the students on their individual needs.

"We'll have to give more thought and do further research on how this will best work. I suggest it for the second year of this plan, not the first, because we have enough on the burner right now to sort out."

That makes sense, Dina thought. This way, we can provide tutoring for those students who want it. And I could hold my administrator colleagues at bay. She knew that if they didn't have a plan for those forty-five minute periods, chaos would result.

Team two's job was to write a plan for developing a culture in which students became empowered. Research indicated that students who were involved in processes instead of being the targets of them were more apt to learn responsibility. Mr. Carlton Rodgers headed the group, which was unique because it was composed mostly of students.

The team leader was Stu Serlutons, a high school junior. Their first activity, they decided, was to write a statement of purpose. After weeks of intense thought, this is what emerged: *We will help students become the solutions to their own problems.*

They developed a vision statement, which they believed would guide them in fulfilling their purpose. Their vision was to support students in creating an environment in which they could learn, and also where they could make learning fun so that they, the students, would want to be in school.

"We want students to be able to plan a bright future," Stu proclaimed. "We'd like to see that students are part of the solution to all problems."

"We need to find out what students want and need," said a senior student on the committee.

Dina recalled a session that she joined with the group. Stu had asked the students to think about why students should become empowered.

The team of students called out: to make our voice count . . . so teachers would listen to us . . . to make school more fun and educational at the same time . . . to help develop positive attitudes among students and staff . . . to have students be part of the education process . . . to have students help students . . . to increase the time the staff stays here.

They called their focus group Students United with Teachers. One week, they discussed how they could reduce discipline infractions. They looked at the reasons for the infractions and something else, something Dina might never have considered. The students observed that a great many of the infractions happened while changing periods, when kids went to their lockers. They suggested if the school dispersed the lockers around the school, instead of in one central location as it was now, infractions would be reduced.

They had a theory: crowded areas of students were places where problems festered and then ballooned. But lockers dispersed in single rows against the buildings were more easily visible. Teachers could easily monitor them by standing outside their doors during passing periods.

They were right . . . and referrals declined by 15 percent after this change was implemented.

The job of Mr. Munn and team three was to review the Alternative Learning Center. The ALC operated in partnership with a local state training facility. Completion of this program allowed students to graduate at a minimum of two and a half years, while receiving on-the-job training. Students accepted into the program had to be at least sixteen years old with a minimum of one year of high school credits.

ALC students entered a job-based environment where they were taught how to work cooperatively with coworkers and bosses. They had to learn good work habits. They had to report to the job site on time and call their supervisor when absent. Each student in the program had to remain drug and alcohol free. In return, they could graduate with a diploma and the promise of further apprenticeship training.

"After interviewing the students in the program, we found that we had need for an additional component tailored specifically to family support structures and goal orientation," Mr. Munn said. "We're still researching how to approach the problem without additional monies."

Team four developed a plan to keep teen parents in school. Mrs. Mo Hubbard, the home consumer and science teacher, chaired this group. It included a preponderance of teen parents and their parents, community members, and members of the clergy.

"Our group has reviewed the research on children with children. We learned that unless the teen parent remains in school, chances are high that her children will also be dropouts," Mrs. Hubbard informed the Democratic Council.

She continued: "The group is working on a plan that would provide teen parenting skills, career education, and a place for their children during school time. The program will have a job skill component, focusing on care-giving skills. At the end of three years in the program, a student could get college credit and a certificate as a child care professional.

"We already had two rather rousing meetings with the community about this. They are beginning to support it, especially with the career orientation and the idea about breaking the cycle of children having children. Of course, we have to have the input of a wider segment of the community. There are those out there who maintain that a program like this only encourages teen pregnancy."

Now that they had plans on the drawing board, the Democratic Council discussed a strategy for disseminating the school improvement plan to a wider audience. They learned that, for a plan to work, they needed buy-in from all the groups that were involved in the teaching-learning processes.

"It would be a good idea to get input from the whole school community about these ideas that we have for changing the school, especially the plan regarding the opening of a child care center," Dina said. "The community will have a lot to say about this." They concurred.

In an unprecedented move, the school suspended classes for a day. They substituted workshops for classes and rotated students, their parents, and members of the school board and community through the various sessions. During the First General Session, Dina reviewed the work that the faculty, staff, parents, and students completed during the year to restructure the school for student success. Participants then attended various workshops where they heard more details about the restructuring plan.

Each team summarized its work, reporting its research, data, and outcomes. They conducted interactive secessions, inviting the audience to participate. Most did.

At the Second General Session, they asked the participants what they thought about the restructuring ideas. Seventy-nine percent of them said they concurred with the school improvement plan. One student echoed the sentiment of many. "We'll never know until we try it."

In May, they took the program to the school board. They listened to all the explanations and nodded their approval. The quantum box had been opened. Would what they found inside work?

Vignette

THE COLLECTIVE APPROACH
TRIGGERS SUCCESS

In his book, *The Brain Has a Mind of Its Own*, Richard Restak cites Zen master Dainin Katagiri.

> Let us imagine you are climbing up a mountain cliff. That situation is just like being on the verge of life and death. There is no way to escape; you cannot complain. If you are there, all you have to do is just be there. If you act instinctively, you could die. If you are nervous, you could die. Should you depend on the intellect, you could also die. So you have to depend on the mountain, your mind, and all the circumstances. You have to watch carefully and understand. Your consciousness must be clear and know what is going on there. Then after using your best understanding, your body and mind should depend upon just one step. This is action. . . . There is nothing to think about, nothing to depend on. All we have to do is just be there using all the things we already have: consciousness, mind, mountain and the weather. Just one step. (Restak, 1991, p. 97)

And that's what Principal Dina Macksy and the school were now ready for, the one step. A plan of action was proposed that provided opportunities for students and teachers to work together as interconnected parts of an interrelational system.

"This new plan accommodates the hazy spectrum of schoolhouse human connections," Mrs. Edna Lightment told the faculty. "I feel as if we are now continually improving student potential in a democratic setting."

"I think of what we are doing as the yin-yang system of education," Mr. Henry Berg added. "We are all dependent upon each other to achieve forward momentum for our students, not always knowing what will happen."

As the faculty attempted to assimilate in their own minds what they were doing, something vexed Dina. During the next school year, the plan of action would become a reality. She envisioned her leadership in working with each step of the plan—checking milestones, mapping routes, analyzing processes. However, what would happen when Newton's world crashed into the quantum one? Could both worlds exist side by side? When the crash occurred, who would be its victims?

She didn't know why she asked this question. Maybe because her daily proximity with the voices in the library had become tenuous.

She also didn't think she really understood what Mr. Quintin Waver had been reciting from his quantum physics books about popping open quantum boxes. Or maybe it was this amorphous heckler who abruptly settled itself inside her, assuming a space she couldn't avoid. The heckler was cold, cacophonous, intermittently jabbing her mind, asking her what would result from the work she had initiated.

In August, the start of the next school year, plans were implemented for the extended class periods. As she walked through classrooms, Dina noticed teachers attempting different instructional strategies as a result of the longer class periods. Many of them had attended summer workshops, brushing up on their pedagogical skills. At faculty and departmental meetings and in the teacher's lounge, they shared these strategies.

As a result of Dina's negotiations with a local college, computer education for both teachers and students expanded. In some classes, students were invited to become a working partner with the teacher.

Mrs. Mo Hubbard and her team worked on securing the necessary funding and licensing for the child development lab after receiving community approval. Mr. Jeb Plowfield decided to transform his agricultural science classes into a problem-solving center. Mrs. Minsey Well proposed that students in her English class negotiate learning activities with her so that they could see the importance and reason behind each activity.

"What they will learn is up to the state standards and the curriculum. How they will learn can be up to them, with me being the facilitator," she explained.

Mr. Berg was concerned about the amount of work he had to do in facilitating the practice state assessment tests. He came up with a plan that encouraged students to seek clarification of instructions from one another before giving up on the test.

The Students United with Teachers focus group became a class of problem solvers. When Dina asked them how they might unravel the graffiti problem, they proposed a practical solution by working with the students in the art department.

As Dina was trying to decode the obscure message of the inner heckler, new ideas were emerging all over the campus. School and process improvement was coupled with the ideas. The talk on campus among the professional staff was about teaching and learning.

She overheard one teacher say to another "I have to constantly reassess what I'm doing as I practice new teaching techniques. I don't tell kids as much. And my assessments are not a one-shot deal. I really think that if students are failing, there may be something wrong with what I am doing. What's the sense of continuing to chapter two when chapter one has not been learned?"

Students United with Teachers received conflict-resolution training from the student counselor Mr. Carlton Rodgers. Then they taught other students what they had learned.

But not everything was rosy. Mr. Sid Munn was having problems with the Alternative Learning Center. Even with the addition of help from social services, the students were unmotivated, he told Dina.

"Students tell me that they are bored. They are losing interest and the program is losing momentum. I wish we had the money to hire an aide to assist me. But I know we don't."

He paused as he gathered his thoughts. "Only a few students have fully embraced the idea that they have a say in what they do. I am finding that other students would rather have me tell them what to do. Right now, I don't have a whole lot of improvement theories. I have asked Students United with Teachers for help. We'll see what happens."

As teachers were implementing their action plans, the Student Council began implementing theirs, seeking feedback from teachers about their activities.

"How would you rate the pep rally we had last week before the football game? Did you observe if students were interested in the activity, bored, disruptive, tried to escape? Do you feel having activities after holidays will influence attendance? Do you like the way we organized the event? Could we have done better?"

Dina noticed that, after the Student Council began distributing their surveys to teachers, she no longer had to remind teachers that they had to be at the assemblies. For some reason, in the past, some teachers thought that it was someone else's job to monitor their students while they were in assemblies.

In October, the Democratic Council reviewed with the Student Council their school improvement efforts. This project was dubbed "The Big Picture Show."

"Our goal is to ascertain how students were handling the changes," Dina informed everyone. The students were engrossed in listening to her as she carefully reviewed the reasons for starting a continuous improvement plan and the various action plans they were implementing. At the end of the session, Dina asked them to evaluate the meeting. She received comments such as these:

"The presentation was very helpful. It made me realize how this school is helping the students. Before, I wasn't ready for the new bell schedule. Even though I was told it would be more exciting, I asked myself how it could be more exciting with the same old boring teachers. Then, as the days passed I found the class periods going by faster. I was getting a lot done. I had fewer classes to worry about. I would like to thank the school for including me in this thing called school improvement."

"Having students come to this presentation shows how much the staff wants student input and wants to work with students. I enjoyed the presentation. It got me to think about the freshman class and their higher dropout and failing rates. We need to do something about that."

"To tell the truth there is stuff you can do, but it's not going to change things. In general, the people who drop out are drug-confused kids, or girls who get pregnant, or kids with screwed up family lives. School just adds extra pressure. I hope I'm not being too negative, but I'm willing to try and help to change whatever I can to improve this problem."

"It was fun to see the results of all the surveys we take . . . and also those our parents and teachers take. I believe that the whole student body should see how important it is to become a contributing member of society. Show the Big Picture Show to everybody."

The faculty followed the Student Council's suggestion. They shared "The Big Picture Show" with the entire student body. Over a period of a week, they showed all the students what was important at their school and why it was important. They told them that they had no numbers to project as goals. But they would be looking at the numbers the system was producing and tweak, change, or even abandon plans if they were not producing the desired positive effects.

Responses were positive. Students thought they were losing their anonymity. They were learning that the school cared about them. Many said in their responses that they now thought their teachers wanted every student to succeed. They were glad that the school was including them in the planning of school improvement.

"The Big Picture Show" was presented to the parents. Dina made this entry in her diary.

> We had a large audience and the parents seemed supportive. They said that their children were actually doing their homework. They seemed less stressed. The school board president was there. He said that his sons were doing their homework after school but remained noncommittal about the changes. He worked the crowd, interested in hearing what the people had to say. Next year was the school board election.

From September to November, they continued their efforts to share "The Big Picture Show" with parents and students. The overwhelming opinion was positive. Students and parents said they liked the direction in which the school was going.

During November, they also had their first indicator of how their processes were reacting to the plans. They received the forty-day attendance report. Attendance averaged 94.74, up from 88.35 the year before. The faculty and staff were overjoyed.

Dina cautioned them about getting too excited. Because of the new bell schedule, the state formula for computing the average daily attendance had changed. The state computed average daily attendance a little differently for schools that were on a block schedule.

However, Mrs. Well echoed the sentiments of the staff: "Who cares, students are coming and the amount of rework we have to do is declining."

Students United with Teachers conducted a survey to see why the ninth-graders still had the lowest attendance, even though their attendance had improved from the previous year. They randomly selected ninth-grade students from a computer-generated list and, after practicing interview procedures with Mr. Rodgers, found that the students liked the new schedule but felt less safe at school than the rest of the student body.

The district had conducted a survey the previous year to ascertain from students, teachers, and parents how safe they felt at school. At the high school level, students felt safe. At the middle school level, they felt less safe. The new ninth-graders had come from a climate of gangs and violence.

Students United with Teachers decided that more communication with ninth-grade parents was necessary to help these students feel safer about being in school. Mr. Rodgers and Dina decided to conduct focus group meetings with these parents and students.

Students United with Teachers began using their peer mediation skills to counsel students accused of drug violations. They suggested that Dina avoid suspending those students from school. Instead, they wanted to work with them.

She reviewed their in-depth project plans and agreed to support this approach on a trial basis. But she told them that she would have to get school board permission to suspend temporarily the discipline code penalties for drug violations.

In December, she recorded in her diary:

First semester has ended. The grades are in. Are more students passing? First semester's pass rates were compared to first semester pass rates last year. This year a semester is nine weeks. Last year it was eighteen weeks. The results showed that at the end of the first semester, 40 percent of the students failed one or more subjects. This year, 17 percent of the students failed. More students are passing. In addition, the ninth grade increased its pass rate by more than 10 percent.

Something that we had not anticipated occurred . . . a kind of quantum effect. The number of students on the honor roll rose significantly. Some of these students had never been on it. We need to celebrate this achievement. And we can't allow cynicism to enter our mindscape by saying, as I have heard Mrs. Trench exclaim, "Sure more kids made the honor roll . . . they are taking fewer subjects."

At the end of January, the one hundred–day attendance report was completed. When Superintendent Mac Avelli saw it, he smiled enthusiastically. "Making a gain of half a percent in attendance was great. However, your school made a gain of 3 percent. That's terrific!" His smile warmed Dina. She usually felt chilly in his presence.

The end of the second semester pass rates were holding. Eighty-two percent of the students passed all their subjects. The ninth grade's pass rate increased by 2 percent.

For a second time, the students completed a survey regarding their perceptions about school. Results were compared to the year before. Mr. Rodgers summarized the results.

"Students were still undecided about their feelings about school. However, they perceived that they were doing more exciting things in the classroom, probably due to the fact that there is more time in class to do exciting things. Students felt they were being allowed to do things their own way sometimes, possibly because teachers were giving them more options. It may also be due to teachers having more time and fewer students, which allows for more flexibility.

"Students perceive less favoritism by teachers possibility because more students are succeeding rather than just a few kids getting all the attention. I spoke to Students United with Teachers and they concluded that more follow-up needs to be done to determine if students still like the new schedule . . . and they think they do . . . and we also need student input about improving the schedule."

Dina recorded this entry in her diary:

I asked teachers to complete the same survey they took last year so I could compare satisfaction levels. Last year, teachers were uncertain whether students were learning the required material. This year they felt they were. This year, they also perceived that the curriculum was flexible enough to adjust for needed changes.

However, all other areas regarding satisfaction with how students manifest their abilities remained the same. While it is encouraging that teachers feel students are learning the required material and they, the teachers, now have time to teach it, it is less encouraging that they still perceive that students are not interested or responsible for their learning.

Could it be that teachers have raised their expectations for student learning? Or had the teachers not diversified their forms of delivery to the degree that provokes student interest. Perhaps the subject matter itself needs to be examined.

Teacher satisfaction with support levels showed the most positive gains. Teachers were more satisfied with collegial interaction, staff development, the quality of their educational experience, and the amount of time for planning, parent involvement, student learning, and workload assignment.

And as I visited classrooms, lecture was not as singularly prevalent as it used to be. Students were using computers more than ever before, working on group activities, or doing individual projects. I saw more discussion going on in more classrooms. I was particularly impressed that working in groups no longer included discussion of the football scores.

What she concluded from both the teacher and student survey results was that both students and teachers supported the new schedule because it supported them. But teachers were still not satisfied with the level of student achievement, and students were reserving judgment about school.

In March, Dina again studied the pass rates. They were holding! What was of particular interest was that the ninth-graders did not have the highest number of failures as in former years. In terms of referrals, they had decreased significantly.

They had many theories about this. The most salient one was that the students met with fewer students during the day. There was less of a chance that they would impact one another in negatives ways. Also, dispersing the lockers around campus had been a valuable and viable solution.

In June, after school was out, the Democratic Council met to review the results of the first year. The initial results overwhelmed them. Pass rates and honor roll rates had increased, while retention and discipline referral rates had declined. Ninth-grade students increased their pass rates but continued to have a high number of students failing one or more subjects over the year. They knew that they had more work to do.

"The number of infractions involving violent behavior such as verbal abuse, weapons, gang association, threats, fighting, and assault were the same," Dina reported. "While these numbers are extremely small, the behaviors in this area are serious and these infractions need constant monitoring and interventions. What is very exciting is that the number of referrals for drug use has dramatically decreased by over 50 percent."

"The fact that peer counselors were on hand to handle problems," Mr. Rodgers said proudly, "made everybody's job much easier and aided greatly in helping students keep their drugs at home."

The faculty and staff applauded the fact that over 40 percent of the students were on the honor roll. "There's a lot more self-esteem walking around here," Mr. Berg noted.

They were especially delighted with the baseline data for students who dropped out of school. The annual dropout rate had declined by about 3 percent.

In late June, Dina, sitting at her desk, began asking herself what change meant. She came to realize that she perceived it meant practicing something Cousin Michael talked about . . . learning how to learn together.

The faculty was pleased but knew that they were just beginning. They were standing at the base of the mountain, looking up at the distant peak. By using their collective minds and forming theories of improvement based on data and research about systems, they could begin the climb up as they worked, reworked, and expanded their repertoire.

Vignette

THE FLAW IN EVERY PLAN

"We can predict how many atoms in a piece of radium are going to disintegrate in the next hour, but we have no way of knowing which ones are going to disintegrate" (Zukav, 1979, p. 60). How true Gary Zukav's statement turned out to be.

Once upon a time, a principal, who had etched in her mind something that was said by someone a long time ago . . . something like the price of liberty is eternal vigilance . . . explored a theory of education. The theory said simply that in the absence of theory, we merely copy and do the same things over and over again. The theory said that without a model of democracy in the schools, the basic tenets of our Republic would eventually erode just as the great Roman Empire did because people lost sight of what their Republic was about.

Once upon a time, a principal began to explore the idea that people weren't widgets, that schools did not have to treat them as if they were, and that once she explored the reasons for why she did things the way she did them, she would throw out the reasons.

Once upon a time, a principal discovered that schools existed in the old Newtonian world but operated in the new quantum one.

Once upon a time, a principal learned that if she constantly looked at processes and their variation, she could begin creating positive change over time.

Once upon a time, a principal learned that, until she continually questioned herself about why she was doing what she was doing, she would find that what she was doing made little sense so much of the time.

Once upon a time, a principal learned that no matter how well things seemed to be going, there was always someone lurking in the shadows who had a great deal of power and could topple democratic practice in the schoolhouse.

In the case of widgets, the principal came to understand that working with widgets and working with human beings was not the same. You may laugh at this statement, but every time a principal assigns a teacher to a new room on the campus map without consulting him or her, or takes a block of students from point A to point B without consulting them, she is treating them like widgets.

Widgets are machine outcomes, tangible products that can be drawn on a piece of paper, detailing exact specifications. Processes that produce widgets can be carefully charted and improved on in order to produce the best possible widget.

Everybody working on the widget in the factory knows what it is going to look like when it reaches the end of the assembly line because its "look" is predetermined and controlled by the processes that produce it. If the widget fails to meet specifications, it is because the people working in the processes are faulty. Fix the people, and the widget will meet specifications.

Within the mechanical physical world of widget manufacturing, the principal found that chaos can be controlled by fixing the parts in the process that were not doing their job. But that was widget production, and the principal realized that she did not run a factory. Or at least she didn't think she did anymore.

The principal knew that the goal of education was not the manufacture of inanimate objects. The goal was to guide a child, channeling his or her mind and body to the knowledge and critical thought necessary for the journey on to the next stage of life within a backdrop called democracy.

There were no exact specifications for this, even though the politicians declared that statewide assessment tests could fill this vacuum, at the expense of true knowledge. What the principal didn't know was that the processes that were used to produce the educated adolescent expanded way beyond the parameters that Mrs. Edna Lightment had suggested.

During the beginning of third year of the school improvement plan, Superintendent Mac Avelli retired. The school board appointed a new superintendent. His name was Dr. Nick Chez, former principal of Berlin High School. Yes, we met him before at the library . . . he was the guy who thought that people had to be controlled for reform to occur.

Shortly before the beginning of the new school year, he summoned Principal Dina Macksy to his office.

"I see that your school has a schedule that is different from the other schools in my district," he said, his tone mellow, almost avuncular. But somehow, Dina sensed this was not to be a tranquil dialogue.

As he sat there behind the cherry wood desk, she saw before her a broad shouldered and powerful looking man whose face twitched from time to time. It made her feel like the next twitch would find her entrenched in the thick of a flock of vultures, their stooped necks and twitching beaks looking over the slowly decaying body on the ground, the body that looked very much like it belonged to her.

"Whose idea was this schedule?" he demanded to know, gentility eroding from the voice, a steely look in his eyes. "Why do you have it? I have also heard that your teachers work together to change the school. That's your job, not theirs.

"Are they doing your job for you? And is it true that students have a say in what happens at the school? What kind of a school are you running? Maybe you're not running it."

Dina saw immediately that they were not going to get along. She informed him that the bell schedule was implemented last year after much work was completed the previous year in assessing the needs of the high school.

"The school and community selected the schedule as a way to change the teaching-learning environment to improve learning outcomes and student achievement. The school and community were looking for ways to actively engage students in school so that dropout, retention, and failure rates would decrease, while attendance increased.

"We have in place this year a child care center to keep kids in school and curtail the cycle of failure. We have an alternative school program for those needing more support. We have a group called Students

United with Teachers to provide solutions for teen problems. We work together as a team to solve our problems. Results have been better than expected."

Dina asked him if he wanted to see "The Big Picture Show." Over the summer, she had evaluated the data and included the results. They were very good. They were making progress. Kids were staying in school.

He provided no response to her question. It was as if he didn't even hear it. He just looked up at her from behind the cherry wood desk, his arms folded, and his elbows resting on the sports section of the newspaper.

In distant, cold, and clipped language he said, "I don't like this bell schedule. It just doesn't seem to me that students are fully applying themselves with only four subjects a day. The program of study does not seem rigorous enough. At my last school, there was a seven-period day and it worked well in producing successful graduates.

"This bell schedule needs serious work. Too many kids are on the honor roll. It appears that you have lowered the standards.

"We need to increase graduation requirements immediately or we will start losing students to early graduation. Do you think a child is ready to enter the world at sixteen? It's not surprising that so many of our high school students don't go to college. We don't spend enough time instructing them.

"And we are losing money when our seniors only attend school for half the time that other students do. There is some feeling among parents that teachers did not adjust their instruction and much of the period is spent on homework. And I have heard parents say that the child care center increases teenage pregnancy.

"Please supply for me in report form the benefits you see for continuation . . . attendance rates, graduation rates, failure rates, absentee rates. I want to weigh the positives and negatives.

"As I see it, we are not providing the kind of quality high school experience parents demand. I have confidence you have all the tools to make the necessary changes. You can make a difference to those students at the high school now and not have to wait a year to realize little success. Let's make a difference. I know you will do the right thing in getting this problem fixed.

"I'd like the report Monday morning . . . and don't make it more than two pages. If you can't say it in two pages, it's not worth saying." Then his sardonic eyes retreated to the sports section.

She left his office feeling very, very uneasy. He was interested in quick fixes. He would have loved her first school improvement plan, she thought. He could have lived off her success until he moved up to a larger district. And there went her weekend. It would take all day Saturday, working in the office, to compress "The Big Picture Show" into the wee little one.

On Monday morning, she provided him the data he requested. The data showed results of the school's first year and compared those results to five years of data prior to its implementation. The results were excellent and trends were positive. She included in her report several comments in response to the remarks he had made. She had to use eight-point font to squeeze it all on the page.

"There is no evidence," she wrote, "as of yet, that we will have an influx of sixteen-year-old graduates. Few students have applied for early graduation. Most students prefer to graduate with their class and appear to enjoy the high school experience. In addition, the parents who pushed for this bell schedule wanted to make the decision themselves about early graduation.

"School policy in my view is an interactive process between the teacher, parent, and student. I cannot make some decisions about change without collaboration with the people who live in the processes. I feel that we have to look at how all the processes in our school are working together and we need everyone's help in evaluating them.

"It is true that we lose money due to seniors leaving early. With the seven-period day, seniors left after four periods. The state counts this as a full day. With the new bell schedule, the state calculates attendance using a different formula. Two periods do not equate to four periods and we only receive three-quarters credit. There are things we can do about this . . . require seniors to stay three periods unless they have a job. But I feel that when our attendance increases and our dropout rate declines, we are offsetting the money lost by the seniors who leave school after two periods . . . for now at least.

"I don't know how to react to your comment that there is some feeling among parents that teachers did not adjust their instruction and much of the period is spent on homework. I find it common for parents and superintendents to take what they hear from a few people, aggregate the statement as being said by all the parents, and come to false conclusions.

"We survey our parents. The majority are not unhappy because their students are not unhappy. I would suggest you refer the parents whom you have spoken to, to me, so that I may understand their perceptions and adjust them."

Yes, Dina was exhibiting more than a little lack of judiciousness in her response, but she was angry, really angry, that the new guy on the block was diminishing the work their school had done, and without any data of his own or theories about why their program should be changed.

"To reiterate," she wrote, "the results we are getting from the school improvement plan show promise. We are keeping kids in school. Based on these facts, we are making a difference. I hope after reading this report, you are better able to weigh the positives and negatives."

There are some principals who will speak differently about whether a glass filled halfway with water is half empty or half full. Dina always fell into the latter camp.

But this time, the inner cautionary heckler was telling her to put her guard up, watch her back, beware of administrators who had power and control. She was experiencing fear in the workplace, fear moving up and down her spine, flooding the nerve endings with uncontrollable terror. But the cup was half full she reiterated to herself. We all want the best things for students . . . and the best things for democracy . . . even superintendents.

The faculty was beginning to discover that the control center of a school resides in all its members, an indivisible body of people who had discovered that education was an interconnected affair. Teaching and learning were about feeding, nourishing, nurturing, and delivering new knowledge to guide students on their educational journey.

They were beginning to understand that the organization had a life of its own, connected by the relationships among people. They were an organic body, housing within them the seeds for new potential.

As school ended for another year, Mr. Newt Owen told Dina, "For the most part, our faculty and staff are unified and in sync. As a result, the students feel empowered and are in school. The past two years have been great. We accomplished a great deal for our students."

A week after delivering her report, the superintendent again summoned Dina to his office. She could see the page of the local newspaper showing the state test scores sitting side by side on his desk with the two-page report she had written.

"I read your report," he began, his anger so intense that she could see the tightness of his skin stretched across his face. "And then I looked at the state scores in the paper. The public doesn't see the numbers in your report. But they see these numbers here," he scowled, pointing at the newspaper, his abrupt fortissimo jarring her nerve endings.

"Why aren't you more focused on raising these numbers instead of this other nonsense? Yes, yes, I know your scores showed improvement, but had you focused all your resources on the state tests, those numbers might look even better." His fingers were jabbing the newspaper as he shouted words into her face.

"All the other principals focus their goals and objectives on increasing the scores . . . all, that is, but you. Why taint your mind with inferior ideas Principal Macksy, conjured up by the banal minds of individuals who occupy space in your organization? Their only motives are self-interest. They don't know how to learn cooperatively . . . nor want to take the time to work together. *Just leave me alone and let me do my job* is their mantra as they shut their doors in your face.

"Teachers need to be controlled. Control must be utilized to educate students. It's the only answer for the students and the teachers. It's the way it has always been done. It's the way test scores go up.

"After weighing all the facts, I want you to change the bell schedule and return to a seven-period day. You are to submit your goals and objectives based on the state test results. The tests are all that matter. It's what people see in the newspapers.

"I don't want poor scores humiliating me. We must show the public we are making a difference. And close the child care center. Of course, I can only make suggestions. It's your choice. Either you play on my team or you get off it."

And that was it. Either she played on his team or got off it. It was at that moment Dina understood what Mr. Quintin Waver apprehended about the potentialities lying in every quantum box. It was only when she opened the box that the actuality was revealed.

So when she did open the box, which actuality popped out? Guided by the rules and lessons learned, there could be only one. The Republic had to be saved.

EPILOGUE

Two roads diverged in a wood, and I—
And I took the one less traveled by
And that has made all the difference.

—"The Road Not Taken," Robert Frost

A headline came across the authors' computers via the electronic world of e-mails: *Study Finds Federal Stimulus Funds Not Driving School Reforms as Intended.* The article reported: "Federal stimulus money from the American Recovery and Reinvestment Act has not generated the kind of educational reforms the law sought, according to a new study released. Nearly two years after the act provided more than $100 billion in stimulus funding for public education nationwide, its impact on student achievement has largely been muted, the study by the nonprofit Bellwether Education Partners in Washington, D.C., argues."[1]

Coincidentally, at the same time, another headline grabbed the attention of educators. The founder of Facebook, Mark Zuckerberg, created a flurry of excitement when he contributed $100 million to improve the public schools of Newark, New Jersey. Despite fifteen years of state control and an infusion of state aid, the district's test scores and graduation rates continue to be below the expectations of the educational community.[2]

School reform continues to be the mantra of federal and local governing bodies throughout our country. Was it Einstein who said doing the same thing over and over expecting different results is a sign of insanity?

The shareholders in the school you just read about had a theory that with the right processes in place, the scores would rise, the climate would improve, and the culture would be refocused on common values. The results would create a new beginning and bountiful opportunities for the students. Yes, they disaggregated the data from the tests in order to evaluate skills in need of improvement, but they did not do this at the exclusion of the main thrust of their planning. They used a democratic and intellectual approach instead of a mechanical mindset. They wanted school to be a place where students—and adults—could do as Cousin Michael had suggested, they wanted them to dream. Having good test scores was a by-product of that dream.

Anyway, back to the Superintendent Mac Avelli types, these types of people don't understand Einstein's theory of relativity, but neither did Principal Dina Macksy. What she did understand—and they didn't—is that by grasping how we and everything around us is interconnected, we can begin to work in our schools on what our students need, not what politics dictates.

Politics, we know, is not about what's best for the common good anymore. It is about groups pushing their own agenda, their misrepresentations and untruths, their righteousness, onto the people. Perhaps our political leaders should venture to take a national exam that will measure their abilities to read, compute, reason, evaluate, and apply knowledge to the work in which they are engaged? Let us demand they have their scores published on electronic bulletin boards throughout the country. Those who do not meet the cut-off scores, established by a noted panel of educators, must resign their positions. Yes, what's good for educators should be good for politicians!

Every person could be better than he or she is because democracies allow us to grow. Every person who must abide by decisions we make as a group should have a stake in making those decision. Superintendent Mac Avelli and the politicians do not believe in this. They would rather that teachers sign in using time clocks so they can control them.

There are lessons to be learned from all this. The authors challenge you to make your decisions from these lessons, being fully cognizant that the threads among schooling, education, and democracy are interwoven and paramount in preserving our public schools and ensuring freedom for generations to come. Now is the time to become the educational leader of your school. Now is the time to rethink democratic schools.

NOTES

1. N. Gonzales (December 2, 2010). Study finds federal stimulus funds not driving reforms as intended. MercuryNews.com. Retrieved December 3, 2010. http://www.freerepublic.com/focus/f-news/2636156/posts.

2. R. Perez-Pena (September 22, 2010). Facebook founder to donate $100 million to help remake Newark schools. New York Times. Retrieved December 3, 2010. http://www.nytimes.com/2010/09/23/education/23newark.html.

REFERENCES

Ackoff, R. L. (1981). *Creating the corporate future.* New York: Wiley.

Arendt, H. (1963). *Eichmann in Jerusalem.* New York: Penguin.

Bendell, T., Kelly, J., Merry, T., & Sims, F. (1993). *Quality: Measuring and monitoring.* London: Century Business.

Bolman, L. G., & Deal, T. E. (2001). *Leading with soul: An uncommon journey of spirit* (revised and updated).San Francisco: Jossey-Bass.

Brookhiser, R. (2006). *What would the founding fathers do?* New York: Basic Books.

Burke, J. (1985). *The day the universe changed.* Boston: Little, Brown.

Carrol, J. (1990). *The Copernican plan: Restructuring the high school.* Andover, MA: Regional Laboratory for Educational Development of the Northeast and Islands.

Chirichello, M., & Richmond, N. (2007). *Leading to lead: Ten stories for principals.* Lanham, MD: Rowman & Littlefield Education.

Counts, G. S. (1931). *Dare the school build a new social order?* New York: Jonn Day Company.

Cremin, L. A. (1980). *American education: The national experience 1783–1876.* New York: Harper & Row.

Cuban, L. (1990). Reforming, again, again, and again. *Educational Researcher, 19*(1), 3–13.

Delavigne, K., &Robertson, J. (1994). *Deming's profound changes.* Englewood Cliffs, NJ: Prentice-Hall.

Deming, W. E. (1986). *Out of the crisis.* Cambridge, MA: Michigan Institute of Technology.

Deming Library, 1987–1989, Volume XXI. Washington, DC: CC-M Productions.

Dewey, J. (1938). *Experience and education.* New York: Macmillan.

Dewey, J. (1961). *Democracy and education.* New York: Macmillan.

Dicker, G. (1993). *Descartes, an analytical and historical introduction.* New York: Oxford University Press.

Doyle, W. (1976). Education for all: The triumph of professionalism. In O. L. Davis, Jr. (Ed.), *Perspectives on curriculum development 1776–1976.* Washington, DC: Association of Supervision and Curriculum Development.

Einstein, A. (1954). *Ideas and opinions.* New York: Bonanza Books.

Famous Quotes. Retrieved October 20, 2010, www.quotes-famous.com/quotes/Albert-Einstein/13592.htm.

Fior, J. (2000). *Alice in wonderland.* New York: Dorling Kindersley Publishing.

Fullan, M. G. (1987). Implementing the implementation plan. In M. F. Wideen & I. Andrews (Eds.), *Staff development for school improvement* (pp. 213–222). New York: Falmer.

Fullan, M. G. (1991). *The new meaning of change.* New York: Teachers College Press.

Gibboney, R. (1994). *The Stone trumpet: A story of practical school reform, 1960–1990.* New York: State University of New York Press

Gilmore, R. (1995). *Alice in quantumland.* New York: Copernicus.

Heil, G., Bennis, W., & Stephens, D. (2000). *Douglas McGregor, revisited: Managing the human side of the enterprise.* New York: Wiley.

Hobbs, T. (1996). *Leviathan.* Kindle Edition. Oxford, NY: Oxford University Press.

Hopkins, L. T. (1941). *Interaction, the democratic process.* Boston: D.C. Heath.

Hunter, R. (2004). *Madeline Hunter's mastery teaching: Increasing instructional effectiveness in elementary and secondary schools.* Thousand Oaks, CA: Corwin Press.

Isaacson, W. (2007). *Einstein, his life and universe.* New York: Simon & Schuster.

Jowett, B. (1973). *The Republic and other works.* New York: Anchor Books, Random House.

Kohn, A. (1986). *No contest: The case against competition.* New York: Houghton Mifflin.

Kohn, A. (1993). *Punished by rewards.* New York: Houghton Mifflin.

Kozol, J. (1995). *The lives of children and the conscience of a nation.* New York: Crown Publishers.

Lieberman, A., & Miller, L. (1984). *Teachers, their world, and their work.* Arlington, VA: Association for Supervision and Curriculum Development.

Lindberg, L. (1954). *The democratic classroom.* New York: Columbia University Press.

Locke, J. (1947). *On politics and education.* Roslyn, NY: Walter J. Black.

Loomis, L. R. (Ed.). (1995). *Aristotle: On man in the universe.* New York: Gramercy.

Marshall, I., & Zohar, D. (1994). *The quantum society.* New York: Morrow.

Montgomery, D. (1987). *The fall of the house of labor.* Cambridge: Cambridge University Press.

Mueller, H. (1993). *The land of green plums.* Evanston, IL: Northwestern University Press.

Ouchi, W. (1981). *Theory Z.* New York: Avon Books.

PBS. *Rediscovering George Washington.* First annual message to Congress, January 8, 1790. Retrieved February 11, 2009, from http://www.pbs.org/georgewashington/collection/.

Pulliam, J. D. (1982). *History of education in America* (3rd ed.). Columbus, OH: Charles E Merrill.

Restak, R. (1991). *The brain has a mind of its own.* New York: Crown Trade Paperbacks.

Sandel, M. J. (2009). *Justice.* New York: Farrar, Straus and Giroux.

Sarason, S. B. (1971). The *culture of the school and change.* Boston: Allyn/Bacon.

Sarason, S. B. (1990). *The predictable failure of school reform.* San Francisco: Jossey-Bass.

Senge, P. M. (1990). The *fifth discipline: The art and practice of the learning organization.* New York: Doubleday Currency.

Sergiovanni, T. J. (1987, May). Will we ever have a true profession? *Educational Leadership, 44*(8), 41–49.

Tarnas, R. (1991). *The passion of the western mind.* New York: Ballantine.

Taylor, F. (1915). *The principles of scientific management.* New York: Harper & Brothers.

Todes, D. (2000). *Ivan Pavlov: Exploring the animal machine.* New York: Oxford University Press.

Tyack, D., & Hansot, E. (1982). *Managers of virtue.* New York: Basic Books.

Walker, S., & Walker, V. (1993). Using SPC in the principal's office. *Quality Digest, 13*(9), 57.

Walker, S. (1995). Using statistical process control to improve attendance. *Quality Digest, 15*(9), 36–42.

Walker, S. (1997). Customer feedback from the classroom. *Quality Progress, 30*(3), 99–102.

Walker, S. (1999). Implementing the 4x4 block schedule: Is it worth it? *Rural Educator, 20*(3), 40–45.

Weber, M. (1968). *Economics and society.* New York: Bedminster Press.

Wheatley, M. (1992). *Leadership and the new science.* San Francisco: Berrett-Koehler Publishers.

Wilbur, K. (ed.) (1985). The holographic paradigm and other paradoxes. Boulder, CO: Shambala Press.

Wolf, F. A. (1989). *Taking the quantum leap.* New York: Harper & Row.

Zohar, D., & Marshall, I. (1994). *The quantum society.* New York: Morrow.

Zukav, G. (1979). *The dancing Wu Li masters.* New York: Morrow.

ABOUT THE AUTHORS

Sharron Goldman Walker began her experience with education as a Peace Corps volunteer in the bush of West Africa and has worked as a public school teacher and high school principal for over three decades. Her public school experience extends from kindergarten to twelfth grade in both rural and urban areas. She earned a doctorate in education from the University of Arizona, Tucson.

In 1986, the U.S. Department of Education awarded her school the National Secondary Education Award. Her school was among the 286 exemplary secondary schools in the nation receiving this recognition, celebrated by the president of the United States in a Rose Garden ceremony for principals. The Arts and Humanities Council made a film about the school's improvement efforts. *Instructor* magazine featured her as an outstanding principal, and she was a Chase Bank Outstanding Principal for the state of Arizona in 1991. Dr. Walker has presented workshops nationally on school improvement through democratic methods and written articles about the topic, especially on how principals can use data to improve their schools.

Active in her community as well as schools, Dr. Walker has served as a mayor and police commissioner in a small town in California. In 1995, the Board of Examiners for the Governor's Awards for Quality in Arizona appointed her as an examiner.

She and her husband, Virgil, a retired teacher and administrator, live in Mesa, Arizona, with their two dogs, Harry and George. Sharron continues to write books about the practice of democracy in public schools, in order to save the Republic.

Michael Peter Chirichello began his experience in education as a teacher in the Bronx, New York, forty-three years ago. He also served as an assistant principal in the New York City public schools. Michael was a principal, district and county superintendent, and university professor in New Jersey. He was the department chair at William Paterson University and developed programs for aspiring principals and supervisors. Currently, he is a visiting professor in the Ed.D. program at Northern Kentucky University.

Michael has coauthored *Learning to Lead: Ten Stories for Principals* and coedited *Exemplary Leadership Development: A Handbook for New Jersey Educational Leadership Interns*. He has published articles on topics related to leadership and curriculum design. His consulting work has brought him to five continents and many states throughout the United States.

Michael was the recipient of the Educational Leadership Award from the New Jersey Coalition of Educational Leaders; the Dale Reinhardt Excellence in Education Award from the Sussex County School Administrators and Supervisors Association; the Distinguished Achievement Award from the Sussex County, New Jersey, Education Association; the Distinguished Dissertation Award from Seton Hall University; and the PTA Honorary Life Member Award. He was also a Hayes-Fulbright Award recipient.

Michael is married to Carol, a retired first-grade teacher. He has two daughters, Deborah and Teri, and three granddaughters, Amanda, Taylor, and Contessa. He is an avid cyclist and has spent the past two summers biking in Italy and the Netherlands.

Michael believes that leadership matters, and great leaders lead from within.